Contemporary Italian Women Poets

Contemporary Italian Women Poets

■

A Bilingual Anthology

Edited & Translated by
Cinzia Sartini Blum
&
Lara Trubowitz

Italica Press
New York
2001

Copyright © 2001

by Cinzia Sartini Blum & Lara Trubowitz

ITALICA PRESS, INC.
595 MAIN STREET
NEW YORK, NEW YORK 10044

LIBRARY OF CONGRESS CATALOGING-IN-PUBLICATION DATA

Contemporary Italian women poets : a bilingual anthology /
edited & translated by Cinzia Sartini Blum & Lara Trubowitz.
    p. cm. — (Italica press dual-language poetry)
    English and Italian.
    Includes bibliographical references.
    ISBN 0-934977-17-8
    1. Italian poetry—Women authors. 2. Italian poetry—Women authors—Translations into English. 3. Italian poetry—20th century. 4. Italian poetry—20th century—Translations into English. I. Blum, Cinzia Sartini. II. Trubowitz, Lara, 1966- III. Italica press dual-language poetry series.

PQ4225.E8 B54 2001
851'.9140809287—dc21

                                                            2001024424

Printed in the United States of America
5 4 3 2 1

Cover Art: From the Collections of the Capitoline Museums at the Montemartini Power Plant, Rome. Photo: Italica Press Archives.

CONTENTS

CONTENTS

PREFACE

In the last few years, several book-length studies and collections of critical essays have introduced the English-speaking public to Italian women's voices and to the extraordinarily heterogeneous Italian feminist movement. Focused primarily on women's contributions to critical theory and prose, such investigations have largely ignored developments in poetry. Our anthology redresses this lack of attention by introducing audiences to the aesthetic and thematic diversity of contemporary women's poetry published in Italy during the past five decades. Our main goal is to make evident the broad range of ways in which Italian women poets have contributed to the field of contemporary literature, and to Italian culture in general.

To introduce women into Italy's poetic landscape we link each writer's work to changing literary and cultural trends. We do not, however, focus only on women's poetic practices as they evolve in relation to given literary histories. We are also concerned with the ways in which individual practices diverge from such histories. Thus, we chart formal and thematic developments as they occur within each poet's work. We hope that this anthology will expand debates about women's writing by exposing readers to a previously inaccessible body of work, enabling them to make cross-cultural connections between Italian women's poetry and poetry written in English. We aim, in other words, not only to explain the political and aesthetic forces that have influenced Italian women's literary production but to bring their poetry into a transnational network of literature and literary theories.

We wish to thank the following people from the University of Iowa for their invaluable assistance: Elizabeth Aubrey, Nancy Byers, Deborah Contrada, Helena Detmer, John E. Grant, Mary Lynn Johnson, Robert Keterer, Rosemary Stenzel, Michelle Visser, and Gay Zoldesy. We are grateful also to Iolanda Sartini, Anna Laura Zani, Elisabetta Novello, and the women at Libreria delle donne in Milan for their help contacting writers and collecting materials that were unavailable in the United States. This project benefited from the intellectual support of many individuals: in particular, we are indebted to Suzi Morrison for her early contributions to the project, David Wittenberg for his thoughtful reading of the introduction and suggestions on the poems, and Jocelyn Emerson for bringing to the book an attention to the breath, tone and voice of poetry wherever it threatened to be lost. In addition, our *grazie* goes out to the poets in this collection who helped us with biographical information, generously answered our questions, and offered comments on the translations: Mariella Bettarini, Anna Cascella, Elena Clementelli, Rosita Copioli, Biancamaria Frabotta, Jolanda Insana, Vivian Lamarque, Gabriella Leto, Dacia Maraini, Giulia Niccolai, Luciana Notari, Rossana Ombres, Piera Oppezzo, Gabriella Sica, Maria Luisa Spaziani, and Patrizia Valduga. Special thanks too to those whose encouragement, support and love of literature have shaped and inspired our work: Naomi and Sidney Trubowitz, Charles and Evelyn Klenetsky, Tom Blum, and the Sartini and Blum families. It is to them that this book is dedicated. Lastly, we would like to express our gratitude to the following publishers, institutions, and individuals for permission to reprint the poems included in this volume: Adelphi Edizioni, Bastogi Editrice Italiana, Campanotto Editore, Anna Cascella, Centro Manoscritti dell'Università di Pavia (Fondazione Rosselli), Edizioni Città di Vita, Elena Clementelli, Crocetti Editore, Edizioni Empiria, Fermenti, Biancamaria Frabotta, Garzanti, Guanda, Jolanda Insana, Lalli Editore, Vivian Lamarque, Lanfranchi Editore, Edizioni del Leone, Gabriella Leto, Professor Agostino Lombardo, Dacia Maraini, Marsilio Editori, Nardini Editore, Neri Pozza Editore, Giulia Niccolai, Piera Oppezzo, Dubravko Pusek Editore, Salvatore Sciascia Editore, Gabriella Sica, Maria Luisa Spaziani, Stamperia dell'Arancio, and Edizioni Tracce. We are especially grateful to Giulio Einaudi Editore and to Rizzoli, who hold the copyrights for a large number of the texts.

INTRODUCTION

Despite the flourishing of Italian women's poetry during the twentieth century, women continue to be conspicuously underrepresented in both Italian anthologies and English translations of Italian writing. Two of the most frequently cited anthologies of Italian poetry are Edoardo Sanguineti's *Poesia del Novecento* and Pier Vincenzo Mengaldo's *Poeti italiani del Novecento.* Mengaldo's book includes only Amelia Rosselli, while no women are anthologized in Sanguineti's work. More recent anthologies show little improvement: eight women are included in Maurizio Cucchi and Stefano Giovanardi's *Poeti italiani del secondo Novecento: 1945–1995* (out of sixty poets) while only two women are featured among the eighteen poets in Roberto Galaverni's *Nuovi poeti italiani contemporanei*. In English translations of Italian poetry women fare no better: Rosselli is the only woman among the twenty-one poets in Lawrence Smith's *The New Italian Poetry*. Similarly, there are only five women out of forty-four poets in Alessandro Gentili and Catherine O'Brien's *The Green Flame*; five women among the thirty-four poets in Gayle Ridinger and Gian Paolo Renello's *Italian Poetry, 1950–1990*; and four women among the thirty authors in *The Promised Land,* edited by Luigi Ballerini, Beppe Cavatorta, Elena Coda, and Paul Vangelisti.

The marginal presence of Italian women in the annals of literary history can be explained, in part, by the fact that, as Ann Hallamore Caesar notes, "cultural histories of post-war Italy have characteristically taken schools or movements as the organizing principle of modern literature, often giving short shrift to works that resist assimilation."[1] Such cultural–historical methods of categorization encourage critics to focus on poetic features that are already well classified and on poets who are already canonized. Indeed, consideration is given to the approaches of poets who diverge from canonical forms only if, ironically, their departures from tradition anticipate future movements in predictable ways. As Dana Gioia succinctly puts it, "[l]ike parents who dress their younger children in hand-me-down clothes,… critics frugally refurbish old theories to describe new poets."[2] In this context, the marginalization of women poets is perpetuated by an

---

1. Ann Hallamore Caesar, "Post-War Italian Narrative: An Alternative Account," *Italian Cultural Studies: An Introduction*, ed. David Forgacs and Robert Lumley (New York: Oxford University Press, 1996), 248.
2. *New Italian Poets,* 4.

insidious logic: it is difficult for critics to categorize or describe women's work precisely because such work resists typical categories and descriptions.

Discussions of Italian women's writing have been further hindered by critical tendencies to adopt the label "feminine" as a derogatory qualifier for inferior, minor poetry, as well as by reactions against the notion of classification itself. Indeed, the position of Italian women in the field of poetry has remained uncertain because of a reluctance by critics and poets, male and female alike, to accept gender as a vital, or even relevant, critical category.[3] In the 1970s, prompted by debates about the viability of the category of gender — the most heated of which arose out of the Italian feminist movement — women authors and critics began to publish their own anthologies dedicated solely to women's poetry.[4] Some of the poets included in these anthologies rejected the notion of a women's poetic ge-nealogy or practice, preferring to think of themselves as writers subject only to their own individual aesthetic choices. The term "women's poetry," they believed, could result only in the ghettoization of women's writing.[5] For those writers who argued that gender crucially shapes one's work, the prosperity of Italian women's poetry, evident in journals even if unacknowl-edged by the editors of more canonical anthologies, indicated a great an-thropological, cultural, and political change, the slow dismantling by the women's movement of the effects of centuries of subjugation. The problem thus remained one of a subtle but crucial negotiation: how to describe women's poetic practices and the history of Italian women writers without erasing the very differences that make women's poetry so interesting.

Anglo–American scholars intent on bringing Italian women's writing to the attention of English-speaking audiences have had to contend with similar difficulties and ambiguities. Only two anthologies that significantly address the work of twentieth-century Italian women poets have ever been published in English, and these offer very different answers to the question of how to describe Italian women's poetry. The editors of the first of these anthologies, *The Defiant Muse*, provide us with a transhistorical compendium of protest poetry, focusing on a female poetic voice inflected by feminist tones. With seventy-six poems by over fifty Italian women

3. North American scholars of Italian literature have been, in general, more open to the question of gender than Italian literary critics. See, for instance, Picchione's "Poesia al femminile(?)."
4. These include *Donne in poesia, Poesia femminista italiana, Care donne, Poesie d'amore*, and *Donne in poesia: Incontri con le poetesse italiane*.
5. See the responses to Frabotta's "Inchiesta poetica," *Donne in poesia*, 137–76.

from the medieval period to the mid 1980s, the collection offers an important survey of women's writing and presents the "many common themes and threads that connect women beyond differences of class and culture, time and place."[6] In the second anthology, *Italian Women Poets of the Twentieth Century*, the editor Catherine O'Brien eschews such historical genealogies. Paying close attention to the unique and specific accomplishments of eleven women poets, she focuses on the ways in which modern women poets "chose not to be part of...prevailing literary fashions or trends."[7]

Our work in this anthology combines the two approaches these previous editors have adopted, offering both a survey of a marginalized body of work and an analysis of women's deliberate divergences from established poetic histories. In addition, we suggest that while it is productive to discuss how women have existed outside conventional literary history, it is also fruitful to consider ways in which they have been integral to that history, as overt inhabitants and architects of its designs. Thus, as we attend to the particular textual nuances of each poet's work, and more generally, to the range of poetic forms that women have produced, we underscore the relationship of women's literary production to the myriad currents of Italian poetry since World War II.

While our selection is not determined by thematic criteria, we identify a series of crucial, recurrent issues: the quest for identity and self-representation; the interwoven experiences of loving and writing; the tense and often painful connections between textuality, sexuality, power, and intimacy; metaphysical reflections on everyday life; and the trauma that can result from daily existence, including the extreme challenge of living with physical and mental illness. The authors we have chosen come from different generations and regions. Some have received international acclaim, while others are known primarily to those within women's literary circles.[8] This anthology is organized with the oldest poets first and the youngest last and includes only work published after the Second World War. The ordering of the poems within each poet's oeuvre is chronological. We hope that this arrangement will give readers a sense of the changes that have occurred in women's writing over the past fifty years.

6. *The Defiant Muse*, vii.
7. *Italian Women Poets of the Twentieth Century*, 16.
8. Given the quantity and quality of women's poetic production in the last few decades, many other poets could have been included in this book. Among the poets unrepresented in this anthology are Margherita Adda, Mara Alessi, Pina Allegrini, Cristina Annino, Daniela Attanasio, Rita Baldassarri, Marilla Battilana, Silvia Batisti,

Many of the poetic approaches and concerns we identify can be linked to developments in Italian culture at large. Such developments are not reducible to linear or schematic simplifications. However, it is possible to give a basic outline of prominent issues and events that have occupied Italian women writers in the last half century. The following pages are intended to offer some points of reference to readers who are unfamiliar with the complex landscape of twentieth-century Italian poetry. We begin with a brief overview of the literary canon, a canon that has excluded women and yet has often also constituted the background of their work. Following this overview, we discuss specific developments within women's poetry over the course of three main historical periods: 1940s–1960s, the 1970s, and the 1980s–1990s. Against the backdrop of major sociopolitical and literary trends, we outline the practices of individual poets as they have evolved during each period.

The Twentieth-Century Canon: From Symbolism to the Neo-Avant-Garde

From the turn of the twentieth century until World War II, the most prominent poetic practices in Italy were characterized by a belief in the evocative power of symbols to illuminate the individual's precarious understanding of his or her existence. Shaped by the poet, words could lend form to the most complex psychological processes and transform even the most intimate of autobiographical details into universal truths. Such an approach evolved from nineteenth-century French symbolism and crystallized during the inter-war years into the methods of the hermetic school (*ermetismo*).[9] Hermeticism was also influenced by efforts to renew the Italian poetic language that were begun before World War I, in particular by the "twilight poets" (*crepuscolari*) and the futurist movement, and that re-emerged in the

---

Giovanna Bemporad, Marella Bentivoglio, Rosa Berti Sabbieti, Carla Bertola, Elena Bono, Edith Bruck, Marianna Bucchich, Paola Campanile, Laura Canciani, Livia Candiani, Lea Canducci, Serena Caramitti, Franca Maria Catri, Agata Italia Cecchini, Annalisa Cima, Silvana Colonna, Maura Del Serra, Milli Graffi, Marica Larocchi, Elia Malagò, Gabriella Maleti, Marina Mariani, Biagia Marniti, Elsa Morante, Gilda Musa, Anna Oberto, Sandra Petrignani, Maria Pia Quintavalla, Raffaella Spera, and Patrizia Vicinelli. Also missing are women writing in dialect. For anthologies focused on dialect poetry, see *Dialetti d'Italia, Via Terra: Antologia di poesia neodialettale,* and *Via terra: An Anthology of Italian Neodialect Poetry.*

9. The trajectory from French symbolism to hermeticism, which played a major role in shaping the literary landscape of twentieth-century Italy, is highly complex,

work of the so called *lirici nuovi* (new lyricists), Umberto Saba, Giuseppe Ungaretti, and Eugenio Montale. The new lyricists, in turn, played a crucial role in the development of the hermetic movement during the 1930s. Ungaretti is the poet most closely linked with hermeticism. Referring to the alchemic, occult, and mystical writings attributed to Hermes Trismegistus, the term "hermeticism" was coined by the critic Francesco Flora to describe "the symbolic density and the linguistic difficulty" of Ungaretti's work.[10] Applied to a generation of writers (including Alfonso Gatto, Mario Luzi, Sandro Penna, Salvatore Quasimodo, Vittorio Sereni, and Leonardo Sinisgalli) who, like Ungaretti, focused on the alienated modern individual, *ermetismo* would eventually became synonymous with poetry that was enigmatic in content and complex in style. Of course, specific differences between poets did exist. Poets such as Sandro Penna, Attilio Bertolucci, and Giorgio Caproni, for instance, departed from the prevailing emphasis in hermeticism on abstraction and lyrical compression in order to pursue a narrative simplicity that would later characterize major trends in post-war poetry. Common to all the hermetic poets, however, was a tendency to focus on existential truths rather than on historical or social issues.

Because their work appeared to be divorced from the difficult sociopolitical realities of the inter-war years, the hermetics were eventually accused of having tacitly supported fascist rule. Such accusations were sparked by fervent debates about the political function of poetry and the responsibility of poets to political causes, debates that followed the collapse of the fascist regime and the end of World War II. Emerging in this period was a new figure of the writer committed to social change, inspired by a sense of moral responsibility, and dedicated to communicating with those outside literary circles. The exemplar for such a figure was Antonio Gramsci, the prominent anti-fascist intellectual who theorized the need for a new historical, political, and popular literature, and was imprisoned for his beliefs. Drawing on his writings, left-wing intellectuals denounced as elitist and reactionary the apolitical stance they saw embodied in hermeticism and called for a reconstruction of culture in reaction to fascism and based on Marxist principles. This project gave impetus to a new realist movement (*neorealismo*) in the late 1940s and early 1950s. Although neorealism is generally identified with developments in cinema and fiction, it also shaped

characterized by disparate and often contradictory developments in poetic theory and practice. For a survey of these developments, see *Twentieth-Century Italian Poetry* (1993), 3–17.

10. *The New Italian Poetry*, 11.

the work of many poets, including Franco Fortini, Giovanni Giudici, Pier Paolo Pasolini, Rocco Scotellaro, and Paolo Volponi. Building on Gramsci's pronouncements and inspired by the early example of Cesare Pavese's narrative poems in *Lavorare stanca* (1936), these writers rejected hermetic notions of the "pure word" in favor of a poetry of and for the common people.[11] By 1956, however, interest in realism as the pre-eminent movement of social and cultural change was waning. The year sparked a new ideological crisis for many intellectuals, as their faith in Marxist ideals was undermined by the Soviet invasion of Hungary. At the same time, Italy was undergoing widespread social and cultural transformation, caused in large part by the so-called "economic miracle," an unprecedented boom, which nonetheless left both old and newly emerged social problems largely unresolved. Facing this new world without the support of the political vision that had initially inspired them, many socially committed writers lost hope in their ability to play a leading role in Italy's reconstruction.

Disillusionment, frustration, and disorientation pervades the works of many poets during and after this period. These traits are particularly evident in the poetry of the *neosperimentalisti* (new experimentalists) associated with Pasolini's journal *Officina* and in the work of the northern poets who became known as the *linea lombarda* (Lombard line). The latter group, whose most famous practitioners include Luciano Erba and Nelo Risi, viewed the world as essentially chaotic and alienating. Among their attempts to engage this chaos was the development of "corporeal" poetry, poetry that could "be seen and touched" because it focused on the physical object, "always a free, unforeseen construction, an intense charge of internally organized forces."[12] Some of the methods of the *linea lombarda* involved the revival and transformation of hermetic practices. In contrast, Pasolini and the new experimentalists (including Roberto Roversi and Franco Fortini) subordinated hermetic interest in style and symbolic expression to a project of explicit cultural regeneration. Such a project, their work suggested, could only assume an oppositional stance.

To a large extent, this oppositional stance would inform later developments in Italian poetry, in particular the work of neo-avant-garde writers Nanni Balestrini, Alfredo Giuliani, Elio Pagliarani, Antonio Porta, and Edoardo Sanguineti (named *I Novissimi* after the title of the 1961 anthology that launched their careers, and known also as *Gruppo 63* after the year of their first official meeting in Palermo). However, this new avant-garde,

11. On post-war debates and the impact of neorealism on poetry see ibid., 13–24.
12. Luciano Anceschi, quoted in *From Pure Silence to Impure Dialogue*, xvi.

seeking a radical break with the past, rejected the historicist premises still crucial to the project of the *Officina* group, shifting its programmatic focus from content — the ethical and political message of the text — to language itself as a locus of power and conflict. Luciano Anceschi's *Il Verri* provided a forum for the movement, whose practitioners were influenced by current semiological, phenomenological, and psychoanalytic theories. Central to their program was the belief that conventional language is the vehicle by which those who hold power perpetuate empty values. By disturbing syntax and mixing registers and diction, these neo-avant-garde writers pursued a strategy of shock and provocation that challenged established codes and reflected the violence and irrationality of the contemporary world. Their aim was to undermine the complacency of their readers, most of whom, they believed, had been dulled by official rhetoric. In some cases their strategy served a political project whose ultimate goal was the creation of a new kind of subjectivity. In this respect the neo-avant-garde movement can be viewed as the most extreme and conspicuous manifestation of a phenomenon that underlies the entire poetic landscape of the second half of the twentieth century in Italy: a widespread cultural malaise that often resulted, first, in the belief that conventional language could not express the poet's vision, and second, in the desire to find a primal language untainted by hegemonic political and cultural power. *Gruppo 63* rapidly unraveled due to theoretical dissentions among its members, but its beliefs and methods led to a further series of vital poetic experiments. Adriano Spatola and Lamberto Pignotti, for example, incorporated techniques of the mass media and built on the groundbreaking work of the historical avant-garde in order to develop new and provocative forms of visual and concrete poetry. In the work of other poets, the radical concerns advocated first by the neorealists and later by the neo-avant-garde were expressed in more subtle forms, for instance, in the broadening of conventional poetic dictions and metric schemes.

Despite a tradition of critical neglect and marginalization, women's contributions to these developments has been vast, as we shall show in the following pages. Indeed, if we look back to the 1950s, we see the presence of women already apparent in the anthology *Quarta generazione*, which was dedicated to the so-called "fourth generation," the young poets who made their literary debut in the decade following World War II. Included in the anthology were works by Margherita Guidacci, Alda Merini, and Maria Luisa Spaziani, poets whose practices and innovations often paralleled, or even pre-dated, major historical trends in post-war Italian poetry.[13] Yet even today these women are only sporadically included in discussions of Italian literary history. They share the fate of women poets of the first half of the twentieth century, such as Annie Vivanti, Ada Negri, Sibilla Aleramo, and Amalia Guglielminetti, whose work has also been too frequently ignored by scholars.[14]

Women's Poetry from the 1940s to the 1960s

As already noted, the predominance of hermeticism was not challenged until after World War II, when neorealist writers began advocating for politically committed literature against what they saw as the obsolete and parochial traditions of the hermetic canon. This new realist trend affected even the least political of poets, for it suggested a practice of thinking that encouraged writers to make their work accessible to a larger audience. The result was a new vitality within the previously ossified lyrical tradition and a vibrant exploration of previously neglected poetic forms and concerns.

Guidacci was among the first to depart from the literary models offered by the hermetic school. Rejecting the school's solipsistic tendencies, she pursued a precision and simplicity predicated on a belief in the communicative function of language and the need to be "a player and a witness in God's universe and in other men's society."[15] While tending toward religious and specifically eschatological meditation in her work, she also commonly linked autobiographical and historical events to metamorphoses in the natural world. In her early collections, *La sabbia e l'angelo* and *Paglia e polvere*, Guidacci saw poetry as a means of redemption and the poet as an interpreter of the dead, whom she viewed as God's messengers. Her theological understanding of the social and ethical relevance of poetry placed her at odds with the poetics of political commitment advocated by the left-wing intellectuals of the *Officina* group, as well as with the iconoclastic program of the *Novissimi*. Inspired by the work of the writers she studied and translated — in particular Emily Dickinson, John Donne, T. S. Eliot, Henry James, Mark Twain and, in later years, Elizabeth Bishop — she

13. Biagia Marniti and Luciana Guatelli were also among the thirty-three poets featured in the anthology.
14. For a selection of works by Vivanti, Negri, Aleramo, and Guglielminetti, see *The Defiant Muse.*
15. For more on Guidacci's stance against hermeticism, see her responses to the journal *Poesia Nuova*'s questions on post-war Italian poetry, published in March 1955 (reprinted in Frattini, *Poesia nuova in Italia,* 153).

developed a distinctive poetic practice and found unique ways of "casting light where previously darkness had been found."[16]

Spaziani's first collection, *Le acque del Sabato*, shows a greater debt than Guidacci's work to the hermetic school: rarefied poetic language is a conspicuous feature, as is her preference for lyricism and confession. Early in her career critics considered Spaziani's precursors to be Montale, Rainer Maria Rilke, and Dylan Thomas. French literature, especially symbolist poetry, was also identified as one of her primary influences; indeed, Arthur Rimbaud's "Bateau ivre" epitomizes for Spaziani the aim of modern poetry, juxtaposing a carefully wrought formal control with thematic attention to the irrationality of modern life. In her own practice Spaziani aims for similar juxtapositions.[17] During the 1960s, with the collections *Il Gong*, *Utilità della memoria*, and *L'occhio del ciclone*, Spaziani establishes a poetic persona that is at once tragic and ironic. As her lyricism gives way to a more concrete personal history, her metric repertoire broadens to include rhythmic schemas and cadences beyond the endecasyllable predominant in her early poems.[18] She appears to have been influenced by the experimental climate of the 1960s, yet refuses to rely on experimentation for its own sake, aiming for harmonious forms of language that reflect her belief "in the restorative powers of poetry."[19] Thus Spaziani echoes the hermetics' faith in the poetic act, even as she departs from hermetic concerns by declaring poetry a social remedy against the commodification of culture.

Like Spaziani, Merini cannot be clearly identified with any single Italian school or trend. Her work has been linked both to the poetry of Walt Whitman and to an anti-modern tendency exemplified by Rilke and Stefan George. Merini's early collections, *La presenza di Orfeo*, *Paura di Dio*, *Nozze romane*, and *Tu sei Pietro* are characterized by a striking mixture of erotic and religious imagery and already contain themes that will be central in her later poetry: the fusion of pagan and Christian worlds; a belief in the prophetic power of the poetic word; reliance on the language of love to describe friendships; and expressions of pain, fear, and anxiety — hints, perhaps, of Merini's incipient mental illness. *Tu sei Pietro* concludes the first creative phase of Merini's poetic career. As noted by critic Maria Corti, the collection focuses on unrequited love evoked in terms that recall, on one hand, the impassioned prophesies of early women mystics, and on the other

16. *Italian Women Poets of the Twentieth Century*, 85.
17. See Lettieri and Marchegiani Jones's preface to Spaziani, *Star of Free Will*, 9–10.
18. See Baldacci's introduction to Spaziani, *Poesie*, 13–18.
19. *Italian Women Poets of the Twentieth Century*, 129.

hand, the fatalism of Greek tragedy.[20] And yet, the book moves away from the metaphorical density and mystical reflection of Merini's early poetry to a lyric that is characterized by lighter, more playful tones, anticipating future developments in her work. *Tu sei Pietro* was followed by a long period of silence, coinciding with the onset of the poet's mental illness; she published no more poetry for twenty years.

Formal and thematic concerns of the "fourth generation" women also appear in the work of poets such as Cristina Campo. As with Guidacci, religion and the search for a spare style assume fundamental importance for Campo. Natural elements are sacred to her, restorative as well as destructive: rivers, rain, tears, and other water images run through her poems, as do images of blood and fire. Campo's later work, exemplified by the poem "Canone IV," is characterized by liturgical tones, as the poetic voice, in physical as well as spiritual pain, assumes the inflection and rhythms of prayer. This voice directly addresses the objects it contemplates, beckoning them to come close, warning them away, pleading with them for compassion. As Campo explains in an interview, poetry "is born of liturgy," which is the supreme form of beauty.[21] Her concerns — the landscape, language, myth, and ritual — express her belief that beauty is the sole means by which the self is "centered" in a time dominated by vulgarity and indifference.[22] In her last poems, influenced by her readings and translations of seventeenth-century mystics, Campo's assessment of the relationship between the poet and beauty is specifically theological in nature. She views the poet as endowed with a "terrible" awareness of the beautiful: terrible because beauty is a double-edged sword, dispensing consolation while inflicting mortal wounds.

Campo's reflections on the degradation of modern culture and on the ethical and spiritual implications of writing were not directly influenced by the wave of polemics and literary experiments first generated by the intellectuals gravitating around the journals *Officina* and *Il Menabò*, and later by the neo-avant-garde *Gruppo 63*. With few exceptions, women poets were not active participants in these groups' debates and programs. Yet, their work suggests

20. See Corti's introduction to Merini, *Fiore di poesia*, x.

21. Campo, *La Tigre Assenza*, 302. In a 1959 letter, Campo wrote of an obsession with perfection that prevented her from writing; in a 1974 letter, she reiterated her fear ("timor sacro"). Her reluctance to write was commensurate with her belief in the supreme importance of poetry and beauty, which she expressed through Dostoyevsky's words: "beauty will save the earth" (ibid., 304).

22. In a 1958 letter in which she refers to the world as "sick with narcosis," Campo calls for a return to the "center" (ibid., 291).

that they shared with both groups a number of concerns and approaches to culture and literary experimentation.

Rossana Ombres's interest in poetic experiment is clear in *L'ipotesi di Agar*; published in 1968, it marks a stylistic and thematic break in her thinking and practice. From the elegiac recollections of her early verses, the poet shifts to an exploration of woman's history, drawing caricatures, disrupting syntax, and merging genres. Two long poems of "poetry-theater" are included in the book, followed by "support texts" that suggest how to stage the works, and make clear the collection's central concern: the impact of our cultural and linguistic past and present on woman's psychic history. The title poem is described by the author as a "hypothetical anamnesis": it combines mystical, esoteric, and scientific vocabularies in tones that shift from the sentimental to the prophetic, chatty, and erotic. The second long poem, "Progetto di tricromia sonora," uses colors to dramatize transformations between the oracular, religious and esoteric, and the revolutionary. Ombres's earlier work had shown the impact of neorealism on post-hermetic trends, specifically the influence of the prose-like poems of Pavese. *Le ciminiere di Casale*, Ombres's nostalgic reexamination of the places, people and objects of her youth in Piemonte, echoes Pavese's efforts to escape an alienation he associates with the city and to recover a mythical life he identifies with childhood. Recalling Pavese's mythical geography, Ombres's landscape is inspired by the hilly Langhe area; and yet, as announced by the collection's title (The smokestacks of Casale), the world she evokes is overshadowed by the sights, sounds, and smells of industrialization. In the last section of the book, her poems take the form of biblical songs, tales, and prayers: they draw upon the author's Jewish heritage and anticipate, both stylistically and thematically, her later more experimental work, which combines elements of daily life with talmudic and cabalistic traditions.

Experimental concerns likewise inform the work of Amelia Rosselli, who, although a member of *Gruppo 63*, maintained a marginal and even critical stance toward the group's programmatic positions.[23] Although her innovations are in keeping with the neo-avant-garde's approach to language, Rosselli introduces another kind of practice into Italian poetry: her work on poetic language is shaped by her training as a musician and by her knowledge of psychoanalytic theory, specifically Jung's theories of creativity as the organization of impulses emerging from the collective unconscious.[24] Like *Gruppo 63*, Rosselli uses extensive alliteration, puns, and

23. Rosselli, *Antologia poetica*, 149–63; and idem, *Variazioni belliche*, 212–18.
24. *Poesia degli anni settanta*, 66.

neologisms. These are signs, she says, of a "logical experience," which can be "mirrored" in all languages and which is based on associations and sounds.[25] Rosselli's assertion is in accord with certain theoretical assumptions of the neo-avant-garde, particularly its belief in the global translatability of the artistic experience, which emerged from a need to build a postwar order from the ruins of two world wars. However, her multilinguistic experiments, the distinguishing feature of *Primi Scritti (1952–1963)*, and the rhythmic metrical strategies characteristic of all her work are clearly the product of her polyglot education and her scholarly interests in musical ethnology. Rosselli further distinguishes herself by the sentiments that her techniques express: an irrepressible and unfulfilled "hunger" for goodness, coupled with an anguish brought on by the unjust conditions of living — in her words, "the world's evil," "the common fraud," the "general paralysis of opinions and hopes."[26] Rosselli's poetry becomes violently expressive in *La libellula*. A lengthy and impassioned monologue, the poem weaves references to such literary "fathers" as Dino Campana, Montale, and Rimbaud into a turbulent and paradoxically "libelous" panegyric on freedom, justice, and love. Besides playing on the words *libertà* (freedom) and *libellare* (to libel), the poem's title refers to the rotating motion of a dragonfly's wings, which Rosselli takes as a model for the "delirious course" of her early writing.[27] In *Variazioni belliche*, the tumultuous stream of the poet's thought is ordered by the uniformity of the poems' "block" form. Through repeating rhythms and the deformation of grammatical conventions, these poems, which are "variations" or meditations on the conflicts that ravish worlds both within the self and without, enact a dramatic clash between a desire for love, peace, and faith, and the fatigue, disorder, and violence that plague society. Rosselli's testimony to spiritual and material suffering was the prelude to a grave illness, which caused her to withdraw into isolation and which transformed her poetic practice. The poems collected in her later *Serie ospedaliera* reflect, in the poet's words, a "melancholic deprivation of life" but also a "greater linguistic rigor."[28]

25. See "Spazi metrici" for Rosselli's theoretical discussion of her metrical experiments, which range from the free verses of her early poems — fitting for a "psychological, musical, instinctive time" — to the closed, "block" form of *Variazioni belliche*, which aims for the "universality" of a predetermined, uniform space (*Antologia poetica*, 75–81).

26. Rosselli, *Diario ottuso*, 39, 41.

27. Rosselli, *La libellula*, 33.

28. *Antologia poetica*, 157.

Giulia Niccolai joins Rosselli as the only other woman whose work has been critically linked to the neo-avant-garde. She was associated with *Gruppo 63* and founded, with Spatola, the experimental journal *Tam Tam*. Despite her fruitful relationship with *Gruppo 63*, philosophical differences led her to distance herself from the movement. In particular, she struggled with the notion, advanced in the meetings of *Gruppo 63*, that "poetry was one thing and the poet another" and concluded that such a formula was at odds with her own practice.[29] However, Niccolai continued to value the neo-avant-garde for its revitalizing effect on literature and for its insistence that the reader be made to struggle, like the author, with the text. Niccolai's early work includes concrete poems (*Humpty Dumpty*) and a series of verses composed entirely of place names (*Greenwich*). A playfulness characterizes the linguistic experiments in both books. As John Picchione and Lawrence Smith note, hers is a poetry "of puns, etymological games, and multilingual pastiches that conveys a world at once ironic, absurd, and joyously whimsical. Like the *Novissimi*, Niccolai explores the possibilities of liberating language from its fossilized accretions and linguistic stereotypes."[30] In the end, however, her poetic experiments, with their international, polyglossic emphasis and their stress on female desire, far exceed the interests of the neo avant-garde.

The surge in experimentalism that occurred in the early 1960s was tempered during the latter part of the decade. The dissolution of *Gruppo 63* coincided with a wave of international political activity and civil unrest, culminating in Italy in the anti-establishment protests of the so-called *Sessantotto* (1968) movement, which tended to sweep aside highbrow literary matters. Having advocated the transformation of society through linguistic disruption, the neo-avant-garde proved unable to suggest a direction for the protests erupting in the streets. The years of the "Italian Miracle," the rapid economic growth and industrialization that unfolded from the mid-1950s to the late 1960s and which turned Italy into the seventh most industrialized country in the world, did not result in equivalent improvements in the living conditions of the working class or in an adequate modernization of the country's social structures. Discontent peaked in what is now referred to as "hot autumn" (Fall 1969), a period of militant unrest that resulted in fundamental sociopolitical changes and brought attention to previously neglected issues and modes of activism. Students protested against

29. See Niccolai, "Niccolai, Giulia," in Piemontese, *Autodizionario*, 237–39.
30. *Twentieth-Century Italian Poetry* (1993), 15.

school systems whose authoritarian organization dated back to fascist rule; committees dedicated to environmental and women's concerns were formed; and a more democratic, grassroots labor movement developed. In turn, this flurry of political activism led to the creation of a New Left unwilling to subordinate its demands to traditional leftist platforms. For instance, it proposed a radical critique of the traditional Left's emancipationist approach to the "woman question," which, while it had aimed for the insertion of women into the work force and for their legislative protection as workers, had nonetheless neglected broader philosophical questions and concerns. Italian feminism developed as part of the New Left's general movement to pursue changes outside of formal political structures and institutions. The traditional strategy of emancipation for women was replaced by a program of activism that sought, beyond equality under the law, "new ways of being" for women, ways made possible only by bringing about a total transformation of society.[31]

"Flusso e riflusso": The 1970s

The year 1968 is generally identified as a defining moment in Italian history by those who chart social, political, and cultural developments in postwar Italy. The enthusiasm that characterized the protests of *Sessantotto* was followed, in the 1970s, by an ideological crisis, the manifestations of which ranged from a neo-conservative backlash to a surge in terrorist activity. Enzo Siciliano has called the seventies "a decade of bereavement, of terror, a decade of blood," referring to the disappointing and violent aftermath of the "progressive dawn of 1968."[32] Yet, in the wake of the protest movement, which in the name of revolutionary praxis had proclaimed the death of art, a renewed interest in poetry was emerging. As Alfonso Berardinelli notes in the preface to his important 1975 anthology *Il pubblico della poesia*, it was out of the rubble of revolutionary ideologies that poetry began again to blossom.[33]

---

31. On Italian feminism, see Hellman, "The Originality of Italian Feminism," in Testaferri, *Donna*, 15–23; Hellman, *Journeys among Women*; Birnbaum, *Liberazione della donna*; Bono and Kemp, *Italian Feminist Thought*; Bono and Kemp, *The Lonely Mirror*; and Jeffries, *Feminine Feminists*.
32. *Poesia degli anni settanta*, 13.
33. "Effetti di deriva" is the title of Berardinelli's preface to *Il pubblico della poesia*. Attending to the "drifting effects" of the 1968 protests, the essay marked the beginning of critical interest in the various poetic discourses that emerged after 1968.

A surge in enthusiasm for poetry's "rebirth," which took place at the end of the 1970s, appears to confirm Berardinelli's assertion. Faith in the expressive force of the poetic subject and a "falling in love" with the poetic word were showcased in programmatic statements and anthologies from the 1978 *La parola innamorata* to the 1985 *Viva la poesia!* In addition, the late seventies witnessed an anti-establishment "carnivalesque explosion of vitalism" that filled the void left in the aftermath of 1968.[34] One effect of this new outburst of anti-establishment sentiment was the writing of so-called "spontaneous" or "wild" poetry by marginalized figures: students, homosexuals, women, prison inmates, and workers. In their poetry, one sees a desire for private communication, a search for individual space, and a concern with existential issues over sociopolitical concerns.[35] As Isabella Vincentini notes, once these disenfranchised groups had claimed a universal right to creativity, poets who had been ignored because of their lack of commitment and political action began to follow suit, reemerging from their private enclaves to contribute to the wave of poetic activity that was gripping Italy.[36]

The most significant characteristic of Italy's "return to poetry" was the appearance of an unprecedented variety of poetic practices, the diversity of which fueled ongoing debates about the status of poetry's revival. Many young poets launched their careers under the banner of a "neo-orphic" defense of poetry,[37] while others rejected traditional literary concerns for a practice of spontaneous self-expression termed "scriversi addosso" (to write on one's body). Still other poets exhibited the continuing influence of the

---

34. Vincentini, *La pratica del desiderio*, 33–37.

35. See the anthologies *La letteratura emarginata* and *Dal fondo*.

36. Vincentini, *La pratica del desiderio*, 37–42.

37. Dino Campana's spiritual voyage in *Canti orfici* (1914) became representative of the view that poetry has a memorial, redemptive function, an "orphic" notion, which plays a fundamental role in twentieth-century Italian poetry, from Ungaretti to the most recent "neo-orphic" trends. Ancient orphic religion provides a mythical framework for modern lyrical orphism: in particular, the myth of purification or metempsychosis leading to salvation; the ritual descent into the underworld; the salvific power of the word; and a striving for absolute insight through memory's omniscience. F. J. Jones explains the fundamental difference between ancient and modern orphism as a shift from an absolutist to an existentialist perspective: "The aim of the modern orphic poet…is to recapture the multiple elements of life in their totality, but at the particular time and the particular place in which he lives." In other words, the "orphic goal of revealing the One through the Multiple changes subtly into a revelation of the perennial through the multiple, which amounts to the creation of a myth of 'absoluteness within change'" (*The Modern Italian Lyric*, 34–35).

neo-avant-garde's metapoetic practices and the impact of postmodern theory. At the same time, poets showed an increased concern with the relationship between poetry and its audience. Indeed, the seventies saw a proliferation of readings, performances, and festivals aimed at closing gaps between poets and the public, and between high and popular culture.[38] For some, this heterogeneity of expression was proof of a crisis in poetry, a state of instability and confusion at best, or "consumption and death" at worst, which mired any analysis of poetry in chaos. The strongest criticisms were made by writers who, faithful to the ideological premises of the neo-avant-garde, fought against poetic practices that seemed detached from any ideological project.[39] These writers were especially opposed to the *poeti innamorati*, who adopted a mystical-spiritual and "neo-romantic" approach to poetic expression. Mario Lunetta, for instance, takes issue with the "naive,""spontaneous" approach of a poetry fetishistically in love with itself and lacking self-irony and critical awareness, a poetry he perceives as striving for an eternal and imponderable essence.[40] Although many represent this period as one of literary and ideological crisis, it is, in fact, an extremely productive time for women, many of whom were influenced by the feminist movement's rejection of patriarchal stereotypes in the 1960s; the destruction of old notions of subjectivity became critical for women seeking to create, within and through literature, new ways of being female.

The anthologies *Donne in poesia* and *Poesia femminista italiana* offer ample evidence of the impact of the feminist movement on women's writing of the 1970s. The effect critics most often note is a so-called "feminist realism," which, characterized by a programmatic resistance to florid or highly stylized uses of language, sought to express a new female consciousness and women's desire. However, this label does not capture the complexities of the work of the poets anthologized in this period, several of whom are also present in our work: Mariella Bettarini, Biancamaria Frabotta, Armanda Guiducci, Jolanda Insana, and Dacia Maraini, who is perhaps the best known internationally of Italy's feminist activists.

38. This phenomenon led to a series of heated debates in venues such as the communist newspaper *L'Unità*. For a selection of such documents, see Lanuzza, *L'apprendista sciamano*. On the "theatricalization" of poetry in the 1970s, see Barbuto, *Da Narciso a Castelporziano*.

39. The main theoretical statements of the proponents of this ideologically oriented approach to literature are collected in Bettini and Muzzioli, *Gruppo '93*. This approach informs the work of the young poets grouped around the journal *Baldus* and of writers included in the anthology *Poesia italiana della contraddizione*.

40. *Poesia italiana oggi*, 10.

Maraini's early work (*Crudeltà all'aria aperta*) predates the rise of Italian feminism and yet addresses themes that will become central to the movement. These poems take us on a journey into the poet's psychic history, a journey driven by love for and resentment toward a father who embodies the violent and seductive practices of the patriarchal system. Maraini demonstrates the painful strain to which the poetic "I" subjects itself in remembering and understanding its history through fragmented syntax and startling, often surreal images. The formal disconnectedness of Maraini's poetry suggests the central theme of *Crudeltà all'aria aperta*: the inner "split" caused and perpetuated by the patriarchal family's demands for conformity. In *Donne mie*, the poems shift from an individual's recollection and expression of loss and alienation to a communal testimony of suffering. Maraini's feminist stance, animated by solidarity with society's silenced and marginalized victims, is expressed through a plurality of voices, including the monologues of underprivileged women who confide their daily miseries in a "spontaneous, robust, popular" language[41] and the poet's didactic, impassioned, and lyrical address to "her women." *Mangiami pure* again develops feminist themes: an ambivalent relationship with the mother figure (traced back to the mythical paradigms of Demeter and Persephone); a call to sisterhood, which identifies woman's historically determined self-hatred as the cause of divisions among women; the valorization of the revolutionary potential of woman's "thinking" body; and the fundamental ambiguousness of love, which is viewed as indispensable but also as a source of extreme violence and pain. The collection's most distinctive feature is an oscillation of registers and tones: didactic and explicitly political admonishment shifts into lyrical effusion, coarse and realistic descriptions give way to figurative expression.

Giuseppe Zagarrio, in his study of post-1968 poetry, says of the political in women's writing of the 1970s, that it is shaped by introspective analysis, philosophical meditation, and dialectic reasoning.[42] In Bettarini's poetry this is particularly evident: seething "rage," political in nature, is contained by analytical reflection. Her early work, from *Il leccio* to *Diario fiorentino*, shows the influence of the period's turbulent youth movement. In these books, she voices the rebelliousness, frustration, and hope of a generation "raised / on fire and smoke…air intake / and gas intake, life born from the blackness / of bombs, gaping oceans / and dead pigeons — without many hopes but already / no longer despairing."[43] Bettarini founded and was an active

41. Wood, *Italian Women's Writing*, 221.
42. Zagarrio, *Febbre, furore e fiele*, 403–24.
43. Bettarini, "Biografia," *La rivoluzione copernicana*.

contributor to the alternative journal *Salvo imprevisti*, which advocated a poetics based on Marxist theory, Catholic activism, psychoanalysis, and linguistic experimentation. Like Maraini, she brings to Italy's literary landscape a dynamic heteroglossia: feminist concerns and notions of civic commitment, interest in the individual unconscious, and an experimental approach to language.

Frabotta's early poems, collected in *Affeminata* and *Il rumore bianco*, are similarly characterized by the interplay of differing voices. Contemplative reflection is combined with political fervor, while rebellion against present conditions turns into a search for new ways of writing and being female. As the selection in our anthology illustrates, Frabotta often strikes a polemical note, emphasizing her ambivalent stance toward literary tradition. She discusses this ambivalence and the intellectual turmoil of the "cacophonic" 1970s in a number of critical writings, in particular her essay "Il rumore bianco" (White noise), named after her 1982 collection of poetry.[44] The piece begins with Frabotta's reflections on the essay's synesthetic title and its relation to the often contradictory characteristics of her poetic practice. "Noise," she tells us, represents the political and psychological forces dominant in her own writing and in the marginalized and anti-institutional poetic practices (rooted in the body and the emotions) common to the period. "White" represents her aspiration to silence, to the purity of a poetry dissolved into music. It is this aspiration that links her to established poetic traditions and to contemporary reactions against "noise" that re-emerged in the second half of the 1970s and were most forcefully expressed by poets such as Milo De Angelis and Giuseppe Conte. For Frabotta, these tendencies are a response to the degradation of the poetic voice, or its transformation into a noise that ultimately kills poetry.

Guiducci, in the introduction to her second collection of poems, *A colpi di silenzio*, alludes to a similar tension manifested, in her case, as a split between her poetic work, inspired by love and gratitude for the "miracle" of life, and her "stern" essayistic writings behind which she "hides," presenting herself "all clad in bronze like Athena armed from head to toe."[45] Her first collection, *Poesie per un uomo,* is the diary of a love story and celebrates the gifts of love and life in a "time / of senseless haste, foolish myths, / and vulgar joys" ("Un giorno"). Love is experienced as both truth and lie. While "relentless tenderness" ("Il sogno della ragione") is the overriding sentiment of the poems, there are references to the "shadows" that

44. See *Poesia oggi*, 242–54.
45. Guiducci, *A colpi di silenzio*, 7–11.

hover over and within relationships: bitter separation, loss, and solitude, all themes that become central in *A colpi di silenzio*. In the last part of *A colpi di silenzio*, Guiducci shifts from her own experience to that of all women, "born to the gods' disappointment / under a hesitant, impure star / in a world of knife-men," and loved "according to the laws of profit, / of power, and abuse" ("Sotto una stella impura"). While denouncing such abuse as a "dissipation" of life, she also hopes that we will eventually find different ways to love "in less aggressive fashion / in the eternity of the temporary" ("Forse un giorno ci saranno maniere"). Stylistically, Guiducci's poetry is characterized by an elegance and clarity that critics have called classical, a term often associated in Italian literary criticism with masculine virility. However, she recognizes a feminine specificity in her imagery, born of her experience as a woman. Noting, in addition, that poetry may reflect traditional gendered roles, and that such roles may produce self-censorship in choices of diction and subject matter, she acknowledges her desire to subvert conventions of "lexical modesty."

Making the body and sexual passions the central foci of their poetry, other poets in this period reject lexical modesty in order to denounce women's traditional roles in relationships. In Insana's case, emphasis on the body is related both to a feminist political call for the liberation of libidinal drives and to popular folk culture. The mocking, impertinent "phonic stabs" of her early collections, *Sciarra amara* and *Fendenti fonici*, exemplify yet another response to the disappointments and frustrations that followed 1968 and characterized the 1970s: here discontent produces a poetry of invective, an invective that draws on the rhythms and rituals of exorcism and incantation. Insana's powerful, cutting, and often scurrilous verses convey a fury that transforms language: neologisms, alliterative and paronomastic variations, and the frequent attachment of the pejorative or intensifying prefix "s" to words — close to the English "dis" but also functioning as a superlative — all contribute to the deformation of language. Although influenced by neo-avant-garde practices, Insana's poetry is rooted more specifically in the vernacular of her native Sicily.

Niccolai's work of the 1970s (which includes two collections of visual poetry and photographs, *Poema & Oggetto* and *Facsimile*, and *Harry's Bar e altre poesie*, a compilation of previously unpublished poems and reprints from *Greenwich*, *Substitution*, and *Russky Salad Ballads & Webster Poems*) demonstrates even more explicitly the continuing impact of the neo-avant-garde on women's poetic practices. This work mirrors the neo-avant-garde's anti-mimetic tendencies while demonstrating Niccolai's ongoing interest in the materiality of her media — film and photography as well as language. However, through her playful dismantling and expansion of common language, Niccolai moves away from the negative impulses of the neo-avant-garde and toward the affirmative vision she will embrace in her most recent work. In *Russky Salad Ballads & Webster Poems*, for instance, she weaves together English, French, German, Italian, and Spanish, dismantling boundaries between languages to create an *insalata linguistica* (language salad) that verges on nonsense. The poems pay explicit homage to Gertrude Stein and recall the philosophical work of Ludwig Wittgenstein, the nonsense poetry of Lewis Carroll, and children's nursery rhymes. Also exemplifying her playful practice is *Francobolli francobolli*, a brief and whimsical book that takes its readers around the world using international stamps as guideposts. The transnational expanse of the book, and the wandering it represents, are in keeping with Niccolai's description of herself as "an immigrant of the soul."[46]

Characterizing Rosselli's work of the 1970s, collected in *Documento*, is the poet's sense of emptiness against which words, destined to fall on indifferent ears, provide only the most fragile of shields. *Documento* can be read as Rosselli's dialogue with the dead, a dialogue she continues in the long poem *Impromptu*, which she wrote in 1979, but only published in 1981. Among those she seems to address in this highly complex and often allusive poem are the poet's dead father, a hero of the anti-fascist movement, and contemporary intellectuals, the "pseudo-living." Rosselli's style and subject matter in *Impromptu* recall her poetry from the 1950s and early 60s. Yet the poem also expresses the poet's desire for "lighter," more whimsical verse, an "other / history."[47] Unfortunately, this other history remains unwritten: the only books Rosselli published between 1982 and 1996, the year in which she committed suicide, were collections of earlier works.

The poets we have just discussed are generally experimental and often overtly feminist in their concerns. However, there were also many poets in the 1970s who, inspired by lyrical and ancient classical traditions, adopted more conventional approaches to poetic expression. Daria Menicanti exemplifies such a tendency. Throughout her work, Menicanti focuses on death and the transience of all connections, for instance, old lovers whose presence is now a "fantastic aura" or animals who "threaten us / but with their disappearance."[48] In keeping with classical traditions, she attaches great importance to the commemorative function of the poetic word and the

46. See Rebecca West, "Giulia Niccolai," in Russell, *Italian Women Writers*, 302–12.
47. Rosselli, *Antologia poetica*, 161 and 148.
48. Menicanti, "Di te resta," *Un nero d'ombra* and "Felini," *Altri amici*.

ability of poetry to keep the dead from fully dying: "The only ones truly dying are those / you are forgetting."[49] Inspired by the work of Catullus and the Roman Neoterics, she uses elegantly sculpted forms to express her compassion for nature and a wide range of responses to personal experiences and historical events. Although seemingly unaffected by contemporary movements and trends, Menicanti's poetry occasionally strikes a feminist chord, for instance, in poems addressed to the poet's ex-husband, a philosopher engaged in "many feats / with Thought on rarefied cliffs" and in "Contro il matrimonio," in which she denounces marriage as a crime against women.[50]

Luciana Frezza's political views emerge through her private and nostalgic reflections on childhood and home. These individual longings and recollections pave the way for her critical assessment of the bourgeois establishment, particularly in poems such as "Requiem per Sylvia Plath," "A Allen Ginsberg & C.," and "Il lavoro," which focuses on the devaluation of women's work. In "A Allen Ginsberg & C.," Frezza compares her own controlled manner of expression to methods of writing and living practiced by the Beat generation, contrasting the Beats' "storms of obscenities… / blasted splashed vomited" with the impulse of the poet who, like "the prudent fisherman… / casts the net everyday and selects / from a loot of small fish / an almost invisible spark of phosphorous."[51] Here Frezza suggests that even the most divergent poetic practices originate from the same general concerns, in particular a preoccupation with death: death due to war, the "death" of love, the "death" of childhood, the global degradation of nature, and the postmodern demise of art.

For some of the poets in this anthology, this preoccupation with death can be related to the post-1968 despondency that afflicted politically committed intellectuals. Often, however, the roots of such a preoccupation are only indirectly historical, evolving instead from more personal struggles with depression and even psychosis, as exemplified by the work of Vera Gherarducci. Central to Gherarducci's diary-like collection of poems (*Le giornate bianche* and *Giorno unico*) is the woman who suffers alone, alienated from others even as she desires connections. Gherarducci's themes include the monotony of solitude and the insignificant yet often unbearable events of daily life, which keep the poetic subject trapped in a house that is "a

49. Menicanti, "Non dire," *Poesie per un passante.*
50. Menicanti, "Epigramma XI (Contro il matrimonio)" and "Di te resta," *Un nero d'ombra.*
51. Frezza, "A Allen Ginsberg & C.," *Un tempo di speranza.*

prison" and a world that is "fear."[52] Formally, Gherarducci blends often divergent styles, moving from lyrical, romantic images of the "dusty deserted" moon, "the great calm sea," children playing on a beach — all of which evoke a past no longer accessible — to self-deprecatory descriptions that echo the work of Sylvia Plath. Gherarducci's "30 giugno" (*Giorno unico*) reads "maybe I am an idiot / maybe I am little / and still in a stroller / they ought to push me / maybe I am exhausted," recalling the following words from Plath's "Poem for a Birthday: Witch Burning": "If I am a little one, I can do no harm. / If I don't move about, I'll knock nothing over ... / Sitting under a potlid, tiny and inert as a rice grain."[53] This oscillation of styles expresses on the level of form the themes of which the poems frequently speak: the deterioration and fragmentation of the psychotic mind and a despair that is eased only by the memory of childhood, or by thoughts of death. Death is often introduced into the poems as an escape, the only available "cure" for loneliness, illness, or tedium. As the poetic subject says in "5 aprile" (*Giorno unico*), "to descend / is death / death / is bléssed."

Loss and alienation are also central themes in the poems of Patrizia Cavalli. Trapped in a world that "arrives like a quotation," Cavalli's poetic subject "vanish[es] from [herself] like an object / looked at too long."[54] Her heightened attention to fleeting, isolated images, and her sudden and often startling juxtaposition of one image with another convey her belief in the ephemerality of all things: "Of all the huntresses / the most beautiful. A candy / wrapper like a bird / without blood."[55] A recurring motif in Cavalli's work is the sky, which evokes both a "promise of light," or happiness, and "ephemeral light," the impossibility of finding contentment.[56] Fearful of disappointment, the poet struggles to maintain a safe distance from the very objects she desires, while still searching for magical encounters with which to "start [her] dreaming."[57]

52. Gherarducci, "5 aprile," *Giorno unico*.
53. Plath, *The Collected Poems*, ed. Ted Hughes (New York: Cambridge University Press, 1981). Both Gherarducci and Plath share a thematic emphasis on psychosis; more importantly, each forces us to witness the progressive deterioration and fragmentation of the poetic subject's mind. For further comparisons, see Plath's "The Ravaged Face" and "Tulips," ibid.
54. Cavalli, "Fuori in realtà non c'era cambiamento" and "Poco di me ricordo," *Poesie*.
55. Cavalli, "Di tutte le cacciatrici," ibid. The translation is from *My Poems Will Not Change the World*.
56. Cavalli, "Questa volta non lascerò che l'azzurro intravisto" and "Fra tutte le distanze la migliore possibile," *Poesie*.
57. Cavalli, "A voce dolce tu mi metti a letto," ibid.

Guidacci's work can be characterized generally by a cautious optimism, which emerges in overtly religious terms. However, in her 1970 *Neurosuite*, even this poet's optimism wanes: mother and child are irrevocably divided, the poetic subject is detached from both its body and its soul, body and soul are similarly severed from one another. Such waning is particularly evident in *Il vuoto e le forme*, which focuses on the arduousness of daily living and the poet's struggle to find reasons to exist. However, *L'altare di Isenheim* shows the poet's renewed faith in the possibility of salvation. This renewal establishes the groundwork for the religious ecstasy of *Inno alla gioia*, which was inspired by the Renaissance masterpiece, the polyptych of Isenheim by Grünewald. In the collection, Guidacci meditates on the meaning of Christ's Death and Resurrection, shifts into a dialogue with her dead husband, and concludes by announcing the rebirth of humankind from the "dust" of World War II, which was the "original sin" that spared no generation.[58]

For Spaziani and Elena Clementelli, reflections on death and dialogues with the dead occur in ancient or pre-Christian landscapes. Spaziani's poems of the 1970s serve as her "prayers"; with collected fragments of the past she seeks to replenish the present. Thus the past fills us; it is a "clamant voice in the desert, lament / ultrasound, light-year, cry of redeemed tribe."[59] Clementelli's works of this period similarly describe the poet's pilgrimage to a past which, although buried, offers a guide to those who suffer upon the confusing "surface" of the present.[60] Many of the poems suggest a state of renunciation: the poet shuts out the din of contemporary life and turns instead to a past animated by the voices of dead friends, relatives, and writers such as Rilke, "whose lights have lit [her] own."[61] As with so many poets in the 1970s, both Clementelli and Spaziani characterize the present as a void that must be filled. However, for them despair is coupled with hope as they find, in the richness of the past, seeds of a new poetry and a new present. This is particularly evident in Clementelli's work. Although she describes the poet's craft as a solitary endeavor, a "rite of silence" ("Lettere a un giovane poeta"), her journey back through time — "where the sunken silence has voices / which are not of death" — ties her to the places she inhabits and to the objects and creatures that come to surround her. In them she recognizes a "sign persisting / from stone to shore," a "long chain" linking past and present ("Quaderno etrusco").

58. Guidacci, "Plus: Poema per una nascita," *L'altare di Isenheim*.
59. Spaziani, "Ultrasuono," *Transito con catene*.
60. Clementelli, "Quaderno etrusco," *Così parlando onesto*.
61. Clementelli, "Tierras adentro" and "Lettere a un giovane poeta," *Vasi a Samo*.

Other poets of this period invent imaginary worlds as an alternative to the present, often using ancient sources to depict modern events. Ombres, in *Bestiario d'amore*, draws on classical music, Jewish folksongs, and the Talmud, as well as medieval, Renaissance, and baroque literature and art, to create fabulous realms populated by magical creatures. Fragmented narratives, tense shifts, and the breakdown of syntax make these worlds appear grotesque, absurd, and violent. And yet, Ombres's invocation of ancient cosmologies and practices also allows her to express her belief in the potency of the word and, by extension, in the power of poetry, as exemplified by her story of Bella who destroys the golem, a figure from Jewish folk history, by pronouncing its name ("Bella e il golem").

Rosita Copioli's *Splendida lumina solis* can be read as "a prehistoric dream: a dream born before the unity of conscience, of family, of state, of monotheism."[62] The book "reflect[s] a vision of female auto-erotic fantasies of generation without copulation,"[63] and depicts "the emergence of a non-human world of births and rebirths" or the "feeling of a *diffused divinity*."[64] Copioli builds her worlds from the composite Mediterranean roots of Italian culture, in particular Latin and Greek mythology. In "The Vegetative Soul," for instance, the poet, who is "the most vegetable 'I,'" invokes the Graces Aglaia (Splendor) and Euphrosine (Mirth), as she expresses her desire for "soul" and "being." Copioli's mythopoetic approach and her valorization of poetry and beauty link her to the neo-orphic practices identified with the anthology *La parola innamorata* and the journals *Niebo* and *Altro versante*, the latter edited by Copioli from 1979 to 1989.

Similar efforts to recuperate poetry from the peripheral status to which it had been relegated by activists of the 1960s occur in the journal *Prato pagano*, which published Frabotta, Gabriella Sica, and Vivian Lamarque. The editors introduce the first issue by embracing the diversity and multiplicity of emerging poetic styles, "a multitude of gods, for the lack of a god,"[65] and by refuting claims of poetry's demise. Porta, in his influential anthology of the 1970s, similarly praises the increasing heterogeneity of modern poetic movements. Any recuperation of poetry, he explains, involves a search for new definitions of literature and, as such, new literary practices. Such developments, he continues, were deeply affected by the "spirit of 1968," a spirit he identifies with the demand for modes of analysis

---

62. See Giuseppe Conte's preface to Copioli, *The Blazing Lights of the Sun*, 15.
63. Treitel, "Translator's Note," ibid., 11.
64. Conte, ibid., 16.
65. *Prato pagano* 1 (1979): 5.

beyond the boundaries of reason, new ways of conceiving of politics, and an increased interest in the concepts of "persona," "privato," and "immaginario."[66] One can certainly view the plurality and vitality of women's poetry, not only in the 1970s, but also in the 80s and 90s, in relation to this spirit. Such vitality can also be seen as proof of the lasting impact of the neo-avant-garde, both in the practices it encouraged and in the reactions it provoked. And yet, these positions are not universally embraced by scholars of Italian poetry.[67]

Crisis or Flourishing? The 1980s–1990s

In one of the more recent canon-forming anthologies, *Poeti italiani del secondo Novecento: 1945–1995,* Giovanardi offers a positive view of the heterogeneous landscape of the 1970s and 1980s. Yet, he also argues that "the diffused creativity" of the 1970s and 1980s gave way to a "devastating aridity" during the 1990s.[68] Falling back on familiar critical categories, in particular neo-avant-garde experimentalism and neo-crepuscular minimalism, he dismisses the poetry of the 90s as derivative of earlier poetic practices. As a result, he fails to capture the complexity of recent poetic developments, specifically the remarkable flourishing of women's poetry.

An entirely different picture of this evolution emerges in a recent survey of women's poetry published by Bettarini in *Poesia.* The survey celebrates the 1980s, at least for women, as a decade of "myth, irony, and a stronger [sense of] identity." As Bettarini writes, "If poetry in the 80s is characterized by a loss of Energy, a loss of the Ideal (the ideal energy) that had characterized the late 60s and, even more so, the 70s, then there is no doubt that women and their poetry appear not to have suffered from such a loss." Common to the approach of women writers, Bettarini notes, is the idea of poetry as "counter-power, [an] *other* (powerless) power against the excessive power of ease, banality, the 'quantifiable,' the cynical conviction

---

66. *Poesia degli anni settanta,* 23–30.

67. See, for instance, Carlo Bo, who argues that the diffuse styles of post-1960 poetry led to the general state of confusion and bewilderment that plagued the 1970s ("Ma dove va la poesia?" *Corriere della Sera* 11 March 1987; quoted in Vincentini, *Colloqui sulla poesia,* 8–9). See also Giorgio Manacorda's comments in "Di che reggimento siete fratelli" and "Risposte per le rime" (*La Repubblica* 1 July 1989 and 22 July 1989) on the "stagnation" that followed the confused, yet vital "drifting" of the 70s (quoted in Vincentini, *Colloqui sulla poesia,* 13).

68. *Poeti italiani del secondo Novecento: 1945–1995,* lviii

that everything can be sold (and therefore bought)."[69] From this perspective, poetry in the 1990s can be seen as even more rich and varied than that of the previous decade, "charged with stylistic force, mature, self-ironic, visionary, learned, fertile, restless, in motion."[70] Several poets included in our anthology offer evidence in support of Bettarini's assessment. Spaziani and Merini, women of the so-called fourth generation, have been especially prolific, joining Guidacci, also a fourth-generation writer, as among the most important poets of the second half of this century.

After not publishing for two decades, Merini reemerged on the poetic scene with *La Terra Santa*. The book initiated a new creative phase in Merini's career, marked by her mixing of poetry, prose, aphorisms, and improvisational writings. In texts such as *La palude di Manganelli o Il monarca del re*, poetry and prose exist side by side; the poems in *La volpe e il sipario* were improvised as they were performed and then transcribed by others; *Titano amori intorno* is conversational in style and represents a departure for Merini away from her usual emphasis on lyricism and metaphor. In *Ballate non pagate,* however, Merini again focuses on the figurative and melodic power of the word. She dedicates one of the collection's poems to Campana, underscoring the clear affinities between the two poets: both view poetry as a descent into the underworld comparable to the journeys of Dante, Orpheus, and Persephone, and describe suffering as a mythical experience. Many of Merini's poems are directly addressed to loved ones — relatives, friends, lovers, and other poets. In her most recent book, *La poesia luogo del nulla*, she calls her writing a "gift" to others, born of an irrepressible "natural force" similar to maternal, erotic, or religious love, and a "hymn to life" that bridges the distance between "dream and reality."[71]

Spaziani's work of the 1980s and 90s is also eclectic in its range of styles. *Geometria del disordine* moves her away from the rarefied atmosphere of the hermetic canon, which had earlier influenced her work, to a more open, communicative style. And yet, she remains interested in poetry's ability to bring to the contemporary world a measure of formal control, a "geometry of disorder," as the oxymoronic title of the collection suggests. *La stella del libero arbitrio* and *I fasti dell'ortica,* in particular, are characterized by the geometrical precision of their forms, a precision in keeping with Spaziani's

69. Bettarini, "Donne e poesia: Seconda parte — Dal 1980 al 1989," *Poesia* 11.121 (October 1998): 61.
70. Bettarini, "Donne e poesia: Terza parte — Dal 1990 al 1997," *Poesia* 12.124 (January 1999): 45.
71. Merini, *La poesia luogo del nulla*, 11–26.

belief that "[Beauty] is an arrow… / it is the flour you are given to / invent your own bread."[72] She addresses such topical concerns as Italy's political scandals and the war in Sarajevo alongside her most recurrent themes: the fragility of human existence and the reaffirmation of such existence through love, memory, and the poetic word. In "Alle vittime di Mauthausen" (*I fasti dell'ortica*), tears are transformed into "flags, obstinately fluttering," while an "emaciated rose shoot" blossoms "at Mauthausen behind barrack fourteen." The poem is filled with descriptions of rebirth: like the image of the blossoming rose, each rebirth suggests the rejuvenating power of poetry. Thus Spaziani reasserts her understanding of poetry as "the sole remaining space of freedom."[73]

Guidacci's work of the 1980s, from *L'orologio di Bologna* to the posthumously published *Anelli del tempo*, also points to a renewed faith in the redeeming power of poetry. Guidacci views poetry as the only means of pursuing truth and as an antidote to the noisy superficiality of contemporary life. She believes that truth becomes more accessible the more direct the form that expresses it, a belief that leads her to experiment with Japanese haiku.[74] However, Guidacci's characteristic modes of expression remain lyric contemplation and dramatic lament, as illustrated in the speeches of the Sibyls with which *Il buio e lo splendore* opens. Thematically the most striking feature of Guidacci's later poetry is her interest in the celestial bodies, a reconfiguration of the image of light central to all her work.[75] She uses the metaphor of the heavens to describe both the distance that separates lovers and the power of destiny, a power that allows her lovers to transcend their isolation. Natural images, such as the century plants of "Anniversario con Agavi" (*Anelli del tempo*), likewise serve as the poet's symbol for death, which is, for Guidacci, the common fate that unites all living things.

In Menicanti's last work *Ultimo quarto*, death is also a recurring theme while poetry is figured as an uncertain shelter against silence, "a handful / of syllables and vowels and consonants / and alliterations" through which a "dark song" can occasionally be heard ("Per una poetica"). In "Horror vacui," Menicanti explains the "necessity of all writing" as "that / of filling

---

72. Spaziani, "La mia calma che alleva nel suo seme," *I fasti dell'ortica*.
73. See Spaziani's answers to Notari's questionnaire in the anthology *Oltre il mare ghiacciato*, 40.
74. These are collected in *Una breve misura*.
75. Other central images include water (the principle of life), sand/dust (the essence of metamorphosis, emblematic of the composing and decomposing of forms), and flight (the desire for metaphysical transcendence).

the spaces of man." In other poems, she meditates explicitly on the approach of death, turning away from the personal details of her own life to the world around her. The survival of animals is a particularly prominent theme in Menicanti's work. Indeed, most of the poems in *Altri amici* are dedicated to non-human "Other Friends," viewed as similar to, or better than, the people who now threaten the animals' survival.

Animals play an even more prominent role in the work of Luciana Notari, for whom the meaning of life reveals itself in nature. Notari's poetry expresses her hope that the human spirit, stifled by a contemporary obsession with appearance and by consumerism, may find its animal roots and live "on familiar terms" with all living things.[76] This desire is premised on her belief that the soul is inextricable from matter and that the essence of existence cannot be found in intellectual abstractions. "Life is not in the answer, / life is in life," Notari declares in "La vita è nella vita." In her most recent book, *Aiuole di città*, Notari eschews the elegiac tones of her earlier work, using concise images to communicate her sympathies with "repudiated Nature" ("Aspra stagione metropolitana") and her belief in the all-encompassing power of love. For Notari, the poet's task is not to engage in polemics or in specific environmental causes but rather to speak with reverence of the breadth of the spirit, the link that connects all beings.

Among the poets who adopt a reverential approach to the poetic word, some, like Clementelli in her recently published *Il conto*, pay homage to poetry by using it as a vehicle to criticize the absurdities of modern life. Clementelli's images and musical cadences are often based on classical traditions (the work of Catullus in particular), but are also inspired by later writers such as Federico García Lorca, Juan Ramón Jiménez, Pedro Salinas, and Antonio Machado. At the same time, her poems address social and political themes, ranging from the disproportionate gap between the affluent West and the so-called third world to the alienating conditions of life in contemporary society, where poetry is exiled and poets have become "zealous accountants…alchemists / at best."[77] In keeping with the collection's title, (The reckoning), the poet takes stock of her life, measuring it against historical changes. She combines irony and parody with a "mobility of register[s]" that corresponds, as she states in the book's preface, to the actual "mood swings" of her "encounters/collisions on the page."

Irony is also an important part of Cavalli's recent work, collected in *Poesie* and *Sempre aperto teatro*. The title of Cavalli's latest collection (Always

76. Notari, "Il corpo e l'anima," *La vita è nella vita*.
77. Clementelli, "Diatriba," *Il conto*.

open theater) suggests the self-reflective nature of her irony, calling attention to the poet's dual role as protagonist and spectator of the drama that unfolds.[78] Throughout the book Cavalli adopts the traditional lyric forms of courtly love and confessional poetry. Yet she also subverts these forms, depicting the poetic subject as a self-conscious performer on an empty stage. Haunted by her own isolation, the poet shifts her "tender gaze" onto herself,[79] turning her love songs into a commentary on her own failures. While there are clear thematic and stylistic links between Cavalli's early collections and her most recent work, her later poetry is characterized by her increasing openness to the outside world. Indeed, the new book begins with an invocation of love ("Oh loves — false or true / be love, happily move / in the void that I offer you") and ends on a note of joyous fulfillment: "What is lost / is returned to me /...I am inside / and the outside enters me."[80]

Vivian Lamarque, author of five collections of poems and a number of children's books, represents an equally original voice in contemporary Italian literature. The uniqueness of her work, already apparent in her first book *Teresino*, stems from her use of nursery-rhyme cadences and fable-like images to convey highly charged, often nightmarish material: a fairy-tale world is tossed into a tornado-like whirlwind; a mailman's hand is severed in a dream; lovers say goodbye unaware that their parting is final; a young girl stitches her mouth closed, unable to speak. Lamarque's three later collections (*Il signore d'oro*, *Poesie dando del Lei*, and *Il signore degli spaventati*), emerging out of the poet's experience in psychoanalysis, are composed of brief, whimsical verses and examine, with an often startling playfulness, a traumatic history of abandonment, isolation, and fleeting joy. Her most recent book, *Una quieta polvere*, alludes more directly to social realities: the difficulties of immigration ("Vù cumprà"), the absurdity of racism ("Di colore"), and the horrors of war ("Ruanda").

In Anna Cascella's work, the contrast between an apparent stylistic "lightness" and thematic gravity is also apparent. Her poetry is filled with epiphanies drawn from a small treasure of daily experiences, as suggested by the titles of her collections, *Tesoro da nulla* (Trifling treasure) and *Piccoli Campi* (Small fields). Giovanni Giudici has likened her work to the poetic practices of Sandro Penna, but, he explains, whereas Penna "caresses" his reader, Cascella "pricks with miniscule thorns, like those of the prickly pear" and

78. Cavalli, "La scena è mia, questo teatro è mio," *Sempre aperto teatro*.
79. Cavalli, "Lo sguardo tutto intenerito," ibid.
80. Cavalli, "O amori — veri o falsi" and "Quel che è perduto mi è restituito," ibid.

"scratches with the claws of a cat."[81] Frustrated love is a central theme in Cascella's poetry and accounts for the "melancholy [that cuts] across the joy of her writing."[82] In poems such as "Il nomade del cielo" (*Tesoro da nulla*), love and pain are inextricably linked and expressed through highly charged, surreal images. Other poems, in more ironic and conversational fashion, address a male "you" who is too concerned with intellectual abstractions and the gratification of his own needs to care for anyone else.[83]

Gabriella Sica's carefully wrought end-rhymes create a similarly productive opposition: on the one hand they give her verses the appearance of sentimentality, on the other hand they demonstrate a deliberateness that underscores the gravity of her subject matter. This opposition is exemplified by the series "Per il mare" (*Vicolo del Bologna*), which contrasts the aspirations of a masculine "you" engaged in the life-long pursuit of his childhood's dreams — sailing on pirate ships and discovering mysterious treasures — with a feminine "I" who beckons him back to "firm ground." Pleasures desired by the feminine "I" are at the core of most of Sica's poems, from her first book, *La famosa vita*, to her most recent work, *Poesie bambine*, which focuses on the distress of a needy "child soul" ("Anima mia candida") and on the joys of a maternal soul in love with the innocence and grace of childhood ("Poesie per un bambino" and "In bicicletta"). In her preface to *Vicolo del Bologna*, Sica describes her intention to celebrate such grace with "courage" and "order"[84] and to indulge in an idyllic depiction of "a beautiful and natural life," even though she is aware that such life may be the dream of a "simple poet out of time."[85]

In general, the poets in this anthology who use traditional meters and rhymes do so to create some "measure of sense" against the "anguished imbalances" of life, as Gabriella Leto explains in "L'amore il sogno il verso" (*L'ora insonne*). Indeed, Leto believes that poetry has a curative power, as is suggested by the title of one of the sections of her *Nostalgia dell'acqua*, "Pharmaca," from the Greek *phármakon*, meaning drug or remedy. Elsewhere Leto compares the "grace" and "strength" of poetry to the force expressed by the fingers of a musician's hand.[86] This analogy is warranted

81. Giudici, "Danzando con le parole," in Cascella, *Piccoli Campi*, 8–9. Giudici calls the movement of Cascella's longer poems "feline" and compares their grace to that of classical dancing.
82. Ibid., 7.
83. See, in particular, "Finanche il tuo fuggire è un po' speciale," *Tesoro da nulla*.
84. Sica, *Vicolo del Bologna*, 7.
85. Sica, "Poesie per le oche," ibid.
86. Leto, "Come le lamine di una corolla," *L'ora insonne*.

by the musical quality of Leto's verses, which she produces with subtle variations of tone and a complex structure of meter and rhyme. Leto's attention to traditional verse forms distances her from the more typical emphasis in contemporary poetry on free verse. At the same time, this traditionalism links her to poets such as Sica, who combine a modern sensibility with a classical handling of structure.

Like Sica and Leto, Patrizia Valduga skillfully uses traditional poetic forms such as the sonnet, *terza rima*, and the ballad stanza. She draws on the most varied sources, from the Petrarchan tradition to baroque mysticism, from Dante to Rilke, conferring literary "dignity" on her often scurrilous themes. Luigi Baldacci has suggested that Valduga's practice of pilfering and rebuilding from the "rubble" of the lyric tradition indicates the existence of an impasse in postmodern literature, one that makes poetry unable to move forward, or capable only of revisiting the past.[87] Yet Baldacci fails to characterize accurately Valduga's primary goal, which emerges most clearly in *La tentazione*: to demonstrate, in a transgressive and ironic manner, the ways in which Western culture has reduced women to an "obscure shadow" and created a universal "nausea" of "emptiness," a "collapse of the dead on [the] living," and a "putrid lethargy."[88] Valduga describes the seductive nature of such a heritage with sarcastic invectives, giving "flesh and blood" to an impassioned female speaker who re-enacts the violence she has suffered at the hands of patriarchal culture.

The revisionist tendency that we see in Valduga is central to women's poetry in the 1980s and 90s. For instance, in *Parabola sub* Frezza revisits the myth of Orpheus and Eurydice with a subversive twist, making Eurydice rather than Orpheus her symbol of poetry. The collection's title describes the experience of one who is "below" water, uninterested in the surface of things and immersed in the obscure dimension of dreams.[89] Such dreams offer a glimpse into the underside of reality, or the essence that is hidden from those "above." Venus, the goddess of love, is another of the mythical figures in *Parabola sub*, as is Isis, the Egyptian goddess who pieces together the dismembered body of her spouse and brother Osiris. As with Eurydice, Frezza makes Venus and Isis the protagonists of their stories. Isis, tired of chasing after Osiris and assisting in his cyclical resurrection, chooses to lose

87. Baldacci, "La parola immedicata," in Valduga, *Medicamenta e altri medicamenta*, vi.
88. Valduga, *La tentazione*, in *Cento quartine e altre storie d'amore*, 138, 141, and 159. In Valduga's work, the diseased body is often emblematic of the degradation of the social and political body.
89. See Pedullà's introduction to Frezza's *Parabola sub*.

him forever in order to assert the "difference of [her] being" ("Iside"), while Venus subverts her seemingly perfect relationship with Adonis, hoping to anticipate and control fate.

Copioli also makes women protagonists of myth and history, freeing figures such as Helen and Eurydice from their traditional roles as objects of male desire by allowing them to articulate their own desires and beliefs. Copioli shares with Valduga the tendency to weave lines from other poets seamlessly into her own work. However, unlike Valduga she draws primarily on the ancient classics, in particular Lucretius and Ovid, and on romantic and symbolist poets such as Giacomo Leopardi and W. B. Yeats. In a recent essay Copioli explains that she revises myths and poetic traditions to make a common heritage more personal and, in turn, to make the poetic self into the "threshold" of a symbolic experience.[90] Such tasks, she says, are especially arduous for women, since traditionally women have been denied an active role in the making or reshaping of myths. In *Furore delle rose* and *Elena*, Copioli searches further for a new woman's voice, using lyrical incantations that recall the speeches of the ancient prophetesses: "And her mute lips murmured: / Yours is the invincible night, / a married death. Your dreams / decay like flesh."[91]

The quest for a new voice is a common concern of those writers whose poetry in the 1970s was shaped by feminism and characterized by a subversive stance toward literary tradition. By 1976 Frabotta had published her now famous anthology *Donne in poesia* in which she argued for the creation of a "third way" beyond the polemics of early feminist literature. The book included statements on the status of women's writing by poets such as Guidacci, Spaziani, Frezza, Gherarducci, Rosselli, Niccolai, Guiducci, Oppezzo, Maraini, and Bettarini. Oppezzo, in particular, while acknowledging the voice given to her by the feminist movement, expressed the need for a further revitalization of women's poetic practices: "Now that silence has turned into words, I find myself using analytical words…and instead I want words that are only expression, that are voice, sound, pause. A word (and a silence) that isn't in the service of confrontation, and therefore instrumental, but simply is. That's enough. Because to be is the most revolutionary of acts."[92] We see Oppezzo implicitly reiterating such claims in the experimentally rich monologues of her 1987 *Le strade di Melanctha*,

90. Copioli, "Occorre tempo per una musica nuova," in Gaeta and Sica, *La parola ritrovata*, 112.
91. Copioli, "Euridice," *Furore delle rose*.
92. See Oppezzo's response to Frabotta's "Inchiesta poetica" in *Donne in poesia*, 166–67.

which portray Melanctha's attempts to escape the artificiality of the contemporary world. In her note to the poem, Oppezzo describes Melanctha, a character she borrows from Gertrude Stein,[93] as one who, tired of conventional forms of communication, speaks to herself elliptically and continuously because "silence is a container." To depict Melanctha's continuous movement and to represent the difficult, even dangerous expression of a feminine desire that exceeds preconstituted roles and boundaries, Oppezzo distorts the syntax of the poem. Such fragmentation is in keeping with her belief that feminine difference is often found in the "fractures, in the reduction of language…that is to say in silence, lived as the sole alternative to an impossible expansion."[94]

The desire to embark on new courses can also be seen in Bettarini's poems of the late 1970s, specifically "Dico che il grillo lo scorpione la cavalletta," in which she rejects the psychological concerns of her earlier work to denounce society's neglect of the world and its obsession with the individual: "plenty has been said about the subject / and it is better to speak of the object / in clear letters clear notes in the clearest / cries / because the woods have already caught fire" (*In bocca alla balena*). In her work of the 1980s and 90s, Bettarini explores a variety of media, themes, and forms, fragmenting syntax and experimenting with puns and sound-play. In one of her most recent collections, *Case, luoghi, la parola*, her interest in experimentation emerges as love for "the word," which is everything for the poet: "mother" and "daughter," "abode — nest — hostel / retreat — relief / shelter — den — umbrella / consolation — pole" ("La casa del poeta"). Like the objects inspiring Bettarini's poems, words function as bridges between the subjective "inside" and the universal "outside," conveying the poet's belief that "form" can have an impact "on life and death / on the collective and plural / on the / individual personal fate" ("Il fotografo").

While Bettarini's latest poetry features the home as a central trope, suggesting the poet's desire to feel "at home" in language and in the world, Frabotta's recent work foregrounds the metaphor of the journey, as announced by the titles of her collections *Appunti di volo* (Flight notes) and *La viandanza* (The wayfaring). In her critical writings, Frabotta explains her revision of the literary trope of the journey as an effort born from her need to discover new, viable forms for self-representation. Indeed, Frabotta believes that women cannot recognize themselves in the images of the traveler

93. For Stein's descriptions of Melanctha, see *Three Lives* (New York: Random House, 1909; rpt., 1987).
94. *Donne in poesia*, 166.

sanctified by Western culture and that thus they should not remain attached to the value systems these images represent. In *Terra contigua*, Frabotta uses the image of a "contiguous land" to ground her poetic project in a humble, precarious space, outside and yet adjacent to the protected "preserve" of literary tradition, a marginal domain in which "one cannot hunt, fish or build," but only plant, cultivate trees, and walk, "listening to the park's echoes and to its invisible life."[95] This juxtaposition between the journey and more rooted endeavors reflects tensions that run throughout her work: the balance between chaotic "noise" and music, "random flight" and ordered patterns, and the "insane reason" (or inebriated passion) of the brain's right hemisphere and the left hemisphere, which analyzes and restrains excess passion or ambition.[96] Frabotta's texts are rich in syntactic and semantic ambiguities and sound-play, all of which are designed to express the movement of the poet's thoughts. Like Gradiva to whom one of the poems is dedicated, her writing is "at once still and in motion, looking ahead and thinking back," "the tip of one foot" touching the ground while the other "scorns it / fermenting among distracted toes the no longer current / gift of a returning path."[97]

Maraini also uses the journey to describe women's experiences of living and writing. Like Frabotta's wayfaring, Maraini's journey is driven by the desire for new beginnings ("to cross the threshold of the house / is to revive from one's own ashes") and by nostalgia for what is left behind ("tomorrow morning I will go / with or without luggage / because waiting for me out there / is nostalgia for the return").[98] Her journey takes her into the recesses of memory where ghosts, such as a "child who died many years ago," materialize ("nel ventre dalle arcate gotiche"). Such memories produce disquieting effects, as when the recollection of a hot August in Spain makes "milk curdle in [the poet's] veins" ("una giostra a Tibidabo"). Maraini's poetic world is populated by cruelly sweet lovers, like the beautiful, jade-eyed man who eats a woman's heart in "ho sognato un porco," and the man with "milk-white eyes and hands" who "slices [the poet's] heart with a knife / then wants to give it compassionate treatment" ("un uomo

95. Frabotta, *Terra contigua*, 5.
96. Frabotta, "Gemina iuvant," *Appunti di volo e altre poesie*.
97. Frabotta, "Gradiva," *La viandanza*. For Frabotta's discussion of Gradiva as a figure for wayfaring poetry, see *Scrittori, tendenze letterarie e conflitto delle poetiche in Italia (1960–1990)*, ed. Rocco Capozzi and Massimo Ciavolella (Ravenna: Longo, 1993), 89.
98. Maraini, "un piede avanti e uno indietro" and "viaggiando con passo di volpe," *Viaggiando con passo di volpe*. Additional quotes from Maraini's poems come from this collection.

bruno"). Each of these male figures recalls the seductive father of *Crudeltà all'aria aperta* whose early betrayals, we learn, continue to shape the experiences of a now grown daughter. From this first collection to the most recent *Se amando troppo*, Maraini's poems connect familial love, friendship, and sexual love, and expose the potential brutality of each. In discussing her reaction to the poetry of earlier writers such as Sappho and Emily Dickinson, Maraini writes that she was intrigued by "the bitter mystical flavor" of Dickinson's poetry and the "happy and ferocious violence" that pervaded Sappho's work.[99] Maraini joins Sappho and Dickinson in a tradition of women poets who combine violence and pleasure, the fantastic and the mundane, the rational and the seemingly absurd.

Insana's work of the 1980s and 90s can be linked to the same tradition. As in her early poems, rage is Insana's *modus vivendi*: "I rage, therefore I am," reads a line in "Perché ti arrabbi tanto" (*Il collettame*). Playing on her family name, which means "insane" or "furious," she speaks in combative, caustic, even raving tones.[100] Such tones are used to describe the traditional silencing of women writers, which Insana casts as a mutilation of the female body: "they cut off my little girl's hand / to write I use a plasticine stump" ("Perché ti arrabbi tanto"). At the same time, she uses sorcery and cooking as figures for a curative writing practice. In "Il magico quadrato" (*Medicina carnale*), the poetic subject's need for "poison" is explained in homeopathic terms: because she loves "the sting of life" she cannot avoid taking daily doses as an antidote against life's "bitter poison." Rejecting the sweetness traditionally associated with the feminine voice, Insana defines her poetry as an "alchemy of enchantments and irony" ("Perché ti arrabbi tanto") and thus refuses the role of the poetess-as-seductress in favor of the "scannaparole," the word-butcher.[101] Insana's latest work, *L'occhio dormiente*, moves away from the verbal jabbing of her earlier "fendenti fonici." The title of the collection, translatable as "the sleeping eye" or "the dormant bud," suggests both the poet's visionary gaze "that knows secrets secretly seeing with other eyes" ("L'urlo di Abû Nuwàs") and the writer who is a careful cultivator of the earth's fruits, experienced in the craft of grafting, sowing, and harvesting.

Overall, as we have seen, the two "opposite poles" of postwar poetry in Italy have tended to converge during the last two decades. On the one

99. See Maraini's response to Frabotta's "Inchiesta poetica" in *Donne in poesia*, 168.
100. Many of Insana's verses recall the poetic duels fought against male rivals by Veronica Franco, one of the most original of Renaissance women poets. See *Women Poets of the Italian Renaissance,* edited by Laura Anna Stortoni and Mary Prentice Lillie (New York, Italica Press, 1997), 196–207.
101. Insana, *Il collettame*, 6.

hand poets close to the hermetic tradition, and hence sympathetic to po-
etry that emphasizes the symbolic, mythical, redemptive power of language,
have recently shown interest in irony, experimental multilinguism, and greater
linguistic play. On the other hand poets influenced by neo-avant-garde and
feminist movements, and thus concerned with the "material" aspects and
critical function of language, have adopted more spiritual stances. Niccolai's
work most clearly reflects the latter development. The goal of her spiritual
quest is, as Niccolai puts it, "a natural, spontaneous equanimity between the
Self and the Other" ("il Sé e l'Altro-da-sé"), which also involves a desire
"to transcend the duality of masculine–feminine."[102] In recent years Niccolai
has tried to repair what she perceives as gaps between the poet, text, and
reader. Explaining the title of her 1994 collection *Frisbees (poesie da lanciare)*,
she writes the following: "I [have] given the title of Frisbees to these poems
in order to communicate the concept of the indispensable interaction be-
tween speaker and listener, a 'game of returns' necessary if we are to knock
down the invisible wall that separates [them]."[103] For Niccolai, *Frisbees* rep-
resents a new receptiveness to the world, to linguistic accidents, and to
coincidences, all of which emerge from a new form of thinking. Her po-
ems suggest that convergences are everywhere: in sounds, history, dreams,
even in the most mundane details of our lives. To attend to such convergences
is, in effect, to throw the frisbee back, to engage in a "game of returns."

The recent surge in publications by women writers demonstrates the
most significant development in late twentieth-century Italian poetry: a
newly emerged inclusiveness and openness to a wide range of literary ap-
proaches, combined with a willingness to turn both to past practices and to
future technologies for guidance and inspiration. From the vantage point
of the end of the twentieth century, one can view the evolution of women's
poetry as a reaction against so-called feminine sentimentality and as a com-
plication of feminist protest poetry. Challenging the dichotomy between
feminist polemics and traditional lyricism, these authors turn their own
cultural and poetic ambivalences into thematic and methodological strengths.

---

102. Niccolai comments on this goal in a statement (dated January 10, 1999), which
appears as a note to one of her recent poems, published in the journal of the Milanese
Libreria delle Donne. See *Via Dogana* 42 (February 1999): 9.
103. Niccolai, "Postfazione," *Frisbees (poesie da lanciare)*, 151.

L

ON TRANSLATION

"I hope that those who know both languages will find some pleasure in my moments of literal fidelity...as well as in those moments when I am unfaithful." With these lines, Agha Shahid Ali introduces his translation of the Urdu poet Faiz Ahmed Faiz.[1] Over the years, lack of fidelity has led to the creation of many beautiful translations. A memorable example is Robert Bly's version of Rilke's "Manchmal steht einer auf beim Abendbrot," from the *Book of Hours,* in which, as Robert Hass notes, Bly opts for the word "stay" instead of the more literal "die" to translate the German *stirbt*: "Sometimes a man stands up during supper / and walks outdoors, and keeps on walking, / because of a church that stands somewhere in the East. / ...And another man, who remains inside his own house, / *stays* there, inside the dishes and in the glasses, / so that his children have to go far out into the world / toward that same church, which he forgot."[2]

When we began our project, a boldness such as Bly's would have been inconceivable to us. We were focused on the pleasures of exactness, primarily because our task seemed more pedagogical than aesthetic: to teach the English reader, through a series of translations, about Italian poetic practices and traditions. Of course, such a direct linking of one language or culture to another is rarely achievable.[3] Often to remain in contact with each poem, we had to draw away from it, focusing not on the ways in which individual words transferred from Italian into English, but on how images, cultural allusions, meter, and rhyme moved or, as was often the case, failed to move from one language to another. In the process we considered the following questions: could the same images used by a poet in Italy be made meaningful to an American audience? If not, how could we alter the image but keep intact the poet's inflections and tone? Was there a particular constellation of images which, when recreated in English, would impart equivalent meaning? Last, but certainly not least, could we communicate the

1. Agha Shahid Ali, "*The Rebel's Silhouette:* Translating Faiz Ahmed Faiz," *Between Languages and Cultures: Translation and Cross-Cultural Texts,* ed. Anuradha Dingwaney and Carol Maier (Pittsburgh: University of Pittsburgh Press, 1995), 87.

2. Robert Hass, "Introduction," *The Selected Poetry of Rainer Maria Rilke,* ed. and trans. Stephen Mitchell (New York: Vintage International, 1982), xviii.

3. As Walter Benjamin famously notes, "no translation would be possible if in its ultimate essence it strove for likeness to the original." See "The Task of the Translator," *Illuminations,* ed. and with an introduction by Hannah Arendt, trans. Harry Zohn (New York: Schocken Books, 1968), 73.

specific ways in which authors manipulated and played with language? These questions remained with us, shaping our choice of language and diction as we struggled to maintain, for instance, the rich puns of Niccolai's "Harry's Bar Ballad" or the neologisms of Insana and Rosselli. In the case of "Harry's Bar Ballad," we opted, as our footnotes indicate, to "mistranslate" words, altering expressions to keep the essence of the puns intact. The relationship we generally sought with the poems was, to borrow the words of Susan Handelman, "intimate but not mimetic."[4]

Because Italian is a naturally rhyming language, the translation of cadence and rhyme turned out to be our most difficult task. The endings of verbs, nouns, and adjectives in Italian — for example, -are, -ere, -ire for the infinitive of verbs and -ato, -uto, -ito for the past participle — means that words commonly echo one another with an ease lacking in English. Consequently, end rhymes in Italian poetry do not sound artificial, or overly crafted, as they might in English. And yet, an abundance of rhymes in our translations would very likely have suggested a naive or precious attention to language on the part of the Italian writers. To avoid this impression, while still approximating the cadences of each poem, we often substituted slant rhymes, internal rhymes, alliteration and assonance for what, in the Italian, were more precise end rhymes. For instance, in Leto's "Davvero troppo tardi sei tornata" we used "late," "heart," and "night" to suggest relationships conveyed in the Italian by the rhyme in "ore" and "cuore." To link words and images in Sica's "Per il mare," we relied on a long chain of slant-rhymes and alliterations: "shout," "shelter," "shores," "ocean," "shun." Our aim in each case was to preserve the overall movement and breadth of the work.

In some instances, the difference between Italian and English led us to make changes we knew would distort the original. Often this entailed simplifying syntax so that the relationship between subjects, objects, and actions would make sense in English. This does not mean that we made the English poems easier to comprehend, but rather that we allowed English syntax to reshape the Italian. In other instances, we wanted the Italian to affect the English more directly. For example, in Maraini's "storie famigliari" we allowed Italian syntax to seep into the English sentence structure, reinforcing the sense of narrative fragmentation so central to the original. Maraini's work taught us many things: "io sono due," for instance, made us

4. Susan A. Handelman, *Fragments of Redemption: Jewish Thought and Literary Theory in Benjamin, Scholem, and Levinas* (Bloomington: Indiana University Press, 1991), 29. See Handelman for an insightful discussion of Benjamin's theories of language and translation.

aware of the difficulties of rendering the gender of a poetic subject from Italian into English. In the original poem the gender of the subject is clearly marked. The verb endings "a" in "nata" (born) and "morta" (died) tell us that the speaker of the poem is female, as does Maraini's use of "una" instead of "uno." In our translation we found no way of alluding to gender until the very end of the piece. Indeed, we could easily have excluded references to gender altogether by changing "she" in the fourth from last line of the poem to "one": "and if one were not two *she/one* would be zero." By de-emphasizing the gender of the speaker until the poem's very end, what we brought to the poem was, we believe, an important delay: added to the apparently neutral gender of the work is the shock of having that neutrality abruptly undermined. In this way we hoped not to ignore questions of gender raised by the poem, but rather to underscore them.

Recent theories of translation assert the centrality of the translator's perception and voice, particularly with respect to poetry.[5] Such centrality does not necessarily obscure the voice of the original writer, but rather creates a framework of language and rhythms in which the poet and translator may converse across cultures and time. In our project, this interaction was further enhanced by the fact that the translations themselves were collaborative acts, involving a process of intellectual and cultural exchange between a native speaker of English and a native speaker of Italian. Our challenge was to develop a method that allowed our two languages to exist simultaneously and that enhanced the intermingling of the translators' and poets' voices. Shaping this process was the wide variety of poetic styles with which we were contending. This variety is what most distinguishes the challenge of translating an anthology from that of translating a single poet. If translating one poet can be likened to crossing a river between languages, with a distinctive poet's style serving as the bridge, then translating an anthology is like having to rely on widely-spaced stones to make the crossing. (In many ways, this parallels the experience of reading an anthology.) Although we began this project hoping to make our leaps without getting too wet, it was often in the moments of tripping, of getting our feet wet, that the pleasures of translating arose. Having said this, we return to Ali's quote, hoping, as he did, that you as our readers "will find some pleasure in [our] moments of literal fidelity…as well as in those moments when [we were] unfaithful."

5. Steve McCaffery, ed., *Rational Geomancy: The Kids of the Book-Machine. The Collected Research Reports of the Toronto Research Group 1973–1982* (Vancouver: Talonbooks, 1992), 29.

Contemporary Italian

Women Poets

Daria Menicanti

Camaleonte[*]

> …he is nothing and he is all:
> he is the chameleon poet
>
> —*John Keats*

Ma sono — oltre che me — sono sul guscio
d'un fiore il mite grillo
dell'estate inquilino —
o l'urlo abbandonato dell'ossesso
sul marciapiede riverso —
o sono cane
lupino che abbaia alla strada
avventato ai cancelli —
o, lungo i cornicioni,
gatta sottile ignara di padroni —
o, ancora, per i viali e gli alberati
la ribalda che vende una sapiente
sfioritura di sé —
o, perché no? — la pioggia
calma e solenne dopo il temporale
d'una giornata cieca —
o la siepe recisa
d'arte a regola in sangue dolorante
atroci amputazioni —
o questa stessa strada che alle soglie
di via Marcello agghinda
di edicole e mercati i suoi cantoni.
Tutto questo e — di nuovo —
la brace che si spegne dentro sé.

aprile 1962

[*]From *Città come* (City as, 1964).

Daria Menicanti

Chameleon

> *...he is nothing and he is all:*
> *he is the chameleon poet*[1]

— John Keats

But I am — other than me — I am the gentle cricket
on the shell of a flower
summer's tenant —
or the forsaken howl of the possessed
supine on the sidewalk —
or I am lupine
dog barking at the street
hurled against the gates —
or, along eaves,
slender cat unaware of masters —
or, again, along avenues and tree-lined roads
the rogue who sells her skillful
withering —
or, why not? — the rain
calm and solemn after the storm
of a blind day —
or the hedge cut off
by expert hand in aching blood
atrocious amputations
or this very street that at the threshold
of Via Marcello dresses up
its corners with kiosks and markets.
All this and — again —
the embers that inside are dying out.

April 1962

Di te resta[*]

aprile 1964
a G. P.

Di te resta sospeso nelle stanze
un leggero sospiro di tabacco
francese,
l'eco delle tante imprese
col Pensiero per balze rarefatte.
Resta di te l'alone romanzesco
degli amori di vecchio Don Giovanni
tenero e stanco, quasi senza impegno
ghermitore di soffici colombe.

Non so[*]

settembre 1964

Non so. Mi chiedo quanto può durare
questa mia vita e intanto mi innamoro
d'ogni cosa e ne seguo con le dita
i contorni e mi specchio nei colori.
Così sono felice di ciascuno,
di costoro con cui sorrido e parlo,
di costui per cui vivo e mi abbandono.
E intanto da ogni cosa e da ciascuno
giorno per giorno mi vo congedando.

Ai lettori che mi scrivono[†]

Ne ignoro bocca odore voci tatto,
ma sono questi miei amici volanti
le loro care lettere
a chiudere sopra di me l'infallibile
colpo di rete e la vecchia farfalla
tutte le volte è presa

---

[*]From *Un nero d'ombra* (A blackness of shadow, 1969).
[†]From *Poesie per un passante* (Poems for a passerby, 1978).

What's Left of You

> April 1964
> to G. P.[2]

What's left of you hanging in the rooms
is a light breath of French
tobacco,
the echo of so many feats
with Thought on rarefied cliffs.
Left is the fantastic aura
of the affairs of old Don Juan
tender and tired, an almost effortless
snatcher of soft doves.

I Don't Know

> September 1964

I don't know. I wonder how long this life of mine
can last and meanwhile I fall in love
with each thing and follow its contours
with my fingers and look at myself in the colors.
So I am happy with everyone
the ones with whom I smile and talk,
the one for whom I live and give myself away.
And meanwhile from everything and everyone
day by day I am taking leave.

To the Readers Who Write to Me

I ignore their mouth smells voices touch,
but it is such flying friends of mine
their dear letters
that close over me the infallible
scoop of net, and the old butterfly
is caught every time.

Epigramma per un verme*

Un verme tranquillo e bavoso
d'un roseo infantile fa il traghetto
del viale.
Mi domando perché poi
mi faccia quasi tenerezza...Ah, sì:
è perché ti assomiglia, mio diletto

Se*

Con l'ultimo giardino la strada
s'insabbia, s'impaluda in un'orchestra
di rane. Steso, chiaro
mi arriva lo stagno con bruschi
cespugli, con piante leggère.
C'è un'aria di abbandono e di rivalsa
intorno alle paludi: se ne vive
ciascuno della vita e della morte
dell'altro: e questo bel verde innocente
della felce ricciuta si fa —
come il resto — da un lungo cimitero.
 E qui ritrovo quel mio divenire
infinito con tutta l'altra terra
e la saggezza ironica: sapere
d'essere sostituibile sempre.
— Se questo, dico all'improvviso, questo
fosse il mio ultimo giorno —
 E subito di tutto m'innamoro
tanto ogni cosa mi risembra bella
nella sua fuga, ogni spiro, ogni insetto.
E quel tuo viso stesso
— che ieri non riuscivo più a vedere —
ecco ridiventarmi fiore e festa.
 O vita, o cara mia felicità.
Mi sento nuovamente buia e calda
come una linfa di pianta nel sole,
come una cosa amata

---

*From *Poesie per un passante* (Poems for a passerby, 1978).

Epigram for a Worm

A worm tranquil and slobbering
rosy like an infant makes the crossing
over the avenue.
I wonder why on earth
it gives me almost tender feelings…Ah, yes:
it's because it resembles you, my darling

If

With the last garden the road
becomes silted, swamped in an orchestra
of frogs. Outstretched, clear
the pond reaches me with brusque
bushes, with light plants.
There is an air of surrender and revenge
around swamps: everyone
lives off the life and death
of another: and this beautiful innocent green
of the curly fern grows —
like the rest — from a long cemetery.
 Here I recover my becoming
infinite with all other earth
and the ironic wisdom: the knowledge
of always being replaceable.
— If this, I suddenly say, this
were my last day —
 And with all things I fall in love at once
so beautiful each thing again appears
in its flight, every breath, every insect.
And your very face
— that yesterday I could no longer see —
now becomes flower and feast to me.
 Oh life, oh my dear happiness.
I again feel dark and warm
as a plant's sap in the sun,
as a thing loved

Felini*

La lunga tigre lucente, il leopardo fiorito
— la guardinga, la silenziosa grazia —
tuttora ci minacciano
ma della loro scomparsa

Gabbiani*

Gabbiani blu gridano ai pesci ingiurie
parolacce. Gridano in Gabbiano
ai pesci: ehi, voi! ehi, voi!
Ci si buttano sopra imprecando.
Ultimamente i cieli
si erano fatti così muti che
perfino quest'ira dall'aria
sembra piacevole cosa se pure
atroce come la vita

Notizie biografiche†

Vuoi notizie biografiche, i fatti
sapere vuoi che abbiano scavato
nella mia vita un fondo di graffiti
che abbiano riarso
una striscia di lungo i miei giorni.
Ma che queste vicende siano parte
di me della mia vita
— inizio fine e nodo —
non pare abbiano questa importanza.
Quello che conta non è l'opinione
l'ideologia il pensiero. Quel che conta
è sempre la parola:
la vita dello scriba è una manciata
di sillabe e vocali e consonanti
e di allitterazioni:

---

*From *Altri amici* (Other friends, 1986).
†From *Ultimo quarto* (Last quarter, 1990).

Felines

The long lustrous tiger, the flowered leopard
— the wary, the silent grace —
still they threaten us
but with their disappearance

Seagulls

Blue seagulls yell insults
swearing at the fish. They yell in Seagulese
to the fish: hey, you! hey, you!
They dive at them cursing.
  Lately the skies
had become so mute that
even this ire from the air
seems an agreeable thing though
atrocious as life

Biographical News

You want biographical news, you want
to know facts that have exposed
a bed of graffiti in my life
that have blazed
a streak along my days.
  But that these events are part
of me of my life
— beginning end and heart —
they don't seem to have such importance.
What counts is not opinion
ideology thought. What counts
is always the word:
the life of a scribe is a handful
of syllables and vowels and consonants
and alliterations:

fra tutto quel sussurro ad ora ad ora
serpeggia appena udibile o sfinisce
una buia canzone, il decanto
del vissuto, lo specchio e la culla

Amore dice*

Oggi — ma anche prima di oggi —
amore dice solitudine dice
separazione strappo.
* Almeno così sembra da quando*
il tempo ha cominciato a menar vanto
di me, delle mie cose, a disfarmi
in famelici morsi

*From *Ultimo quarto* (Last quarter, 1990).

amidst all that whispering now and then
a dark song crawls barely audible
or wanes, the decanting
of life, the mirror and the cradle

Love Says

Today — but before today too —
love says solitude says
separation laceration.
  At least it seems so since
time has begun boasting
of me, of my things, undoing me
in famished bites

MARGHERITA GUIDACCI

From **Meditazioni e sentenze**[*]

II

Il primo banchetto è d'amore. Sugli avanzi d'amore banchetta la febbre.
Infine i vermi, dita sicure della morte, ci spogliano ed aprono
Fino allo scheletro lucente.

IV

La piccola rugiada rinvigorisce la piccola erba
Alla pazienza d'un altro giorno arido;
Mentre l'albero assetato desidera la pioggia o la scure.

Madame X[†]

Io non sono il mio corpo.
Mi è straniero, nemico.
Ancora peggio è l'anima,
e neppure con essa m'identifico.

Osservo di lontano
le rozze acrobazie di questa coppia,
con distacco, ironia —
con disgusto talvolta.

E intanto penso che la loro assenza
sarebbe più guadagno che dolore:
questa e altre cose… Ma mentre le penso,
io chi sono, e dove?

La madre pazza[†]

Noi con gli stracci smessi del passato
ci costruiamo un presente.
Come una bambola piena di segatura
lo stringiamo al petto,

---

[*]From *La sabbia e l'angelo* (The sand and the angel, 1946).
[†]From *Neurosuite* (Neurosuite, 1970).

MARGHERITA GUIDACCI

From **Meditations and Maxims**

II

The first to feast is love. On the scraps of love the fever feasts.
Finally the worms, death's confident fingers, strip and expose us
Down to the shining bone.

IV

The tiny dew reinvigorates the tiny grass
With patience for another arid day;
While the parched tree longs for the rain or the axe.

Madame X

I am not my body.
It is alien, an enemy to me.
Worse still is my soul,
nor in it do I see myself.

From a distance I watch
the boorish acrobatics of this couple,
with detachment, irony —
sometimes with disgust.

And in the meantime I think that their absence
would bring more gain than grief:
this and other things… But while I think of them,
who and where am I?

The Crazy Mother

With cast-off rags of the past
we build ourselves a present.
We clutch it to our chests,
cradling it tenderly

teneramente lo culliamo.
Cosí la madre pazza, mia vicina,
parla con un fanciullo
da molto tempo sparito in mezzo ai fiori,
e intanto volta indignata le spalle
all'uomo grigio, flaccido ed affranto
che quel fanciullo è diventato
e che la supplica invano
di riconoscerlo.

Prima del nostro incontro*

Sottraggo i giorni ad uno ad uno, li sigillo
e metto via, quando sono compiuti,
benedicendo il loro sole, la loro pioggia,
o qualunque sia stato il loro dono;
benedicendo sopratutto la notte
che, seppur lenta, li accolse alla fine.

E prego quelli che ancora rimangono
prima del nostro incontro (ed a contarli
bastano ormai le dita di una mano)
di non smarrirsi in cielo, ma procedere
come i loro fratelli: un po' più in fretta,
se possono, ritmandosi sul vivo
battito del mio cuore.

E tuttavia, neppure troppo in fretta —
perché ancora non so comprendere, adattarmi:
temo il momento in cui sarò chiamata
alla quasi insostenibile gioia.

*From *Inno alla gioia* (Hymn to joy, 1983).

like a doll stuffed with sawdust.
In this way the crazy mother, my neighbor,
speaks to a little boy
long ago lost among the flowers,
while indignant, she turns away
from the flaccid and broken gray man
the little boy has become,
begging her in vain
for recognition.

Before Our Encounter

I subtract the days one by one, seal them
and put them away as soon as they're done,
and I bless their sun, their rain,
or whatever their gift may have been;
above all I bless the night, the night
which finally welcomed them, though slowly.

And I plead with those that still remain
before our encounter (they can be
counted on the fingers of one hand)
not to get lost in the sky, but to proceed
like their brothers: a bit more hurriedly,
if possible, following the rhythm of the living
beat of my heart.

And yet, not too hurriedly —
because I still can't understand, adapt myself:
I fear the moment in which I will be called
to the almost unbearable joy.

Mappa del cielo invernale*

Con la mappa del cielo invernale, che tu hai disegnato per me,
uscirò prima dell'alba in una piazza ormai vuota
d'uomini e alzerò gli occhi ad incontrare
i viandanti stellari che lentamente si muovono
intorno al polo dell'Orsa. Ai più splendenti
chiederò: «Sei tu Rigel? Sei tu Betelgeuse?
O Sirio? O la Capella?», restando ancora in dubbio
(tanta è la mia inesperienza nonostante il tuo aiuto)
su quale sia la risposta. E intanto penserò
a San Juan, perché quella sarà la notte di Dio,
dopo la notte dei sensi e dell'anima; e le stelle,
riconosciute o ignote, saranno per me tanti angeli
il cui volo silenzioso mi conduce verso il giorno.
E penserò anche a te, che da un altro parallelo contempli,
ugualmente assorto, lo stesso firmamento,
sentendo come me un gelo esterno ed un fuoco interiore,
mentre i nostri cuori lontani, che sono ancora imprigionati nel tempo,
lo scandiscono all'unisono.

Fonte†

> Que bien sé yo la fuente que mana y corre
> Aunque es de noche. *(San Juan de la Cruz)*

Io so la fonte che zampilla e scorre
benché sia notte, la so ritrovare
benché sia notte e un grappolo di notti:
notte del cielo e notte
del bosco, notte della lontananza,
notte di tutto il tempo ch'è trascorso
dal primo scaturire…La raggiungo
lungo i bruni sentieri dove mi guida
il suo richiamo d'argento. E vi tuffo
le mani, le sollevo

---

*From *Il buio e lo splendore* (Darkness and splendor, 1989).
†From *Anelli del tempo* (Rings of time, 1993).

Map of the Winter Sky

With the map of the winter sky you drew for me,
I will go out before dawn into a square now emptied
of men, and raise my eyes to meet
the wayfaring stars which are slowly moving
around the pole of the Bear. Of the most splendid
I will ask: "Are you Rigel? Are you Betelgeuse?
Or Sirius? Or Capella?" still remaining doubtful
(great is my inexperience despite your help)
about the answer. And meanwhile I will think
of San Juan,[3] for this will be the night of God,
following the night of the senses and the soul; and the stars,
both known and unknown, will be to me so many angels
whose silent flights guide me toward the day.
And I will think of you, equally absorbed in contemplating,
from another latitude, the same firmament,
feeling, as I do, an external frost and an interior fire,
while our distant hearts, still imprisoned in time,
beat in unison.

Spring

> Que bien sé yo la fuente que mana y corre
> Aunque es de noche. (San Juan de la Cruz)

I know the spring that spurts and flows
though it is night, I know how to find it again
though it is night and a cluster of nights:
night of sky and night
of woods, night of distance,
night of all the time that has passed
since the original gushing...I reach it
along the dark paths where its silvery call
guides me. And I plunge my hands
into it, and raise them

congiunte a coppa fino alle mie labbra
ed alle tue. Riconosci anche tu
nell'arcana purezza che ci disseta
il nostro pianto d'un giovane addio
(disceso ad irrorare le profonde
radici della vita), riconosci
quelle nostre visibili
e invisibili lacrime?

È come una mancanza di respiro*

È come una mancanza
di respiro ed un senso di morire,
quando mi stringe improvviso
il desiderio di te tanto lontano
e nulla può calmarlo, altro pensiero
non può occuparmi, tranne il Paradiso
che sarebbe per me lo starti accanto.
Ma poiché ciò m'è negato, più cara,
molto più cara d'una fredda pace
mi è la stretta indicibile —
quasi marchio di fuoco che proclami
ancora e sempre quanto sono tua.
A nessun costo vorrei separarmi
da questo mio dolore.

Anniversario con Agavi*

Questo giorno, che fu d'amore e lacerazione
tanti anni fa, ci vede ora camminare
insieme su sabbie e rocce, la tua mano
aiutandomi nei passi difficili
e il tuo sguardo orientando il mio, verso l'alta
barriera d'agavi e di canne,
limite di nord-est al litorale.
«Ecco — mi dici — sono queste», e indichi

*From *Anelli del tempo* (Rings of time, 1993).

cupping them to my lips
and to yours. Do you also recognize
in the mysterious purity quenching our thirst
tears of a young farewell
(descended to nourish the deep
roots of life), do you recognize
our own visible
and invisible tears?

It Is like a Shortness of Breath

It is like a shortness of breath
and the sensation of dying,
when the desire for you
so far away suddenly grips me
and nothing can calm it, no other thought
can occupy me, except for the Paradise
that would be mine if I were near you.
But since this is denied, I hold more dear,
much more dear than a cold peace
the unspeakable grip —
like a brand proclaiming
still and always how fully I am yours.
Never would I separate myself
from this pain.

Anniversary with Agave Plants

This day, so many years ago a day
of love and laceration, now sees us walk
together over sand and rocks, your hand
helping me in the difficult steps,
your eyes guiding mine, toward the high
barrier of agave plants and reeds,
northeastern boundary of the coast.
"Here," you say, "these are the ones," pointing to

le cinque agavi ormai pronte,
dopo la quasi centenaria attesa,
all'incredibile fioritura. Racchiuso
nel suo grosso uovo bruno, ogni fiore-fenice
si prepara ad erompere in un volo
estatico: la breve festa nuziale
al sole e al vento, celebrata da sciami
d'api d'oro — poi, subito, la morte.
Osserviamo le agavi protendersi
al loro compimento, nello slancio
degli steli, indomabile, e la resa
delle foglie già esauste, che immolarono
ogni linfa all'unico fine e si ripiegano
come vele ammainate. Qualcosa in noi
profondamente, quasi perdutamente,
risponde a quello slancio, a quella resa.
Io sento un nodo alla gola e rimango
in silenzio. Tu dici piano: «Anche le piante
hanno il loro destino».

the five agave plants now ready,
after almost a century of waiting,
to break into incredible bloom. Closed
in its large brown egg, each phoenix-flower
prepares to erupt in ecstatic
flight: the brief nuptial feast
in the sun and wind, celebrated by swarms
of golden bees — then, immediately, death.
We watch the agave plants straining
toward their fulfillment, in the indomitable
rush of the stems, and the surrender
of leaves already spent, which having sacrificed
every bit of sap to a sole end fold
like lowered sails. Something in us
deeply, almost desperately,
responds to that rush, to the surrender.
I feel a lump in my throat and remain
silent. You say softly: "Even plants
have their destiny."

CRISTINA CAMPO (VITTORIA GUERRINI)

Si ripiegano i bianchi abiti estivi*

Si ripiegano i bianchi abiti estivi
e tu discendi sulla meridiana,
dolce Ottobre, e sui nidi.

Trema l'ultimo canto nelle altane
dove sole era l'ombra ed ombra il sole,
tra gli affanni sopiti.

E mentre indugia tiepida la rosa
l'amara bacca già stilla il sapore
dei sorridenti addii.

A volte dico: tentiamo d'esser gioiosi*

a m. c.

A volte dico: tentiamo d'esser gioiosi,
e mi appare discrezione la mia,
tanto scavata è ormai la deserta misura
cui fu promesso il grano.

A volte dico: tentiamo d'essere gravi,
non sia mai detto che zampilli per me
sangue di vitello grasso:
ed ancora mi appare discrezione la mia.

Ma senza fallo a chi così ricolma
d'ipotesi il deserto,
d'immagini l'oscura notte, anima mia,
a costui sarà detto: avesti la tua mercede.

Amore, oggi il tuo nome*

Amore, oggi il tuo nome
al mio labbro è sfuggito
come al piede l'ultimo gradino...

*From *La Tigre Assenza* (The tiger absence, 1991).

CRISTINA CAMPO (VITTORIA GUERRINI)

The White Summer Clothes Are Folded Away

The white summer clothes are folded away
and you descend, sweet October,
on the meridian and the nests.

The last song trembles on roof terraces
where shadow was sun and sun shadow,
among appeased agonies.

And while the rose is tepidly lingering
the bitter berry is already dropping the flavor
of smiling farewells.

At Times I Say: Let's Try to Be Joyous

to m. c.

At times I say: let's try to be joyous,
and I think I am being discrete,
so hollowed now is the deserted measure
to which grain was promised.

At times I say: let's try to be serious,
let it not be said that the blood of a fattened calf
gushes for me:
and still I think I am being discrete.

But without fail to the one who thus fills
the desert with hypotheses,
the dark night with images, my soul,
to that one it will be said: you had your reward.

Love, Today My Lip

Love, today my lip
has slipped on your name
like a foot on the last step...

Ora è sparsa l'acqua della vita
e tutta la lunga scala
è da ricominciare.

T'ho barattato, amore, con parole.

Buio miele che odori
dentro i diafani vasi
sotto mille e seicento anni di lava —

ti riconoscerò dall'immortale
silenzio.

Ora rivoglio bianche tutte le mie lettere*

Ora rivoglio bianche tutte le mie lettere,
inaudito il mio nome, la mia grazia richiusa;
ch'io mi distenda sul quadrante dei giorni,
riconduca la vita a mezzanotte.

E la mia valle rosata dagli uliveti
e la città intricata dei miei amori
siano richiuse come un breve palmo,
il mio palmo segnato da tutte le mie morti.

O Medio Oriente disteso dalla sua voce,
voglio destarmi sulla via di Damasco —
né mai lo sguardo aver levato a un cielo
altro dal suo, da tanta gioia in croce.

Devota come ramo*

Devota come ramo
curvato da molte nevi
allegra come falò
per colline d'oblio,

su acutissime làmine
in bianca maglia d'ortiche,
ti insegnerò, mia anima,
questo passo d'addio...

*From *La Tigre Assenza* (The tiger absence, 1991).

Now the water of life is spilled
and the long stairway
must be climbed again.

I have traded you, love, for words.

Dark honey fragrant
in diaphanous vases
under sixteen hundred years of lava —

I will recognize you by your immortal
silence.

Now I Want All My Letters White Again

Now I want all my letters white again,
my name unknown, my grace resealed;
that I may unfold myself on the quadrant of days,
leading life back to midnight.

And that my valley rosy with olive groves
and the intricate city of my loves
may be resealed like a short palm,
my palm marked by all my deaths.

Oh Middle East unfolded from his voice,
I want to reawaken on the road to Damascus —
and raise my eyes to no sky
but his, so much joy on the cross.

Devout like a Branch

Devout like a branch
bowed by many snowfalls
happy like bonfires
on the hills of oblivion,

on the sharpest blades
in a white mesh of nettles,
I will teach you, my soul,
this farewell passage...

Estate indiana*

Ottobre, fiore del mio pericolo —
primavera capovolta nei fiumi.

Un'ora m'è indifferente fino alla morte
— l'acero ha il volo rotto, i fuochi annebbiano —
un'ora il terrore di esistere mi affronta
raggiante, come l'astero rosso.

Tutto è già noto, la marea prevista,
pure tutto si ottenebra e rischiara
con fresca disperazione, con stupenda
fermezza...

    La luce tra due piogge, sulla punta
di fiume che mi trafigge tra corpo
e anima, è una luce di notte
— la notte che non vedrò —
chiara nelle selve.

La Tigre Assenza*

        pro patre et matre

Ahi che la Tigre,
la Tigre Assenza,
o amati,
ha tutto divorato
di questo volto rivolto
a voi! La bocca sola
pura
prega ancora
voi: di pregare ancora
perché la Tigre,
la Tigre Assenza,
o amati,
non divori la bocca
e la preghiera...

*From *La Tigre Assenza* (The tiger absence, 1991).

Indian Summer

October, flower of my peril —
spring reversed in rivers.

One hour makes me indifferent to death
— the maple's flight is broken, the fires grow dim —
another hour and the terror of existence confronts me
radiant, like the red aster.

Everything is already known, the tide foreseen,
and yet everything darkens and clears
with fresh desperation, with wonderful
steadiness...

    The light between two rains, on the point
of the river that transfixes me between body
and soul, is a light of night
— a night I won't see —
clear in the woods.

The Tiger Absence

pro patre et matre

Ah that the Tiger,
the Tiger Absence,
oh my loved ones,
has devoured all
of this face turned
toward you! The mouth alone
pure
still praying
to you: to pray once more
so that the Tiger,
the Tiger Absence,
oh my loved ones,
does not devour the mouth
and the prayer...

Canone IV*

Il Tremendo, conoscendone l'animo
pieghevole come il salice al vento dell'idolatria,
trasfuso ch'ebbe nella divina icone
il suo indicibile sguardo sugli uomini,
volle talora sottilmente provarne
l'antico occhio di carne,
un lampo trasfondendo della suprema Maschera
in un volto di carne:
centro celato nel cerchio, essenza nella presenza,
lido inafferrabilmente coperto e riscoperto
della Somiglianza, fermo orizzonte dell'Immagine,
all'incrocio del tempo e dell'eterno,
là dove la Bellezza,
la Bellezza a doppia lama, la delicata,
la micidiale, è posta
tra l'altero dolore e la santa umiliazione,
il barbaglio salvifico e
l'ustione,
per la vivente, efficace separazione
di spirito e anima, di midolla e giuntura,
di passione e parola...
    O quanto ci sei duro
Maestro e Signore! Con quanti denti il tuo amore
ci morde! Ciò che dal tuo temibile
pollice luminoso è segnato
— spazio ducale tra due sopraccigli, emisferi
cristallini di tempie, sguardi senza patria quaggiù,
silenzi più remoti dell'uranico vento —
ancora e ancora, scoperta e riscoperta
la tua Cifra per ogni angolo della terra, per ogni angolo
dell'anima da te è gettata, da te è scagliata:
a testimoniare, a ferire,
a insolubilmente saldare
a inguaribilmente separare.

*From *La Tigre Assenza* (The tiger absence, 1991).

Canon IV

The Terrible One, knowing their hearts
which were pliant like the willow in idolatry's wind,
wished, after having transfused into the divine icon
his ineffable gaze on men,
to subtly test now and then
their ancient eye of flesh,
transfusing a flash of the supreme Mask
in a face of flesh:
center concealed in the circle, essence in presence,
elusively covered and rediscovered shore
of Likeness, still horizon of the Image,
at the crossroads of time and eternity,
where Beauty,
double-edged Beauty, the delicate,
the deadly, is placed
between proud sorrow and holy humiliation,
between the redeeming dazzle and
the burn,
for the living, effective division
of spirit and soul, of marrow and joint,
of passion and word...
    Oh you are so hard on us
Master and Lord! Your love bites us
with so many teeth! That which is marked
by your dreadful luminous thumb
— ducal space between the brows, crystalline
hemispheres of temples, eyes without a country in this world,
silences more remote than the celestial wind —
your Cipher, again and again, discovered and rediscovered
on every corner of the earth, on every corner of the soul
is cast by you, is hurled by you:
to witness, to wound,
to insolubly solder
to incurably divide.

ARMANDA GUIDUCCI

Brevità degli abbracci*

Io giaccio in te, mio spazio d'amore,
e tu giaci in me, con un respiro solo.

Un corpo completo vibra nell'intreccio:
ma a lui è negato di durare.

Perché non esistono le sirene,
né i liocorni, i cavalli marini;
sulla terra esistono solo forme
che si compongono e scompongono

solitarie, come la luce, la neve.

A chiusura di libro*

Quando la cerniera in uno scatto
mozzerà l'ondeggiare del respiro,
io giacerò come un libro appena chiuso:
mille pagine astratte; un senso solo.
Fissa, sfuggente: il nerbo d'un racconto.

E tu — che mi avrai letta per intero,
saprai (per il distacco delle fini)
ciò che ora nega l'occhio irrequieto
respinto in corsa da tronca riga a riga.
Afferrerai il tutto: ciò che io fui
— d'un colpo solo. Senza più esitare,
ammetterai: non raccontò che amore.

Letture*

Ho consumato notti dentro i libri,
lune, e perfino primavere;
chinato il capo, e udito
l'insidiosa eco del pensiero.
Conosco i rischi; le perdite; i furti.

*From *Poesie per un uomo* (Poems for a man, 1965).

ARMANDA GUIDUCCI

Brevity of Embraces

I lie in you, my space of love,
and you in me, with a single breath.

A complete body quivers in the weave:
yet it is denied duration.

Because there are neither sirens
nor unicorns, nor sea horses;
there are only forms on the earth
composing and decomposing

solitary, like light, or snow.

Upon Closing the Book

When in a snap the hinge
will cut off the waves of my breath,
I will lie down like a book just closed:
one thousand abstract pages; a single sense.
Fixed, elusive: the core of a tale.

And you — having read me in full,
will know (through the detachment of endings)
what the restless eye now denies
rushed away from truncated line to line.
You will grasp the whole: what I was
— in one breath. Without further hesitation,
you will concede: she spoke of nothing but love.

Readings

I consumed nights inside books,
moons, and even springs;
bowed my head, and heard
the insidious echo of thought.
I know the risks; the losses; the theft.

Ma neppure la lettura più azzardata
ha messo in dubbio te — come fai tu
ogni volta sull'asse di una pagina
che ti sposti un sistema costruito.
T'ammiro, così astratto, e provo orrore
della tua incerta furia — forza maschile
e debolezza insieme; mancanza di natura
che mi relega in nota — a pié di pagina.

Alla maniera di Emily*

Ignoravo quale estraneazione
possa offendere l'amore dall'amore.
È il delitto inatteso
sempre il più perfetto.
Racchiuso in un bacio,
il giardino
o, nel giardino, la notte
di Getsémani.

Ti guardo così vecchio*

Ti guardo così vecchio ed incompiuto
e provo strazio di te
che fosti, e non sei stato,
quel compiuto angelo ribelle
che porta sulle braccia un mondo nuovo
ed alla donna annuncia
resurrezione in un amore pari.
Eppure il volo si era spiegato
nelle ali tenere e superbe
e, per un tratto di cielo
o di intrepida aurora,
visse quel messaggero,
quell'uomo fiero,
fosti quella forza del diverso
che lungamente e invano

*From *A colpi di silenzio* (By strokes of silence, 1990; 1st ed. 1982).

But not even the most hazardous reading
put you into question — as you put me,
each time on the axis of any page
that shifts your constructed system.
I admire you, so abstract, and feel horror
at your uncertain fury — at once man's
strength and weakness; a lack in nature
relegating me to a note — at the bottom of the page.

In Emily's Manner

I didn't know what estrangement
could from love offend love.
The unexpected crime is
always the perfect one.
Closed in a kiss,
the garden
in the garden, the night
of Gethsemane.

I Look at You So Old

I look at you so old and unaccomplished
and I agonize for you
who were, yet haven't been,
the accomplished rebel angel
carrying in his arms a new world
and announcing to womankind
resurrection in an equal love.
Yet the tender and superb wings
had spread into flight
and, for a stretch of sky
or intrepid dawn,
the messenger lived,
that proud man,
you were the force of difference
which I vainly pursued

per tanti anni ho cercato,
povero angelo crollato
dalle temibili altezze
per un errore nella ribellione,
amore mio giusto, e perduto
lungo le rotte della mediocrità.

Parto*

Si ruppe il buio in vita, e seppi
(come sa un'acqua per cerchi lontananti)
che l'esistere è per vibrazioni
da uno a un altro essere — all'infinito.

Sotto una stella impura*

Nacqui con disappunto degli dei
sotto una stella esitante e impura
in mezzo a un mondo di uomini-coltello.

Avrei raccolto ginestre a braccia piene.
Ma ignoravo che il sole fosse a prestito.
A ogni primavera
venni potata come un bosso delle siepi.
Fui sventrata da uomini distratti
fui tradita da uomini leali
divorata e sputata
insomma amata —
amata come si amano le donne
secondo le leggi del profitto,

del potere, e della sopraffazione.

†From *A colpi di silenzio* (By strokes of silence, 1990; 1st ed. 1982).

for many long years
poor angel collapsed
from dreadful heights
for a mistake in the rebellion,
my just love, lost
along the routes of mediocrity.

Delivery

Darkness broke into life, and I knew
(as water knows through widening circles)
that we exist through vibrations
from one being to another — endlessly.

Under an Impure Star

I was born to the gods' disappointment
under a hesitant, impure star
in a world of knife-men.

I would have picked genista in armfuls.
But I didn't know the sun was borrowed
Every spring
I was pruned like a boxwood hedge.
I was disemboweled by distracted men
I was betrayed by loyal men
devoured and spit out
in short, loved —
loved as women are loved
according to the laws of profit,

of power, and abuse.

Forse un giorno ci saranno maniere*

Forse
un giorno
ci saranno maniere
meno selvagge di queste
o anima a sufficienza
per amarsi in modo meno aggressivo
nella eternità del provvisorio.
Bisognerebbe
inventarsi
tutti daccapo
donna nella donna
uomo nell'uomo
perché fosse mutato corso
alle vene capillari
della sopraffazione.

*From *A colpi di silenzio* (By strokes of silence, 1990; 1st ed. 1982).

Perhaps One Day There Will Be Ways

Perhaps
one day
there will be ways
less wild than these
oh barely sufficient soul
to love in less aggressive fashion
in the eternity of the temporary.
It would take
inventing ourselves
all over again
woman in woman
man in man
to change the course
of the capillary veins
of abuse.

Elena Clementelli

Le tue mani, amore[*]

Le tue mani, amore.
L'ala delle tue mani
e il mio corpo si fa aria leggera di primavera.
Il respiro delle tue mani
e il mio corpo si fa sabbia tiepida di sole.
Il solco delle tue mani nella febbre
e il mio corpo s'inarca, oscura acqua di lago.
Il brivido delle tue mani
e non so più se sono fiamma o neve.
La furia delle tue mani tra i capelli,
la musica delle tue mani sulle labbra,
il silenzio delle tue mani sfinite, sazie, lontane.
La malinconia delle tue mani
sorelle ai tuoi occhi
nel lungo indugio sul mio viso
quando la sera ci diciamo addio.
Le tue mani, amore.

Giro e ossessione di pareti[*]

Giro e ossessione di pareti,
freno e silenzio di soffitti,
l'amore imprigionato non respira,
nelle tue braccia io lo sento morire
ora per ora.
Fresca la schiuma dei tuoi capelli
sotto le labbra che ne sanno il sapore,
morbido il buio
che non inganna con i sensi il cuore.
E siamo già senza parole nuove,
e gli occhi hanno brevi orizzonti d'angoli
dove sbattono cieche le ali
del desiderio che non si libra.

[*]From *Questa voce su noi* (This voice over us, 1962).

ELENA CLEMENTELLI

Your Hands, My Love

Your hands, my love.
The wing of your hands,
and my body becomes light spring air.
The breath of your hands
and my body becomes sun warmed sand
The wake of your hands in a fever
and my body crests, dark lake water.
The shiver of your hands
and I no longer know if I am flame or snow.
The fury of your hands in my hair,
the music of your hands on my lips,
the silence of your exhausted, sated, distant hands.
The melancholy of your hands
lingering on my face
sisters to your eyes
as we say good-bye each night.
Your hands, my love.

Circle and Obsession of Walls

Circle and obsession of walls,
restraint and silence of ceilings,
caged love does not breathe,
in your arms I feel it dying
hour by hour.
Fresh the foam of your hair
under lips that know its taste,
soft the darkness
that doesn't deceive with the senses the heart.
And already we are without new words,
and eyes have brief angled horizons
where wings of desire
flap blindly, unable to soar.

Un orologio ritma cupo i tempi
dei nostri abbracci,
fuori c'è il sole o piove,
non per noi.
Questa nostra stagione c'illuse
e troppo in fretta, avidi di ombre,
abbiamo spento il mondo.
Ma nel mondo è tornata primavera,
l'aria è gentile e nuova,
ed io con te vorrei guardare il cielo.

From **Quaderno etrusco***

(Analisi o prologo)

Geografia sotterranea,
ampie correnti,
contro la superficie che ospita il mio presente.
Da sentieri sommersi
un richiamo penetra il sonno di queste notti,
fra miraggi d'astri cadenti
e inquieti presagi.
Ordine o invito.
Nessuna luce nella mente:
il sangue guida i passi
all'incerta fiaccola dei suoi stimoli
su luoghi d'oggi dove l'ieri veglia.
Pellegrinaggio o sfida?
Il dubbio cede all'avventura
che già mi spinge ai mobili confini
dove il silenzio inabissato ha voci
che non sono di morte.
O forse è il mare che a distanza breve
segue il profilo antico
a suggerire suoni
alla conchiglia del tempo,

---

*From *Così parlando onesto* (Thus honestly speaking, 1977).

A clock sullenly beats the time
of our embraces,
outside it's sunny or rainy,
not for us.
This season of ours beguiled us
and too hastily, eager for shadows,
we extinguished the world.
Yet in the world spring has returned,
the air is gentle and new,
and with you I'd like to look at the sky.

From **Etruscan Notebook**

(Analysis or Prologue)

Subterranean geography,
vast currents,
against the surface where my present is guest.
From submerged trails
a call penetrates the sleep of these nights,
among mirages of falling stars
and restless premonitions.
Order or invitation.
No light in the mind:
the blood guides the steps
by the unsteady flame of its urges
over today's sites where yesterday keeps vigil.
Pilgrimage or challenge?
Doubt cedes to an adventure
that already drives me to shifting borders
where the sunken silence has voices
which are not of death.
Or perhaps it is the sea that closely
follows the ancient profile
suggesting sounds
to the shell of time,

perché l'eco smarrita e frantumata
conosca la sua nascita perenne.

XI

   Ansa del golfo,
dilatato sorriso del mare.
Persistere del segno
dalla pietra alla riva,
reiterata saggezza,
aperto invito
dal passato al futuro
sulle mobili creste del presente.
Non mistero celeste.
Gesto amico,
mano tesa dell'uomo
fra tombe e altari,
anelli anelli anelli anelli anelli
della lunga catena.

Vorrei provare a raccontarti la primavera*

Vorrei provare a raccontarti la primavera,
prima che anche i glicini e le acacie
si accorgano dell'inganno,
nascendo — morendo
alle nevi d'aprile,
alle gelate di maggio.
Vorrei raccontartela a pieni colori,
a pieni odori,
la favola bella che più non c'illude,
perché almeno un'eco ti resti
dell'antico miracolo
dalle statistiche escluso, dai calendari bandito.
Dunque, c'era una volta…

*From *L'educazione* (Education, 1980).

so that the lost and fragmented echo
may know its perennial birth.

XI

   Bend of the gulf,
dilated smile of the sea.
The sign persisting
from stone to shore,
reiterated wisdom,
open invitation
from past to future
on the present's shifting crests.
No celestial mystery.
Friendly gesture,
man's outstretched hand
among tombs and altars,
links links links links links
of the long chain.

I'd Like to Try Telling You of Spring

I'd like to try telling you of spring,
before the wisterias and acacias also
realize the deception,
being born — dying
to April snows,
to May frosts.
I'd like to tell it in full color,
in full fragrance,
the beautiful fairytale which no longer beguiles us,[4]
that you may have at least an echo
of the ancient miracle
excluded from statistics, from calendars banned.
Well then, once upon a time...

Moviola*

La mia mamma è morta che io ero già vecchia.
La mia mamma morì che ero ancora bambina.
I dissidi, le asprezze,
e quindi la pietà, l'insofferenza, il rancore,
di questi anni lunghissimi e pesanti
solo un felice volo di memoria
può forse rinnegare.
Un colpo d'ala ardito
fino al letto della mia scarlattina,
alla camera infetta,
al "vietato l'ingresso" per tutti.
Tranne per lei:
il camice bianco appeso alla maniglia,
la catinella col disinfettante
per mondare le mani sulla soglia.
Quella mamma ho perduto
quando avevo otto anni.
Io la piango da allora.
E nel tempo è sfiorito il suo sorriso,
la sua voce è una vela nella nebbia.
Ore e ore leggeva, la sua voce,
a occhi chiusi io mi vedevo il Tour,
Bartali sempre in testa ai Pirenei.
Brutta! mi disse una compagna a scuola,
corsi fra le sue braccia singhiozzando.
Con dolore e con furia mi serrò,
negando: la sua unica bugia.
ma è troppo lungo questo film,
e monotono, e uggioso,
non ho voglia di proiettarlo tutto.
Basta così.
Lunga è stata la frangia di quel tempo
e fitti i nodi che non so sbrogliare:
inutile il replay,
quella bambina non sono io,
non mi riguarda la sua storia melensa.
Brucia la vita coi suoi specchi ustorî
gli ultimi rami, gli ultimi rimorsi.

*From *Vasi a Samo* (Vases to Samos, 1983).

Moviola

My mother died when I was already old.
My mother was dead when I was still a child.
The dissentions, the difficulties,
and then the pity, intolerance, rancor,
of these very long, heavy years
only by a happy flight of memory
might they perhaps be denied.
A daring flap of the wing
to the bed of my scarlet fever,
the infected room,
the "keep out" to all.
Except to her:
the white coat hanging on the door knob,
the basin of disinfectant
to cleanse her hands on the threshold.
That mother I lost
when I was eight years old.
I have been mourning her ever since.
And over time her smile has faded,
her voice is a sail in the fog.
Her voice for hours and hours reading,
I saw the Tour with my eyes closed,
Bartali[5] always leading in the Pyrenees.
Ugly! a schoolmate told me,
I ran into her arms sobbing.
With pain and rage she held me tight,
denying: her only lie.
But this movie is too long,
and monotonous, and tedious,
I don't feel like screening the rest.
That's enough.
Long has been the fringe of that time
and thick the knots I can't untangle:
useless the replay,
that child is not me,
her doltish story is not my concern.
With its burning glasses life consumes
the last branches, the last remorses.

MARIA LUISA SPAZIANI

Il presente*

Allegri e mesti erano i ricordi,
nebbiosa, misera trama della vita.
Sul futuro si aprivano finestre
ora buie, ora azzurre di palmizi.

Ma qui il tempo fu vivo, fu presente,
fu il tanghero che impone il pagamento immediato.
L'imprecisione delle ore si fece allucinante chiarezza
e il tormento mi rose, instancabile, come una marea.

Ora so cos'è vivere: un gioco crudele
che inchioda profonda ogni fibra alla ruota del tempo.
E mentre il sogno corre le sue pianure sconfinate
noi, come un giovane frutto, sentiamo la linfa salire
e placata al meriggio fermarsi,

mentre il tragico peso cresce, fino a staccarci dal ramo.

La prigione†

Memoria, fiorita prigione,
dureremo vent'anni, quaranta,
a trastullarci in questi giochi d'ombre?
Come un cane ti annuso e ti raspo,
come un guanto ti infilo e ti rovescio,
hai spigoli aguzzi, celesti barlumi,
sei la pioggia di rose che mi soffoca,
l'ancora e la grisella degli spazi
e museruola e zufolo e malaria.
Sei l'aria fresca su un deserto, sei
il deserto d'un cielo senz'aria.

---

*From *Le acque del Sabato* (The waters of the Sabbath, 1954).
†From *Il Gong* (The gong, 1962).

MARIA LUISA SPAZIANI

The Present

Happy and mournful were the memories,
hazy, miserable weft of life.
Windows now dark, now blue with palm trees
were open toward the future.

But here, once, time was alive, was *present,*
it was the lout who insists on immediate payment.
The imprecision of the hours became hallucinatory clarity
and anguish consumed me, relentless, like a tide.

Now I know what living is: a cruel game
nailing each fiber deeply to the wheel of time.
And as the dream rides its boundless plains
we, like young fruit, feel the lymph as it rises
and appeased at noon halts,

while the tragic weight grows, till it pulls us off the tree.

The Prison

Memory, flowering prison,
will we last forty, fifty years,
toying in this play of shadows?
Like a dog I sniff and scratch you,
I put you on like a glove and reverse you,
you have pointed edges, sky-blue glimmers,
you are the shower of roses that suffocates me,
the anchor and ratline of space
and muzzle and flageolet and malaria.
You are fresh air on a desert, you are
the desert of an airless sky.

Utilità della memoria*

Altri guadagneranno ciò ch'io perdo
giorno su giorno, lentissimamente.
Avranno i sensi freschi, morderanno
rabbrividendo nella polpa acerba,
trasaliranno di delizia all'alba
se mai li sfiori un dito d'aria d'oro.

Ma io ricordo tutto, grazie al Cielo,
la memoria l'ho giovane e forte.

Forse che Robinson Crusoe sudando
per trarre una scintilla da due legni
non ricorda benissimo lo stipo
che incontestato a Londra gli appartiene,
dove un tesoro di mille ghinee
sta in saeculorum saecula aspettando?

Dicono i marinai, quegli ormai vecchi †

Dicono i marinai, quegli ormai vecchi
lupi di mare che sugli usci fumano
pipe portoricane, che fra tutti
i ricordi tremendi dei tifoni
e l'ululo di morte dei naufragi,
nulla atterrisce più di quella calma
che per ore si crea al centro stesso
della tregenda: l'occhio del ciclone.
Il mare è un olio, brillano sinistre
luci che paion di bonaccia, e affiora
tranquillo il tonno a respirare. Eppure
quella è una gabbia, quello è un trabocchetto,
lì la morte è in agguato: ché più lungi,
a cento metri o forse meno, infuria
l'uragano più nero. Così avviene,
vero? troppo sovente per noi tutti,
ragni fra i mozzi delle ruote. E avvenne

---

*From *Utilità della memoria* (Memory's usefulness, 1966).
†From *L'occhio del ciclone* (The eye of the cyclone, 1970).

Memory's Usefulness

Others will gain what I lose
day upon day, so very slowly.
Their senses will be fresh, they will bite
shivering into the unripe pulp,
if ever a golden finger of air grazes them
they will startle delighted at the dawn.

But I remember everything, thank Heavens,
my memory is young and strong.

As Robinson Crusoe struggles
to draw a spark from two sticks
doesn't he vividly remember the cabinet
undisputedly his in London,
where a treasure of one thousand guineas
awaits *in saeculorum saecula?*[6]

It Is Said by Some Sailors, The Old

It is said by some sailors, the old
sea wolves who smoke Puerto Rican
pipes on the doorsteps, that of all
the terrible memories of typhoons
and howls of death in shipwrecks,
nothing is more terrifying than the calm
which forms for hours at the very center
of the tumult: the eye of the cyclone.
The sea is oil, sinister lights
shine seeming signs of dead calm and the tuna
peacefully surfaces for air. Yet
it is a cage, it is a trap,
there death lies in ambush: since further on,
one hundred meters or perhaps less, the darkest
storm rages. Thus it happens,
doesn't it? too often to all of us,
spiders between wheel hubs. And thus it

anche a Fabrizio quando conversando
con la graziosa vivandiera, seppe
— più tardi, e con che tragico suo scorno —
che Waterloo, la massima avventura,
si era svolta lì intorno.

Ultrasuono*

Il rumore soffoca il canto
ma il canto è uno spillo che attraversa il pagliaio,
cercalo se puoi con torce e calamite
lui ti punge e trafigge quando vuole —

Voce clamante nel deserto, gemito,
ultrasuono, anno-luce, urlo di tribù riscattata,

inconsùtile varchi i deserti del tempo,
le inutili matasse dello spazio

Il crocevia†

Quell'unghia che raspava contro i vetri
— cane o persona amata, mio padre o il giardiniere —
più non chiama né indugia né si ostina.
Ma esiste, più irrequieta d'ogni mare.

È un rumore schiacciato, una pastiglia di silenzio
che porta ancora un nome, un barlume di vita.
Càpita a volte di trovare in un libro
un fiore memorabile, filigrana e fantasma.

Tutto ciò che ora è denso, un crocevia di linfe,
dovrà passare per quella cruna d'ago.
Ride e piange il presente, e si prepara al rito.
Le maschere bifronti lo guardano passare.

*From *Transito con catene* (Transit with chains, 1977).
†From *Geometria del disordine* (Geometry of disorder, 1981).

happened to Fabrizio[7] when, chatting
with the charming vivandière, he heard
— later, and to his tragic humiliation —
that Waterloo, the greatest adventure,
had taken place nearby.

Ultrasound

The noise suffocates the song
yet the song is a needle that goes through the straw stack,
look for it if you can with torches and magnets
it pricks you and pierces you whenever it wants —

Clamant voice in the desert, lament,
ultrasound, light-year, cry of redeemed tribe,

seamless[8] you cross the deserts of time,
the useless skeins of space

The Crossroads

The nail scratching at the glass
— dog or loved one, father or gardener —
no longer calls or lingers or persists.
Yet it exists, more restless than any sea.

It is a crushed noise, a pill of silence
still bearing a name, a glimmer of life.
At times it happens that one finds a memorable
flower, filigree and phantom in a book.

All that which is now thick, a crossroads of lymphs,
must pass through the eye of the needle.
The present laughs and cries, preparing for the rite.
The dual-faced masks watch it as it passes.

Ai lettori[*]

Stella-libero arbitrio è endiadi di sogno,
anelito patetico che oggi può far ridere.
Teoria, utopia, ipotesi, follia.
Né io né alcuna stella siamo mai state libere.

Questa mia «stella» è un mare che fabbrica i suoi ritmi
riflettendo caverne del più profondo ieri.
La metafora è un velo che cela altri misteri.
Io non ne vedo il fondo. Voi mi state dettando.

Scintilla di verde[†]

Punta le lance ai punti cardinali,
formidabile barbara regina
irta fra i suoi aculei, scintilla
di verde insostenibile, guerriera.

I suoi fasti li sa soltanto il cielo.
Al cimitero li ignora ogni sguardo.
Io l'amo, in lei mi specchio e riconosco
e in lei sprofondo, rustico velluto,
tutta mia, mio radar sensibile,
vessillo, insegna, simbolo invisibile
ai soliti cantori della rosa.

Alle vittime di Mauthausen[†]

Troverò in paradiso le parole non dette,
capitelli di colonne rimaste a metà.
Scaglie di stelle esplose, private di ogni luce,
antiche fontane secche che ritrovano il canto.

Troverò in paradiso quel macilento tralcio di rosa
che a Mauthausen fiorì dietro la baracca quattordici.
Avrà i suoi occhi ogni cosa capace di durare,
miracolata, innocente, ostinata e radiosa.

---

[*]From *La stella del libero arbitrio* (Star of free will, 1986).
[†]From *I fasti dell'ortica* (Glories of the nettle, 1996).

To the Readers

Free will–star is a hendiadys[9] for dream,
a pathos of longing that may be ludicrous today.
Theory, utopia, hypothesis, madness.
Neither I nor any star have ever been free.

My "star" is a sea that forges its rhythms
reflecting caverns of the deepest past.
Metaphor is a veil that hides other mysteries.
I can't fathom its depths. You are dictating to me.

Spark of Green

She aims her spears at the cardinal points,
formidable barbarian queen
bristling among her prickles, spark
of unendurable green, warrior.

Only the sky knows her glories.
In the graveyard all eyes ignore them.
I love her, in her I see and recognize myself
and into her I sink, my rustic velvet,
all mine, my sensitive radar,
banner, insignia, symbol invisible
to the usual bards of the rose.

To the Victims of Mauthausen

In heaven I will find the words not said,
capitals of columns left half done.
Splinters of exploded stars, bereft of all light,
ancient dried–up fountains recovering their song.

In heaven I will find that emaciated rose shoot
which bloomed at Mauthausen behind barrack fourteen.
Its eyes will be the eyes of each thing capable of lasting,
miraculously healed, innocent, obstinate and shining.

Troverò in paradiso la tua e la mia pazienza.
Ne faremo un collage con rendez-vous mancati,
e velieri arenati, e brandelli di scienza,
bandiere intrise di pianto, ostinate a sventolare.

Rovesciamento dei ruoli*

La chiave è sempre nomade.
La serratura è ferma.

Io chiave sì, furiosamente chiave,
farfalla in mille giri
intorno al tuo portale.

Viaggio per non vederti, per pensarti,
e forse amarti meglio.

La chiave è sempre zingara.
Ferma la serratura.

*From *I fasti dell'ortica* (Glories of the nettle, 1996).

In heaven I will find your patience and mine.
We will piece them together with missed rendezvous,
and stranded vessels, and scraps of science,
tear-drenched flags, obstinately fluttering.

Role Reversal

The key is always nomadic.
The lock is still.

I, yes, a key, furiously a key,
butterfly in a thousand circles
around your portal.

I travel to avoid seeing you, to think of you,
and perhaps to love you better.

The key is always a gypsy.
Still is the lock.

LUCIANA FREZZA

Vecchia dedica*

Gingilli di creta che impasto qui sulla soglia
d'una casa alta sul monte alta sui gradini
d'una piazza siciliana silenziosa come avanti l'alba
dove il sole incendia il mio cuore come un tetto brullo
e lo raggiunge con le stregate antenne una chiocciola
di nube che striscia fra i grigi intrighi del vento.
Miei ninnoli, vi metterò sulle consoles coi fragili
giocattoli delle ave intatti sulla cresta degli anni,
ne è pieno il salotto come un cuore d'immote memorie
che fievoli trovano voce se il vento lo cinge
di draghi fischianti e tremano le vetrate.
Allora è dolce per l'ombra tenera camminare piano
guardando i miei ninnoli togliere grani di polvere,
pensando quale si potrebbe in dono mandare
quale affidare al tepore di mani amiche.

Contro corrente*

Contro la mia corrente
che scende alacre senza posa,
contro l'azzurra vorticosa vita
mi porti allacciata:
il sole ormai
nasce e tramonta
dietro il tuo petto, nascondi
con le tue spalle il domani,
non te ne accorgerai
quando le mie braccia
saranno stanche
quando mi si allenteranno le mani.

*From *La farfalla e la rosa* (The butterfly and the rose, 1962).

Luciana Frezza

Old Dedication

Clay trinkets that I knead here on the threshold
of a house high on the mountain high on the steps
of a Sicilian square quiet as the silence before dawn
a square where the sun burns my heart like a barren roof
brushed by the bewitched antennas of a snail
cloud slithering among the gray intrigues of the wind.
My knick-knacks, I'll place you on the consoles with my
        foremothers'
toys, fragile yet intact on the crest of the years,
the living-room is filled with them like a heart of immobile
        memories
that feebly find a voice when the heart is surrounded
by the wind's hissing dragons and windows shake.
Then it is sweet to walk slowly through the tender shadow
to remove specks of dust while I look at my knick-knacks,
while I wonder which might be sent as a gift
which entrusted to the warmth of friendly hands.

Against the Current

Against my current
that briskly descends without respite,
against the swirling blue life
you carry me clasping you:
behind your chest
the sun now
rises and sets, you hide
the future with your shoulders,
you won't know
when my arms
are tired
when my hands lose their hold.

A Allen Ginsberg & C.*

Cari cari cari beat
invidio la vostra deriva
imbarcati su macchine da scrivere elettriche,
i vostri fortunali di sconcezze,
l'oceano di luce
delle vostre bonacce troppo limpide,
colori come frutti pomposi
maturati nei soli delle droghe
o dai semi di pazzia
cresciuti come liane nelle giungle di stanze;
le cacce insensate al vostro Dio che vi spezza
arti e nervi con un colpo di coda:

ma ahimé!
rimarrò il pescatore prudente
che in vista della costa
cala ogni giorno la sua rete e trasceglie
da un bottino di minutaglia
una scintilla di fosforo quasi invisibile
per un boccone di verità.

Cosí la forza del vostro urlo
scoppiato spruzzato vomitato — un urto
in un abbraccio totale —
mi fa arrossire delle cernite
da piantatore di cavoli e insalate:
dei miei onesti concimi
dei miei solchi ordinati
da cui tutt'al piú si solleva
il bombo d'una vespa
o il volo basso d'una cavolaia.

E penso al mio ruscello di pazienza
ai vostri fiumi di lava,
eppur mischiati! nel calderone livido
d'invidia sempiterna di Dio.

*From *Un tempo di speranza* (A time of hope, 1971).

To Allen Ginsberg & Co.

Dear dear dear beat
I envy your drifting
aboard electric typewriters,
your storms of obscenities,
the ocean of light
in the overly clear lulls,
colors like lavish fruits
ripened in the suns of drugs
or from seeds of madness
grown like lianas in jungles of rooms;
the senseless hunting for your God who breaks
your limbs and nerves with a tail stroke:

but alas!
I will remain the prudent fisherman
who in sight of the coast
casts the net everyday and selects
from a loot of small fish
an almost invisible spark of phosphorous
for a bite of truth.

Thus the strength of your howl
blasted splashed vomited — shock
in a total embrace —
makes me blush for my pickings
good for a planter of cabbage and lettuce:
for my honest fertilizers
my orderly furrows
from which nothing rises but
the buzz of a wasp
or the low flight of a cabbage butterfly.

And I think of my stream of patience
of your rivers of lava,
mixed nonetheless together! in the livid cauldron
of a sempiternal envy of God.

Luoghi*

Qui non si perde
la verde polla della vita
nelle spume d'un'alba, non è favola
sinuosa la memoria — non il sogno
del fiume che mi porta all'infinto
sempre alla stessa alba, al latte tiepido
e la capra ancorata fra i cespugli:

ma si raccorcia in prospettiva,
in tempo:
qui la nascita, il punto
cruciale: risalire alle sorgenti
di mille rivi pigri,
trovare l'errore
nel disegno, discernere
mischiati alle figure d'innocenza
i neri semi del male,
questo rifarmi intera
con fatica è l'ergastolo
della mia città.

Ah! Milano era questa
la ragione più fonda
del tuo incanto:
essere nuova, amnistiata, illusione
cresciuta nella tua colonna di smog
con sentore di stazioni,
essere sottratta all'impegno
di rispondere dei miei primi vagiti
come il luogo d'origine comanda.

Là, distrutte le mie carte
mi mossi sgombra e leggera
in un arco di tempo infinito
perché altra vita, vacanza dalla mia,
in direzioni precise, scacciando

*From Un tempo di speranza (A time of hope, 1971).

Places

Here the green vein of life
does not disappear
in the foams of dawn, memory is no
sinuous fairy tale — not the dream
of the river that carries me to the infinite
always to the same dawn, to the warm milk
and the goat anchored in the brush:

but it is shortened in perspective,
in time:
here the birth, the crucial
point: tracing one thousand
lazy streams to their source,
finding the error
in the design, discerning
the dark seeds of evil
mixed with the figures of innocence,
the labor of making myself
whole is the life sentence
of my city.

Ah! Milan this was
the deepest reason
for your spell:
to be new, amnestied, illusion
grown in your column of smog
with the smell of stations,
to be delivered from the obligation
of answering for my first wailing
as the place of origin demands.

There, my papers destroyed
I moved unencumbered and light
in a span of time infinite
because it was another life, respite from mine,
I moved in precise directions, driving off

come un moscerino fastidioso
un vago senso d'irrealtà, trasalendo
di rado, oltre barriere di bambagia
ai richiami soffocati
dall'altra riva

— l'odore della mimosa nel freddo,
nel fruscio delle pagine nel caldo
del lavoro avviato —

    Fossi sorda
ora ai mille segnali, lamentose
voci, bandiere lacere, stracci
da illusionista estratti senza fine:
amebe di glicini, piovre
rosse di mura, meduse di pini:
        Euridice
troppo troppo guardata
la mia città mi chiama a conviti di ombre,
e ancora non finisco di tornare.

Il lavoro*

Il lavoro della donna
che cura la casa
colma i vuoti della fame
della stanchezza, il terreno
accidentato mortale
del disordine spiana,
non ha vette di diamante
né ridenti colline
ma è piatta soffocante pianura.

Nascosto come il lievito
o l'umore della terra
non la conforta che sia
necessario ferreo cerchio

*From *Un tempo di speranza* (A time of hope, 1971).

62

like an irritating gnat
a vague sense of unreality, seldom
startled, beyond wadded walls
by the stifled calls
from the other shore

— the scent of mimosa in the cold,
in the rustle of pages in the warmth
of initiated work —

      If only I were deaf
now to the thousand signals, plaintive
voices, tattered flags, an illusionist's
rags endlessly extracted:
amoebas of wisterias, red
giant squids of walls, jellyfish of pines:
          Eurydice
watched much too long
my city calls me to feasts of shadows,
and still I won't stop returning.

Work

The work of the woman
who cares for the house
filling voids of hunger
and fatigue, smoothing
the rough deadly
ground of disorder,
has neither diamond peaks
nor pleasant hills
but is a flat stifling plane.

Hidden like the yeast
or the sap of the earth
it does not comfort her
that it is the necessary iron hoop

alla botte del mondo
eguale in questo al giro delle stagioni.

Colmare e spianare
riempire e svuotare
negativa fatica
senz'altra mercede
che la vita.

Il sorriso*

Sorridere diventa
sempre più necessario,
non possiamo permetterci
le trafitture degli azzurri stiletti d'un tempo,
ora ci sono le grige piovre d'angoscia
se non si è pronti ogni mattino
all'alzabandiera di quel bianco pennone
a cui si volgono giovani occhi aspettando
di trovarlo là sventolante.

Questo pane della gioia
da distribuire ogni giorno
è cresciuto con i lieviti di gioie
a loro sconosciute,
intense o lievi, pazze o sagge
che sono sempre la gioia
come ogni goccia è mare.

Di fronte a questo sorriso
tutto è secondario e
scrivere più che mai secondario
e futile e rischioso per paura
di lasciarlo cadere in un abisso.

*From *Un tempo di speranza* (A time of hope, 1971).

in the world's barrel
equal in this to the circle of seasons.

Filling and smoothing
replenishing and emptying
negative toil
with no reward
other than life.

The Smile

Smiling becomes
more and more necessary,
we cannot afford
the piercing of the blue stilettos of times past,
now there are gray tentacles of anguish
if one is not ready every morning
for the hoisting of that white banner
to which young eyes turn waiting
to find it there waving.

This bread of joy
for daily distribution
has risen with a yeast of joys
that are unknown to them,
joys, great or small, wild or wise
which are still joy
as each drop is sea.

Before this smile
all is secondary and
writing more than ever secondary
and futile and risky lest
we let it fall into an abyss.

VERA GHERARDUCCI

22 settembre[*]

brutto
chiudermi anche nel corpo
come una palla buttata
sul letto
immobile
le mani sul viso
tutta accartocciata
penso
alla mia vita
fuori le voci
le voci
un incubo di voci
io maledico
la testa mi fa male
ancora voci di fuori
e un motore
l'unico del paese
che non ingrana
e io neppure.

27 ottobre[†]

papà guidava e noi bambini dietro
insonnoliti timorosi di tutto
i viaggi trasloco decisi dall'alto
catastrofi inattese per noi piccoli
da una città all'altra
e da poco mi ero accoccolata
sotto il riparo di una consuetudine
conquistato un pezzetto di calore
di stanza
una striscia di sole il pomeriggio
nel pavimento a rombi

[*]From *Le giornate bianche* (The white days, 1962).
[†]From *Giorno unico* (A single day, 1970).

VERA GHERARDUCCI

September 22nd

awful
even my body closing up
like a ball dropped
on the bed
motionless
hands on my face
all curled up
I think
about my life
voices outside
voices
a nightmare of voices
I curse
my head hurts
again voices outside
and an engine
the only one in town
that won't start
and I won't either.

October 27th

daddy drove with us kids in the back
sleepy fearful of everything
the relocations decided from above
catastrophes we couldn't have expected
from one city to another
and I had just crouched
under the protection of a routine
conquered a small piece of warmth
in a room
a strip of sun in the afternoon
on the tile floor

mi regalava un'abitudine
i visi cominciavano a riconoscermi
qualcuno mi sorrideva andando a scuola
chiedeva qualcuno il mio nome
e quella stanza lì per lì inaspettatamente
non era più la stessa
e il giardino della passeggiata e dei giochi
non era più lo stesso
invece il cielo da una finestra sembrava uguale
forse per rassicurarmi
ma la finestra non era più alta e stretta
ma larga e senza le tende
e le voci e gli accenti dalla strada
suonavano stranieri inquietanti
difficile sapere di chi fosse la colpa
se ero stata abbandonata o castigata
o se invece ero io così cambiata
tanto da non essere riconosciuta

agosto

un silenzio denso
pausato anche se silenzio
profondo
poi parole incerte di tutto
come desiderio concreto
ma anche svuotato
terribile è che si sa
cosa si può simulare
dire e non dire
fare finta
e fare paura
e avere moltissima paura
parole in crisi
che vibrano e cadono

parole

giving me the gift of a habit
the faces beginning to recognize me
someone smiling at me walking to school
someone asking my name
and suddenly unexpectedly the room
was no longer the same
and the garden of daily walks and games
was no longer the same
and yet the sky from a window seemed unchanged
perhaps to reassure me
but the window was no longer tall and narrow
it was large and curtainless
and the voices and the inflections of the street
sounded foreign and disquieting
difficult to know whose fault it was
if I had been abandoned or punished
or if instead I myself had so changed
that I was no longer being recognized

august

a thick silence
paused but still a deep
silence
then words uncertain of everything
like a concrete
though hollowed desire
a terrible thing it is to know
what you can simulate
to say and not say
to make believe
and make afraid
and to be horribly afraid
words in crisis
that vibrate and fall

words

parlano tranquilli
quelli dell'ombrellone vicino
discorsi estivi
dopo l'ultimo bagno
e fanno disegni a spirale
coi piedi allegri
inconsapevoli
nella sabbia del tramonto
parlano
parliamo
il silenzio è una pausa
per questi discorsi avviliti
diversi da ieri
oggi dunque è avvenuto qualcosa?
potresti giurarlo?

i bambini

che giocano ora qui sulla spiaggia
che vivono per otto dieci dodici anni
in uno splendore isolato
per loro
una palla è una palla
(non un ricordo)
e il mare è un gioco
il sole è la luce
i bambini mi ritornano
per risanare
e mi regalano incanto
sempre

e tu parli
io parlo

rispondo
e se oggi non avessi così male
potrei scherzare
e farti capire

people speak calmly
under the next umbrella
summer conversations
after the last swim
and they trace spiraling designs
with joyful feet
unaware
in the sunset sand
they speak
we speak
silence is a pause
for these disheartened conversations
different from yesterday
so did something happen today?
would you swear it?

the children

that play now here on the beach
that live for eight ten twelve years
in isolated splendor
for them
a ball is a ball
(not a memory)
and the sea is a game
the sun is the light
the children return to me
to heal
and they give me the gift of a spell
always

and you speak
I speak

I answer
and if today I wasn't feeling so bad
I would be able to joke
and make you understand

invece rispondo male
cioè ti rispondo
col sole che tramonta
e il mare grande e tranquillo
e la luna che spunta ad oriente

la luna

la stessa che abbiamo visto
due domeniche fa
umiliata polverosa deserta

la luna

parli di
di soluzioni radicali
quando io e te lo sappiamo
niente è radicale
deciso
definitivo
neanche la luna
e i sentimenti
e l'egoismo
la tenerezza
l'estate
l'inverno
la vita

parli categorico
senza pudore
come un condomino ad una riunione
che si protrae troppo a lungo

ed io ascolto

domani alle dieci
oppure tra un mese
o un anno
stiamo tutti per morire
ci pensi?

instead I respond badly
that is I answer you
with the sun that sets
and the great calm sea
and the moon that rises from the east

the moon

the same we saw
two sundays ago
humbled dusty deserted

the moon

you speak of
of radical solutions
when you and I know
nothing is radical
determined
definitive
not even the moon
and the emotions
and selfishness
tenderness
summer
winter
life

you speak categorically
without discretion
like a condominium owner at a meeting
that has gone on too long

and I listen

tomorrow at ten
or else in a month
or a year
we're all about to die
do you think about that?

15 dicembre*

spengiamo la luce
e facciamo l'amore
non parliamo di noi
né prima né dopo
spengiamo
sempre
la luce
anche se non facciamo l'amore
cerchiamo di non trovarci
all'ora dei pasti
o la mattina nel corridoio
spengiamo la luce
perché non ti so guardare
spengiamo la luce
e non facciamo l'amore
io esco in silenzio
torno nella mia stanza

5 aprile*

il cielo
è aria
io sono merda
il mondo è paura
il legno è legno
la preghiera
è parola
l'amore è coito
il figlio
è rimorso
la casa
è prigione
il padre
è odio
credere
è comodo
salire è assurdo
scendere

*From *Giorno unico* (A single day, 1970).

December 15th

we turn off the light
and make love
we don't speak of us
neither before nor after
we always
turn off
the light
even if we don't make love
we try not to see each other
at mealtimes
or in the morning in the hallway
we turn off the light
because I don't know how to look at you
we turn off the light
and don't make love
I leave in silence
I return to my room

April 5th

the sky
is air
I am shit
the world is fear
the wood is wood
the prayer
is word
love is coitus
the child
is remorse
the house
is prison
the father
is hate
to believe
is comfortable
to ascend is absurd
to descend

è morte
la morte
è benedetta

30 giugno*

comincia sempre
un intervallo
chiuso e compiuto
disponibile
alla fine

il silenzio non serve
nemmeno a chiudere gli occhi
e riposarsi
è un involucro vuoto
da riempire
con dischi
o voci
comincia
il pensiero
come una litania
psicoperidol
o psicoril
psicoperidol
o psicoril

decido di andar via
e anche il piede
resta
immobile
freddo
neppure per coprirsi
si muove

decido
che decido?
che posso decidere io?
non vado — mai — via
forse sono invalida

*From *Giorno unico* (A single day, 1970).

is death
death
is blessèd

June 30th

an interval
always begins
closed and completed
available
in the end

the silence isn't even good
for closing the eyes
and resting
it is an empty wrapping
to be filled
with records
or voices
the thought
begins
like a litany
psicoperidol
or psicoril
psicoperidol
or psicoril

I decide to go away
and even the foot
remains
immobile
cold
it won't move even
to cover itself

I decide
what do I decide?
what can I decide?
I don't go — ever — away
maybe I am invalid

e mi dovrebbero portare
in carrozzina

o forse sono ebete
o forse sono piccola
e sempre in carrozzina
mi dovrebbero portare
forse sono stanchissima

non
vado
mai
via
nella stanza buia
nel letto
con tutto il soffitto
da immaginare
e la musica stessa
ricomincia
psicoperidol
o psicoril?

tutto si ripete
tutto è già compiuto
chiuso e disponibile
tutto è fine
tutto è a metà

tempo di quiz
tempo di parole
tempo di prigione
di vera solitudine
tempo di amare male
tempo di invidia
e di nevrosi
di cadute
e ricadute
tempo di medicine
tempo di intervallo
tempo di morte
tempo di morire

and they ought to push me
in a wheelchair

or maybe I am an idiot
maybe I am little
and still in a stroller
they ought to push me
maybe I am exhausted

I don't
ever
go
away
in the dark room
in the bed
with all the ceiling
for imagining
and the music itself
begins again
psicoperidol
or psicoril?

everything repeats itself
everything is already completed
closed and available
everything is conclusion
everything is half-way through

time for quizzes
time for words
time for prison
for true solitude
time for loving badly
time for envy
and for neuroses
for falls
and relapses
time for medications
time for intermission
time for death
time for dying

AMELIA ROSSELLI

Contiamo infiniti morti!
la danza è quasi finita! la morte*

Contiamo infiniti morti! la danza è quasi finita! la morte,
lo scoppio, la rondinella che giace ferita al suolo, la malattia,
e il disagio, la povertà e il demonio sono le mie cassette
dinamitarde. Tarda arrivavo alla pietà — tarda giacevo fra
dei conti in tasca disturbati dalla pace che non si offriva.
Vicino alla morte il suolo rendeva ai collezionisti il prezzo
della gloria. Tardi giaceva al suolo che rendeva il suo sangue
imbevuto di lacrime la pace. Cristo seduto al suolo su delle
gambe inclinate giaceva anche nel sangue quando Maria lo
travagliò.

Nata a Parigi travagliata nell'epopea della nostra generazione
fallace. Giaciuta in America fra i ricchi campi dei possidenti
e dello Stato statale. Vissuta in Italia, paese barbaro.
Scappata dall'Inghilterra paese di sofisticati. Speranzosa
nell'Ovest ove niente per ora cresce.

Il caffè-bambù era la notte.

La congenitale tendenza al bene si risvegliava.

Se l'anima perde il suo dono allora perde terreno,
se l'inferno*

Se l'anima perde il suo dono allora perde terreno, se l'inferno
è una cosa certa, allora l'Abissinia della mia anima rinasce.
Se l'alba decide di morire, allora il fiume delle nostre
lacrime si allarga, e la voce di Dio rimane contemplata.
Se l'anima è la ritrosia dei sensi, allora l'amore è una
scienza che cade al primo venuto. Se l'anima vende il suo
bagaglio allora l'inchiostro è un paradiso. Se l'anima
scende dal suo gradino, la terra muore.

*From *Variazioni belliche* (War variations, 1964).

Amelia Rosselli

Infinite We Count the Dead!
The Dance Is Almost Finished! Death

Infinite we count the dead! the dance is almost finished! death,
the blast, the little swallow lying wounded on the ground, illness,
and discomfort, poverty and the devil are my dynamitard's
tools. Tardy I arrived to pity — tardy I lay among
accountings troubled by a peace that didn't offer itself.
Close to death the ground yielded to the collectors the price
of glory. Tardily peace lay on the ground that yielded its
tear soaked blood. Christ sitting on the ground on
inclined legs also lay in blood when Mary afflicted[10]
him.

Born in Paris afflicted in the epoch of our fallacious
generation. Laid out in America among the rich fields of
                landowners
and the statal State. Lived in Italy, barbarous land.
Fled from England land of the sophisticated. Hopeful
in the West where nothing now grows.

The caffè-bambù was the night.

The congenitalial[11] tendency to what's good reawakened.

If the Soul Loses Its Gift Then It Loses Ground,
If Hell

If the soul loses its gift then it loses ground, if hell
is a certainty, then the Abyssinia of my soul[12] is reborn.
If dawn decides to die, then the river of our
tears widens, and the voice of God remains contemplated.
If the soul is the reluctance of the senses, then love is a
science that falls to the first comer. If the soul sells its
baggage then ink is a paradise. If the soul
steps down, the earth dies.

Io contemplo gli uccelli che cantano ma la mia anima è
triste come il soldato in guerra.

L'alba si presentò sbracciata
e impudica; io[*]

L'alba si presentò sbracciata e impudica; io
la cinsi di alloro da poeta: ella si risvegliò
lattante, latitante.

L'amore era un gioco instabile; un gioco di
fonosillabe.

Un'esile vocina: basta aprire
appena il battente[†]

Un'esile vocina: basta aprire appena il battente
della finestruola, che cangia il mondo e
le sue apparenze sono tutt'uno con le tue
emicranie. Basta appena aprire, aprire, il
tuo sonno si misura con il cielo, di cui
resta tragica immagine.

Apri un muro: ne appare un altro, a tastarti
il polso. Radendo il muro non puoi, non vuoi
salvarti quelle poche ore dello spirito, forzare
quelle sue cellule misteriose. E rimane il
sentirsi pino accasciato tra le pinete nuove
dritto fine a marcia pietà.

Di sera il cielo spazia, povera[†]

Di sera il cielo spazia, povera
cosa è dalla finestra il suo bigio
(ma era verde) ondulare. Oppure

colori che mai speravo riconquistare
abbaiavano tetri al davanzale. Se

---

[*]From *Variazioni belliche* (War variations, 1964).
[†]From *Serie ospedaliera* (Hospital series, 1969).

I contemplate singing birds but my soul is
as sad as the soldier at war.

Dawn Presented Itself Bare-Armed and Immodest

Dawn presented itself bare-armed and immodest;
I crowned it with poetic laurels: it awakened
fledgling, fleeing.[13]

Love was an unstable game; a game of
phonosyllables.

A Feeble Little Voice: All It Takes Is Barely Opening the Shutter

A feeble little voice: all it takes is barely opening the shutter
of the small window, and the world changes and
its appearances are one and the same as your
migraines. All it takes is barely opening, opening, and your
sleep measures itself against the sky, whose
tragic image it remains.

Open a wall: another appears, feeling your
pulse. Grazing the wall you can't, you won't
save those few hours of the spirit, force
its mysterious cells. And what is left is
feeling pine collapsed amidst new pinewoods
straight end to rotten pity.

In the Evening the Sky Roams, a Meager

In the evening the sky roams, a meager
thing from the window its grayish
(once green) undulations. Or else

colors that I never hoped to reclaim
barked gloomily at the window-sill. If

questa tetra verginità non può

rimuovere dal cuore i suoi salmi
allora non v'è nessuna pace per
chi scuce, notte e dì, trite cose
dai suoi labbri.

Non è la casa (cucita con le mattonelle)
a farti da guida; è il mistero
disintegro delle facciate aeree

che ti promette gaudio sottilmente.

Attorno a questo mio corpo*

Attorno a questo mio corpo
stretto in mille schegge, io
corro vendemmiando, sibilando
come il vento d'estate, che
si nasconde; attorno a questo
vecchio corpo che si nasconde
stendo un velo di paludi sulle
coste dirupate, per scendere
poi, a patti.

Attorno a questo corpo dalle
mille paludi, attorno a questa
miniera irrequieta, attorno
a questo vaso di tenerezze
mal esaudite, mai vidi altro
che pesci ingrandire, divenire
altro che se stessi, altro
che una incontrollabile angoscia
di divenire, altro che se
stessi nell'arcadia di un
mondo letterario che si forniva
formaggi da sé; sentendosi
combattere, nelle vacue cene

*From *Serie ospedaliera* (Hospital series, 1969).

this gloomy virginity cannot

remove from the heart its psalms
then there is no peace for
the one unstitching, day and night, trite things
from lips.

It is not the house (stitched together with tiles)
acting as your guide; it is the disintegral[14]
mystery of the aerial facades

that promises you bliss subtly.

Around This Body of Mine

Around this body of mine
bound in a thousand splinters, I
run harvesting, whistling
like the summer wind, which
hides itself; around this
old body which hides itself
I lay a veil of marshes on the
precipitous shores, to come
then, to terms.

Around this body with
a thousand marshes, around this
restless mine, around
this vase of tenderness
poorly answered,[15] I never saw anything other
than fish growing bigger, becoming
anything other than themselves, other
than an uncontrollable anguish
of becoming, other than them-
selves in the Arcadia of a
literary world lavishing itself
with its own cheeses; feeling themselves
battled, in the vacuous dinners

da incontrollabili istinti
di predominio: logori fanciulli
che stiravano altre membra
pulite come il sonno, in vacue
miniere.

Ho sognato visite di parenti*

Ho sognato visite di parenti
maldestre donne e sindacati
mi congiungo a chi vive più vivo di me
sviscerare le piante, emettere un grido.

Poi dimostrarsi inadatti alla causa
mentre balenano pidocchi
scrittore in povertà, la mente
disturbata da nonsensi.

Come una bestia le tue indulgenze, e
i cuscini affondavano comodamente
in una specie di clausola senza causa
senza emettere un suono.

Mentre fiaschi di vino e trappole usuali
strizzavano l'occhio a tanta verginità
ed ora annaspa nel retrocampo
umiliandosi le mani.

un blu che non è nemmeno blu o comunque*

un blu che non è nemmeno blu o comunque
è un blu chiaro chiaro chiaro e la polvere
sembra mischiata all'aria essendo un
poco gialligno il cielo che è stesura
di sabbia.

Le case sono muri che come una lavagna
si cancellano, hanno anch'essi aria di
sabbia.

---

*From *Documento* (Document, 1976).

by an uncontrollable instinct
for domination: worn-out children
who stretched other limbs
clean like sleep, in vacuous
mines.

I Dreamt of Visiting Relatives

I dreamt of visiting relatives
bungling women and unions
I join myself to those who live more alive than me
dissecting the designs, emitting a cry.

Then demonstrating oneself inadequate to the cause
while lice flash
writer in poverty, the mind
disturbed by nonsense.

Your indulgence like a beast, and
the cushions sank comfortably
in a sort of clause without cause
without emitting a sound.

While flasks of wine and the usual snares
were winking at so much virginity
and now it gropes in the backfield
humbling its hands.

A Blue That Isn't Even Blue or in Any Case

a blue that isn't even blue or in any case
is a clear clear clear blue and the dust
seems mixed with the air for it's a
little yellowish the sky that is draft[16]
of sand

The houses are walls that can be erased
like a slate, they also have this air of
sand.

Ma la sabbia non ha voce e tristemente
rovina il paesaggio perché non può lei
stessa volare al cielo, votare quel suo
esistere!

Gli specchi! il*

Gli specchi! il
segreto, l'anima, e il rimedio.

Non v'è rimedio agli specchi!

Il dovere: sagace organizzazione forzata
una promessa di riposo
a turbare il tuo rigore

una tranquilla essenza inattiva.

L'impulso (corporale e insieme logico)
protegge il corpo coi suoi nervi
sottovaluta il male. Il giorno dopo

ne decidono la sua tragicità.

Vizio congenito sembra incorreggibile
segue senza capriccio
una qualsiasi via di ristoro.

La crisi ti mette in congiuntura
ripeti l'avventura.

---

*From *Appunti sparsi e persi* (Lost and scattered notes, 1983).

But the sand doesn't have a voice and sadly
ruins the landscape because it itself
can't fly to the sky, consecrate its own

existence!

The Mirrors! The

The mirrors! the
secret, the soul, and the remedy.

There is no remedy against mirrors!

The obligation: sagacious forced organization
a promise of repose
to disturb your severity

a tranquil idle essence.

The impulse (at once corporeal and logical)
protects the body with its nerves
underestimates the bad. The day after

they decide its tragedy.

Congenital vice, it seems incorrigible
follows without whimsy
any means to relief.

The crisis puts you at the juncture
you repeat the adventure.

questa notte con spavaldo desiderio*

questa notte con spavaldo desiderio
scesi per le praterie d'un lungo fiume
impermeato d'antiche abitudini
ch'al dunque ad un segnale indicavano

melma, e fiato. Solo sporcizia
sì, vidi dall'ultimo ponte, dubitando
d'una mia vita ancora rimasta al
sole, non per l'arrosto ma per

il fuoco è buona: se a tutti divenne
già prima ch'io nascessi — indifferente

la mia buona o cattiva sorte, dall'altr'angolo
che non da questa visione crematorizzata

dalla mia e vostra vita terrorizzata
se resistere dipende dal cuore

piuttosto dalle sottane s'arrota
la Mistinguette, la vita sberciata
per un attimo ancora, se sesso
è così rotativo da apparire poi

vano a questo recitativo che mi
faceva passare per pazza quando
arroteandomi dietro ad ogni scrivania

sorvegliavo i vostri desideri d'essere
lontani dalla mia, rotativa nella
notte specchiata nel lucido del

vetro che copre le vostre indifferenze
alla mia stralunante morte.

*From *Impromptu* (Impromptu, 1981).

Tonight with Bold Desire

tonight with bold desire
I descended through the prairies of a long river
impermeated[17] with ancient habits
that at a signal ultimately indicated

slime, and breath. From the last bridge
I saw only filth, yes, doubting
that a life of mine still remained in the
sun, it is good not for the

roast but for the fire: if everyone became
indifferent — even before I was born —

to my good or bad luck, from the angle
that is not this crematorized[18] view

from my and your terrorized life
if resisting depends on the heart

but it's from the skirts that *Mistinguette*[19]
grinds away, another moment
of hollered life,[20] if sex
is so rotative as to then appear

vain to this recitative that made
me pass for mad when
grinding[21] myself behind every desk

I watched all of you desiring to be
far from mine, rotary in the
night mirrored in the shine of the

glass that covers your indifferences
to my bewildering death.

GABRIELLA LETO

Non fu amore di altri e non il mio*

Non fu amore di altri e non il mio
non fu il rigore di cui ti vanti.
Devi alla cura dell'esistente
l'arida scelta dell'addio.
A una memoria ferma e senza incanti
le poche ore tra suburbani
assimilabili orizzonti
presto vissute cui feci dono
di altere lacrime sottaciute.

Scoscese acquisizioni immobili paure*

Scoscese acquisizioni immobili paure
piú non avrò.
Non piú scarti né fughe e quella che mi assale
felicità insidiata io neppure
saprò se fu.
Tale è il vostro potere odiate rughe.
In cui si compie l'alta mutazione
che ogni costanza ogni evento delude.
Albe di levigati pensieri e impervie in sogno
scale vi dico addio. Né a voi chiedo ragione
pallide macchie sulle mani nude.

non c'è non ci sarà mai tanta e tale*

non c'è non ci sarà mai tanta e tale
ahimè breve e non pura
altra felicità se nel tuo sguardo
né morte né altro male
mi fa paura

*From *Nostalgia dell'acqua* (Nostalgia for water, 1990).

GABRIELLA LETO

It Wasn't the Love of Others or Mine

It wasn't the love of others or mine
it wasn't the rigor of which you boast.
To your concern for what exists
you owe the dry choice of leaving.
To a still memory without magic
the quickly lived few hours
among assimilable suburban horizons
to these hours I gave the gift
of proud unmentioned tears.

Steep Acquisitions Motionless Fears

Steep acquisitions motionless fears
no longer will I have them.
No more deviations or flights and what assails me,
endangered happiness, I won't even know
if it ever was.
Such is your power hated wrinkles.
Here is fulfilled the high mutation
disappointing every perseverance every occasion.
I bid you farewell dawn of smooth thoughts and stairs
impervious in dream. Nor will I seek your explanation
pale spots on my bare hands.

There Is Not and There Will Never Be So Much

there is not and there will never be so much
and such other alas brief and impure
happiness if in your eyes neither
death nor any other affliction
frightens me

Qui dove all'improvviso*

Qui dove all'improvviso
si interrompe il sentiero
per oscuro divieto
non piú non mai reciso
langue in nudo pallore
il fiore del narciso
chiuso nel suo segreto
di voluttà e colore.

Solo che sul divano*

Solo che sul divano
cada una luce privilegiata
che la diafana ampolla sul ripiano
abbia una rosa ardente e atteggiata
trema nella mia mente e si confonde
quasi in acque profonde
immagine riflessa
la realtà dinegata
cosí che la mia vita in quel momento
si arresta da sé stessa dipartita
e dalle vuote finzioni a stento
si ridesta e si scuote.

Davvero troppo tardi sei tornata*

Davvero troppo tardi sei tornata
se diradate sperdute le ore
rintoccavano in diàstole al mio cuore
se un'ansia grigia da poco aggiunta
al respiro inoltrato della notte
con sé mi aveva e io compresi
quella piccola piega rassegnata
l'ombra smunta del viso sul cuscino
e gli altri segni attesi
a dividere il tuo dal mio destino.

*From *Nostalgia dell'acqua* (Nostalgia for water, 1990).

Here Where the Path

Here where the path
is abruptly interrupted
for obscure interdiction
no longer nor ever severed
the narcissus flower
languishes in naked pallor
closed up in its secret
of desire and color.

If a Privileged Light

If a privileged light
falls on the couch
or the diaphanous cruet on the shelf
has an ardent, posing rose
negated reality
like an image reflected
in deep waters
quivers in my mind and blurs
so in that moment my life
having departed from itself halts
and from empty fictions barely
stirs itself and wakes.

Indeed You Came Home Too Late[22]

Indeed you came home too late
if the hours, dispersed, lost,
were striking in diastole at my heart
if a gray anxiety just added
to the late breathing of the night
was holding me and I understood
that little line of resignation
the gaunt shadow of the face on the pillow
and the other signs intent on
dividing your destiny from mine.

La nave attende nel porto*

La nave attende nel porto.
È l'ora — bisogna salpare.
E quando sarò sullo smorto
broccato di seta del mare
quando la riva svanirà inghiottita
con il mondo che si allontana
per l'amore che era e piú non è
lasciate che scriva parole
di nostalgia di cortesia di vita:
mille regretz de vous habandonner.

Quello che resta ormai ridotto a poco*

Quello che resta ormai ridotto a poco
o giorni o giorni che lo consumaste
sopravvive in un nome nel tuo nome.
Ma voi profondi sensi e voi mie virtú nuove
come teneramente invano a lungo
palpitaste! E gli eventi le ragioni
cosí avversate e cosí vive
l'ardito cuore dove altrimenti
sono se non nel segno che ne scrive?

Tra miti e spettri del futuro*

Tra miti e spettri del futuro
in qualche luogo con te mi avrai.
Sarò tra incensi di sigaretta
con quei pensieri che non sai
nella tua cauta memoria il mio
sguardo irrequieto avrà ti giuro
forza e ragione dell'oblío
oh amara oh esangue vendetta.

*From *Nostalgia dell'acqua* (Nostalgia for water, 1990).

The Ship Waits in the Harbor

The ship waits in the harbor
it is time — time to set sail.
And when I am on the pale
silk brocade of the sea
when the shore disappears engulfed
with the world by the growing distance
for the love that was and is no longer
allow me to write words
of nostalgia of courtesy of life:
mille regretz de vous habandonner.[23]

What Is Left and by Now Reduced to Little

What is left and by now reduced to little
oh days oh days that consumed it
lives on in a name in your name.
But you my deep senses and you my new virtues
how long tenderly and in vain
you palpitated! And the events,
the contested and vital reasons
and the daring heart where else are they
if not in the sign that writes them?

Among Myths and Specters of the Future

Among myths and specters of the future
you'll have me with you somewhere.
I'll be immersed in cigarette incense
with thoughts of which you're unaware
in your cautious memory my
restless gaze will have, I swear,
force and power over oblivion
oh bitter oh bloodless revenge.

L'amore il sogno il verso[*]

L'amore il sogno il verso
moduli inesprimibili del senso
hanno in comune — di segno diverso
il loro tempo breve.
Ogni vita cosciente del suo stesso
angoscioso scompenso
dal mobile riflesso
di quella brevità pregio riceve.

[*]From *L'ora insonne* (The sleepless hour, 1997).

Love Dream Verse

Love dream verse
inexpressible measures of sense
though diverse in sign
share the brevity of their time.
Each life aware of its own
anguished imbalance
draws worth from the mobile reflection
of that brief duration.

ALDA MERINI

Dies irae[*]

Tu insegui le mie forme,
segui tu la giustezza del mio corpo
e non mai la bellezza
di cui vado superba.
Sono animale all'infelice coppia
prona su un letto misero d'assalti,
sono la carezzevole rovina
dai fecondi sussulti alle tue mani,
sono il vuoto cresciuto
sino all'altezza esatta del piacere
ma con mille tramonti alle mie spalle:
quante volte, amor mio, tu mi disdegni.

Inno[†]

> a Pietro De Paschale

Se Tu mi hai posto in grembo e nella mente
questo seme dolcissimo d'amore,
versa sopr'esso un'aria che lo allevi
e che gli dia piú facile respiro!

Se mi hai dato l'amore come parte
di Te che sei la Parte della vita,
fa che io trovi il calice piú mio,
il piú vasto, il piú ricco e desolato
per colmarlo di me, fa che io trovi.

> Pietro!

[*]From *Paura di Dio* (Fear of God, 1955).
[†]From *Tu sei Pietro* (Thou art Peter, 1961).

ALDA MERINI

Dies irae

You pursue my figure,
seeking the sanctioned body
and never the beauty
of which I am proud.
I am a beast at the unhappy coupling
prone on a miserable bed of assaults,
I am the caressing ruination
quaking fecundly at your hands,
I am the void raised
to the exact height of pleasurc
but with a thousand sunsets at my back:
how many times, my love, you scorn me.

Hymn

to Pietro De Paschale

If in my womb and mind You placed
this sweetest seed of love,
pour over it an air that will raise it
that will ease its breath!

If You gave me love as part
of You who are the Part of life,
see that I find the chalice that most belongs to me,
the vastest, the richest and most desolate of chalices
see that I find it to fill it with myself.

Pietro!

Genesi[*]

Vorrei un figlio da te che sia una spada
lucente, come un grido di alta grazia,
che sia pietra, che sia novello Adamo,
lievito del mio sangue e che risolva
piú quietamente questa nostra sete.

Ah, se t'amo, lo grido ad ogni vento
gemmando fiori da ogni stanco ramo
e fiorita son tutta e d'ogni velo
vo' scerpando il mio lutto
perché genesi sei della mia carne.

Ma il mio cuore, trafitto dall'amore
ha desiderio di mondarsi vivo.

E perciò dammi un figlio delicato,
un bellissimo, vergine viticcio
da allacciare al mio tronco, e tu, possente
olmo, tu padre ricco d'ogni forza pura
mieterai liete ombre alle mie luci.

Canto di risposta[†]

a Franco Gentilucci

L'essere stata in certi tristi luoghi,
coltivare fantasmi
come tu dici, attento amico mio,
non dà diritto a credere che dentro
dentro di me continui la follia.
Son rimasta poeta anche all'inferno
solo che io cercavo di Euridice
la casta ombra e non ho piú parole...
Ecco, Franco, la tenera risposta
al tuo dilemma: io sono poeta
e poeta rimasi tra le sbarre

[*]From *Tu sei Pietro* (Thou art Peter, 1961).
[†]From *Destinati a morire* (Destined to die, 1980).

Genesis

From you I would love a child who could be a sword
shining, like a cry of high grace,
who could be stone, a new Adam,
yeast of my blood and who might resolve
more quietly this thirst of ours.

Ah, if I love you, I will shout it to the wind
and bud flowers from every tired branch
now all in bloom I am rending
each veil from my mourning
because you are genesis of my flesh.

But my heart, pierced by love
desires to cleanse itself into life.

And thus give me a delicate child,
a most beautiful, virgin tendril
a tendril I may tie to my trunk, and you, mighty
elm, you father, rich with every pure force
will harvest happy shadows in my lights.

Song of Reply

to Franco Gentilucci

That I have been in certain sad places,
that I have cultivated ghosts
as you say, my attentive friend,
doesn't entitle one to believe that inside
inside of me the madness continues.
I remained a poet even in hell
and yet having searched for the chaste shadow
of Eurydice I am now wordless…
Here, Franco, the tender reply
to your dilemma: I am a poet
and a poet I remained between bars

solo che fuori, senza casa e persa
ho continuato mio malgrado il canto
della tristezza, e dentro ad ogni fiore
della mia casa è ancora la speranza
che nulla sia accaduto a devastare
il mio solco di luce ed abbia perso
la vera chiave che mi chiude al vero.

Ah se almeno potessi[*]

Ah se almeno potessi,
    suscitare l'amore
  come pendio sicuro al mio destino!
  E adagiare il respiro
    fitto dentro le foglie
  e ritogliere il senso alla natura!
    O se solo potessi
    toccar con dita tremule la luce
    quella gagliarda che ci sboccia in seno,
    corpo astrale del nostro viver solo
    pur rimanendo pietra, inizio, sponda
      tangibile agli dèi...
    e violare i piú chiusi paradisi
    solo con la sostanza dell'affetto.

L'uccello di fuoco[*]

L'uccello di fuoco
della mia mente malata,
questo passero grigio
che abita nel profondo
e col suo pigolío
sempre mi fa tremare
perché pare indifeso,
bisognoso d'amore,
qualche volta ha una voce
cosí tenera e nuova
che sotto il suo trionfo
detto la poesia.

[*]From *La Terra Santa* (The Holy Land, 1984).

and yet outside, homeless and lost
unwillingly I continued the song
of my sadness, and each flower
in my house still holds the hope
that nothing has happened to devastate
my trail of light and that I have lost
the true key that shuts me from the truth.

Ah If at Least I Could

Ah if at least I could,
    arouse love
  like a sure slope to my destiny!
  And gently lay my breath
    thick among the leaves
  and again take sense from nature!
    Oh if only I could
    touch with trembling fingers the light
    the bold one that blooms in our breast,
    astral body of our lonely lives
    while remaining stone, beginning, shore
      tangible to the gods…
    and violate the most sealed paradises
    only with the substance of affection.

The Bird of Fire

The bird of fire
of my maddened mind,
this gray sparrow
that lives in the depths
and always makes me
tremble with its chirping
because it seems defenseless,
needy of love,
sometimes it has a voice
so tender and fresh
that under its triumph
I dictate poetry.

Lascio a te queste impronte sulla terra*

Lascio a te queste impronte sulla terra
  tenere dolci, che si possa dire:
qui è passata una gemma o una tempesta,
  una donna che avida di dire
  disse cose notturne e delicate,
  una donna che non fu mai amata.
Qui passò forse una furiosa bestia
avida sete che dette tempesta
alla terra, a ogni clima, al firmamento,
  ma qui passò soltanto il mio tormento.

Sono nata il ventuno a primavera*

Sono nata il ventuno a primavera
  ma non sapevo che nascere folle,
  aprire le zolle
  potesse scatenar tempesta.
Cosí Proserpina lieve
  vede piovere sulle erbe,
sui grossi frumenti gentili
e piange sempre la sera.
Forse è la sua preghiera.

Il pastrano*

Un certo pastrano abitò lungo tempo in casa
era un pastrano di lana buona
un pettinato leggero
un pastrano di molte fatture
vissuto e rivoltato mille volte
era il disegno del nostro babbo
la sua sagoma ora assorta ed ora felice.
Appeso a un cappio o al portabiti
assumeva un'aria sconfitta:
traverso quell'antico pastrano
ho conosciuto i segreti di mio padre
vivendolo cosí, nell'ombra.

*From *Vuoto d'amore* (Void of love, 1991).

I Leave You These Imprints on the Earth

I leave you these imprints on the earth,
    tender sweet, that they may say:
here passed a bud or tempest,
    a woman eager to tell who told
    of things nocturnal and delicate,
    a woman who was never loved.
Here perhaps passed a furious beast
an avid thirst that brought tempest
to the earth, to every climate, to the firmament,
    but here passed only my torment.

I Was Born on the Twenty-First in Spring

I was born on the twenty-first in Spring
    but I did not know that to be born mad,
    to open the sod
    could unleash storms.
Thus gentle Persephone
    sees rain falling on the grass,
on the thick kind wheat
and always cries at nightfall.
Perhaps it is her prayer.

The Overcoat

A certain overcoat lived at home for many years
it was an overcoat of fine wool
a light worsted
an overcoat resewn again and again
lived in and reversed a thousand times
it was our father's shape
his silhouette, absorbed or happy.
Hanging on a loop or the hanger
it assumed an air of defeat:
through that ancient overcoat
I learned my father's secrets
living him like this, in the shadow.

*Apro la sigaretta**

*Apro la sigaretta
come fosse una foglia di tabacco
e aspiro avidamente
l'assenza della tua vita.
È cosí bello sentirti fuori,
desideroso di vedermi
e non mai ascoltato.
Sono crudele, lo so,
ma il gergo dei poeti è questo:
un lungo silenzio acceso
dopo un lunghissimo bacio.*

*From *Ballate non pagate* (Unpaid ballads, 1995).

I Open the Cigarette

I open the cigarette
as if it were a tobacco leaf
and inhale avidly
the absence of your life.
It is so beautiful to feel you outside,
eager to see me
and yet never heard.
I am cruel, I know,
but the jargon of poets is this:
a long silence lit
after a very long kiss.

ROSSANA OMBRES

Talin del pastificio*

Il mio amico, l'ho perso.

Mi piaceva veder riposare
nello schermo dei suoi occhi
un giogo tranquillo di buoi.

Mi piaceva ricordare
con lui, i girasoli dell'orto
delle suore e il bastardo spinone
che teneva sotto le sue corse
il pollame del Sumiano.

Verso sera andavamo a cercare
cicoria sui bordi dello stradone;
ci guardavano, le donne di casa:
finché non si diventava
io la bandiera brillante del mio
grembiule di scuola
lui, uno dei tanti respiri di fumo
— erano venti, le ciminiere a Casale —
col suo vestito di telone.

Ma succederà che gli anni
mi faranno dimenticare
d'essere nata in una fabbrica
d'aver camminato le campagne
d'aver giocato da bambina
dentro i bacili di zinco della farina
(fingendomi in una barca a mare).

Così nella pace della memoria tralasciata
diventerà una lapide
la sua ferma testa d'uomo tenace.

---

*From *Le ciminiere di Casale* (The smokestacks of Casale, 1962).

Rossana Ombres

Talin of the Pasta Factory

I lost my friend.

I used to like seeing
a peaceful yoke of oxen
resting in the screen of his eyes.
With him I used to like reminiscing,
about the sunflowers in the nuns'
garden and the mongrel griffon
that kept Sumiano's chickens
under its tracks.

At dusk we used to go searching
for chicory along the edges of the main road;
the women of the house would watch us:
until I would become
the bright banner of my
school smock
and he, one of many breaths of smoke
— there were twenty smokestacks of Casale —
with his canvas clothes.

But of course the years
will make me forget
about being born in a factory
about having walked the fields
about having played as a child
inside the zinc flower bowls
(pretending to be in a boat at sea).

Thus in the peace of neglected memory
the still head of a tenacious man
will become a memorial headstone.

Travaglio sentimentale dell'ostrica di fumo*

non in questo modo, dicevo, trascinando sul fondo la co-
        pertina rosa
non in questo, dicevo, modo
la magnolia soda attraendomi fresca, sgusciando la taran-
        tola
dal tavolo di ferro per sorreggermi
la ferita rosa oblunga molto pateticamente incorniciata
non in questo modo
non in questo — urlando nella più carezzevole delle voci —
        questo modo:
    con tutti quei cocci ti farai male amore
    con tutti quei cocci mi farò male amore
(col più scheggiato dei sospiri, dilungando la più
carezzevole delle voci...)
Cupo di radici di foglie di gesti terribili in un segno di
        terra
garbatamente tiri indietro i tuoi aquiloni:
Lazzaro in veste di yogi
alza il mondo cantabile addormentato con le cosce a fior di
        loto.

Sprofondata nel tuo mondo vegetale
non in questo modo dico arrochita non
in questo modo imploro nell'intrico (rapprendendomi
        dentro
la larga chiazza disposta per l'infrazione delle comete)
non in questo modo non
corpi dilatati enfiati oboe di deformità empite d'acque di
        disgelo
si rimboccano sui miei piedi
lunghi cordoni rosa attorcigliandomi l'alluce
nel ginocchio componendo serpentini la coccarda rosa del-
        le feste femminili,

non in questo modo premendo implorando gemendo il ne-
        ro subíto come una seppia

*From *L'ipotesi di Agar* (Hagar's hypothesis, 1968).

Sentimental Suffering of the Oyster of Smoke

not in this way, I said, dragging the little pink blanket
       along the bottom
not in this, I said, way
the firm magnolia drawing me in its freshness, the tarantula
       slipping away
from the iron table to hold my
oblong pink wound so pathetically framed
not in this way
not in this — screaming in the most caressing of voices —
       this way:
    with all those shards my love you'll get hurt
    with all those shards my love I'll get hurt
(with the most chipped of sighs, protracting the most
caressing of voices...)
Dark with roots with leaves with terrible gestures in an earthly
       sign
politely you pull back your kites:
Lazarus in the cloths of a yogi
raises the singable world asleep with lotus-shaped
       thighs.

Sunk in your vegetable world
not in this way I say hoarsely not
in this way I beg in the tangle (coagulating
       inside
the large stain disposed for the infraction of comets)
not in this way not
bodies dilated swollen oboe of deformities filled with thawing
       waters
long pink cords fold over
my feet entangling my big toe
on my knee composing serpentine the pink cockade of
       women's festivals,

not in this way pressing imploring moaning
       blackness suffered as a cuttlefish

disposta a copertina rosa portandoti trofei di sinuose for-
  me aperte
aquiloni attirando con carezzevole voce e corde oleose
amore, dicendoti, al colmo dello scompenso con brevità
  telegrafica:
non in questo modo non in non in questo modo non in
  questo non in

1965.

Tempo di rondò*

Il trampoliere imperturbabile
placò la terra beante ranocchie:
dopo i giuochi d'acqua del labirinto, s'alzava
un vertiginoso nido
dove le preghiere depongono le uova.

All'Angelo del sognato fui vicina
qualche secondo nella collaretta di un labirinto.
Il grado ultimo del magistero alchimistico
imparai dall'Angelo del sognato,
dimenticata alla sua fosforescenza minerale.

Ora so che davanti alle sue costruzioni
s'intorpidiscono le proterve mani tessute
dei Cherubini dell'Apocalisse:
blatte dal dorso querulo
vengono spazzate via le loro fidule
in bare per infanti si mutano le trombe marine
e i salteri, sedotti dai serpenti e dalle iguane,
diventano sonore acrobatiche tane.

Fui vicina all'Angelo del sognato
dove i pitosfori concentrici
diventano valve sigillate all'esodo.

Un dolore itinerante ha tempo di rondò.

---

*From *Bestiario d'amore* (Bestiary of love, 1974).

disposed like a little pink blanket bringing you trophies
    of sinuous open shapes
attracting kites with caressing voice and oily cords
love, telling you, at the peak of imbalance with telegraphic
    brevity:
not in this way not in not in this way not in
    this not in

1965.

Rondeau Tempo

The imperturbable wader
calmed an earth blissful to frogs:
after the labyrinthian watergames,
a vertiginous nest where prayers lay eggs
took flight.

I was close to the Angel of dreams
a few seconds in the neck of a labyrinth.
From the dream Angel I learned
the ultimate degree of the alchemical magistery
and was left to its mineral phosphorescence.

Now I know that facing its constructions
the insolent woven hands
of the Apocalyptic Cherubs[24] become numb:
roaches with querulous backs
whose shells are swept away
sea twisters turning into infant caskets
psalteries, seduced by serpents and iguanas,
becoming sonorous acrobatic lairs.

I was close to the dream Angel
where the concentric butterburrs
become valves sealed to the exodus.

An itinerate pain has rondeau tempo.

L'angelo che ci separò con la fiamma*

L'angelo che in remoti tempi ci divise
dissaldando la doppia creatura con la sua fiamma feroce
perché ci cercassimo
attraverso estenuanti pause d'attesa e guerre
macinanti prodigi

l'angelo che fra tutti gli animali
nell'acqua sopra la terra e dentro
nelle tane dell'aria e sulle foglie del creato
scelse il bigatto
perché aggrovigliasse in cirilliche sete i nostri passi

oggi è qui
dritto in piedi
a riscuotere la caccia dai suoi guardiani.

I guardiani, brevi, certi, gli han portato
di te e di me
gesti e accenti, e vernici d'oggetti nuovi
e tonfi d'oggetti caduti
paesaggi perduti dal treno, dialoghi, forme armoniose
e forme stravolte
e forme di crescita in crescita;
gli hanno portato
venefici implacabili e gardenie di pensieri:
e, dopo tutto,
sogni — sognati da te e da me —
che l'arsura del giorno faceva dissetanti
mescolati
e legati insieme,
memoria terminale della doppia creatura.

Nessuno li separerà mai più
quei gesti quelle forme quei sogni
usciranno
insieme da questo mondo che somiglia a un vestibolo
mentre l'angelo che ci separò con la fiamma
starà faccia a terra ad ascoltare
una voce che parla.

*From *Bestiario d'amore* (Bestiary of love, 1974).

The Angel Who Separated Us with the Flame

The angel who divided us in remote times
unsoldering the double creature with its ferocious flame
so that we would seek each other
grinding prodigies
through extenuating pauses of expectation and war

the angel who amidst all the animals
in the water above the earth, and inside it,
in the lairs of air and on the leaves of creation
chose the silkworm[25]
so that it would entangle our steps in Cyrillic silks

today is here
standing straight
to collect the game from its keepers.

Of you and me
the keepers, brief, certain, brought him
gestures and accents, and the gloss of new objects
and the thud of fallen objects
views lost from the train, dialogues, harmonious shapes
and distorted shapes
and shapes from spurt to spurt;
they brought him
implacable poisonings and gardenias of thoughts:
and, after all,
dreams — dreamt by you and me —
that the parching day made refreshing
mixed
and tied together,
terminal memory of the double creature.

No one will ever again separate them
those gestures those shapes those dreams
together
will leave this world which resembles a vestibule[26]
while the angel who separated us with the flame
will stay face to the ground listening[27]
to a speaking voice.

Filastrocca su otto strofe[*]

La parola mangia una strada
la strada che va lontano è amore, la parola
mangia l'amore che è una lunga strada
con due linee parallele, e il treno
divora la parola
poi fugge
per oscuri cunicoli di pietra e torna fuori
accerchiato dal cielo, un cielo
sicuro fino all'incredibile.

La parola che ha mangiato la strada
è masticata da un treno in fuga, e il treno
scampato ai cunicoli oscuri
va a stamparsi nella bocca di un cielo
che non permette evasioni!
Ma ecco che il cielo (che sembrava
sicuro fino all'incredibile)
è strapazzato e mangiato dal pesce-indecifrabile
e il pesce-indecifrabile
cade, per disattenzione
nella trappola della sirena che brucia
la sirenafiamma
che mangia il pesce-indecifrabile che ha mangiato
il cielo che ha mangiato il treno che ha inghiottito
una parola che ha divorato una strada
una strada con due linee parallele
che va lontano e dunque è amore.

Alla fine interviene Raziél, custode del sognato,
(che disse ad Adamo i nomi
delle immagini degli Angeli:
quei nomi che da un altro
furono corretti con maligna intenzione…)
«Queste cose» dice Raziél «furono nell'occhio
di un torbido brontosauro,
e l'aquila che le afferrò per portarle ai suoi neonati
fu spezzata dal fulmine
e il fulmine

[*]From *Bestiario d'amore* (Bestiary of love, 1974).

Nursery Rhyme in Eight Strophes[28]

The word eats a road
the road that goes far is love, the word
eats love, which is a long road
with two parallel lines, and the train
devours the word
then flees
through dark stone tunnels, emerging outside
surrounded by the sky, a sky
unbelievably sure.

The word that has eaten the road
is chewed by a train in flight, and the train,
having escaped from the dark tunnels,
imprints itself on the mouth of a sky
that won't permit evasions!
But suddenly the sky (that seemed
unbelievably sure)
is battered and eaten by the indecipherable-fish
and the indecipherable-fish
falls, for lack of attention
into the trap of the siren who burns
the flamesiren
who eats the indecipherable-fish that has eaten
the sky that has eaten the train that has swallowed
a word that has devoured a road
a road with two parallel lines
that goes far and hence is love.

In the end Raziel intervenes, the dream keeper,
(who told Adam the names
of the images of the Angels:
those names that another
corrected with malign intention…)
"These things" says Raziel "were in the eye
of a turbid brontosaurus,
and the eagle that seized them to take them to her newborns
was split by lightening
and the lightening

fu smentito dall'acqua
e l'acqua
fu bevuta da un agnello
che un ladro d'agnelli rubò e uccise
e un castigatore di ladri d'agnelli
sparò al cuore del ladro
e poi fu castigato e assaggiato dal lupo che lo mangiò
e il lupo
morì per il veleno di serpicina
e la serpicina
fu uccisa da una signora
che morì attempata fra gladioli bianchi
e con le sue scarpette ricamate
ruppe la catena.»

Così parlava Raziél, presidente dei nomi
degli Angeli, dei nomi
che il Maligno nell'ora seconda storpiò
e riportò sbagliati ad Adamo,
così dunque parlava Raziél,
quando un grandissimo ondulato animale
venne e lo mangiò:
un animale
mascherato con buffe vetrofanie
inghiottì Raziél e ruttò sconciamente
non si seppe che animale era
perché si nascondeva in un costume da teatro,
un costume tempestato di vetrofanie.

Allora ci fu una pausa nel tempo,
una calma disperante ninfea
che tutto chiuse in una cornice di foglie
che alla sera macerarono in un inchino:
ci fu un silenzio lungo
nutrito del grano velenoso
cresciuto nelle cantine di notte.

Poi il silenzio diventò alto e solenne
e si travestì da spaventapasseri
e fece fuggire l'animale che aveva divorato

was belied by water
and the water
was drunk by a lamb
that was stolen and killed by a thief of lambs
and a punisher of lamb thieves
shot the thief in the heart
and was then punished and tasted by the wolf that ate him
and the wolf
died of a small snake's venom
and the small snake
was killed by a lady
who died elderly among white gladiola
and with her embroidered slippers
broke the chain."

Thus spoke Raziel, president of the names
of the Angels, of the names
that the Evil One in the second hour crippled
and wrongly reported to Adam,
thus then spoke Raziel,
when a very large undulant animal
came and ate him:
an animal
masked with funny decals
swallowed Raziel and burped obscenely
what animal it was, no one ever knew
because it was hiding in a theater costume,
a decal studded costume.

Then there was a pause in time,
a calm despairing water-lily
closing everything in a frame of leaves
that in the evening macerated in a bow:
there was a long silence
nourished with poisonous wheat
grown in the cellars by night.

Then the silence, high and solemn,
disguised itself as a scarecrow
and caused the flight of the animal that had devoured

Raziél, dispensa e presidente di sogni,
l'animale vetrofanico che ancora s'aggirava
eruttando sconciamente tra i crepacci:
e l'animale vetrofanico morì
soggiogato dal silenzio travestito da spaventapasseri
che era uno spaventapasseri
dalle braccia tanto larghe fatte per prendere
— poiché il silenzio
era la sostanza dello spaventapasseri —
vane misure.

Ci sarebbe voluto,
per trafiggere il silenzio-spaventapasseri,
un nome chiamato invocato
gridato in una strada che è parola e si fa amore
un nome forte per uccidere il silenzio
ma
nessuno lo disse, e ancora
sparita la strada-parola nel treno e il treno divorato
dal fulgido cielo
e il cielo, per oscure interpolazioni, finito
nella bocca del pesce-indecifrabile mangiato
dalla sirenafiamma
spariti l'acqua il lupo il ladro il castigatore di ladri
l'agnello l'aquila il serpente il fulmine
la signora dalle scarpette ricamate,
spariti Raziél, patrono dei sogni,
e l'animale vetrofanico
che inghiottì Raziél

ultimo resta il silenzio con gli stracci da spaventapasseri
silenzio per ultimo silenzio
ultimo per ultimo
silenzio, dopotutto
testimone, oh, dopotutto, silenzio.

Raziel, dispensary and president of dreams,
the decaled animal that still roamed
obscenely burping among crevices:
and the decaled animal died
subdued by the silence disguised as a scarecrow
a scarecrow
whose giant arms were made to catch
— because silence
was the substance of the scarecrow —
vane measures.

To pierce the scarecrow-silence,
it would have taken
a name called invoked
shouted in a road that is word and becomes love
a strong name to kill silence
but
no one said it, and again
the word-road disappeared into the train and the train
        was devoured
by the bright sky
and the sky, through obscure interpolations, ended
in the mouth of the indecipherable-fish eaten
by the flamesiren
they disappeared: the water the wolf the thief the punisher
        of thieves
the lamb the eagle the snake the lightening
the lady with embroidered slippers,
they disappeared Raziel, patron of dreams,
and the decaled animal
that swallowed Raziel

the last to remain is the silence in scarecrow rags
silence the last silence
last the last
silence, after all
witness, oh, after all, silence.

Bella e il golem*

Chi ha uno yod nel nome
ha il suono delle galassie future:
e lui era profeta di un mondo venturo
soprattutto per quel piccolissimo yod.

Sapeva i nomi dei basilischi
che popoleranno l'ora cangiante della trasformazione
e del leviatano tortuoso
e del leviatano guizzante
che sporgerà dalle trombe del diluvio di polvere
e di tutti i sauri
suscitati dal grande crogiuolo
sui quali cavalcherà l'esercito
della celeste disinfestazione.

Anche i grifi che ingoieranno grappoli di fuoco
sotto il pergolato che si sarà fatto rovente
sapeva chiamare col loro giusto nome:
che è il nome col quale li chiamerà Sammael
angelo che ha cento occhi per cento morti diverse.

Anche di Metatron, il più impervio degli angeli,
conosceva tutti e nove i nomi e le variazioni dei suoni
secondo la chiarità del giorno
e la tenebra notturna
i movimenti delle maree e la direzione dei venti.

Il giorno ch'ebbe finito
di fabbricare il golem
provò una fitta sulla spalla destra.
Non s'accorse
del tocco furente di Ariel
invidiosissimo principe delle invenzioni
e dei sortilegi,
non vide che la barba lampeggiando
gli era diventata del bianco incandescente
dell'ultimo magistero alchimistico.

*From *Bestiario d'amore* (Bestiary of love, 1974).

Bella and the Golem[29]

He who has a yod in his name[30]
holds the sound of future galaxies:
and it was above all for that smallest yod
that he was prophet of a coming world.

He knew the names of the basilisks
that will people the iridescent hour of transformation
of the tortuous Leviathan
of the slithering Leviathan
that will emerge from the whirlwinds of the dust deluge
and of all the sorrels
quickened from the great crucible
on which will ride the army
of the celestial extermination.

With the right name he could call even the griffins,
they that will swallow clusters of fire
under the red-hot pergola:
the name they will be given by Sammael
angel with one hundred eyes for one hundred different deaths.

Even for Metatron, the most impervious of angels,
he knew all nine names and the variation of sounds
according to the clarity of the day
and the darkness of the night
the movements of tides and the direction of winds.

The day he was done
making the golem
he felt a twinge in his right shoulder.
He did not notice
the raging touch of Ariel
most invidious prince of inventions
and spells,
he did not see that his blazing beard
had become the incandescent white
of the ultimate alchemical magistery.

Così fu che s'alzò
uno spaventoso golem
e percorse le strade stralunate:
scelse il crepuscolo, che più d'ogni altra ora
somiglia alla menzogna e alla confusione.
Le sue deformità erano quelle
d'una stella interrotta e lasciata a macerare
nelle viscide piaghe dell'abbandono:
lo corrodeva una torva acqua siderale.

Il golem condusse
nelle sue mani di lavorante dei cunicoli
astucci dorati e scatole legate coi nastri di seta
perché le vittime innocenti
non vedessero gli oggetti di tortura;
da una finestra tolse un drappo riverenziale
ricamato a pigne d'argento
se ne fece una sciarpa per nascondere
la mostruosa transenna delle spalle.

«Il golem! il golem!» e il ragno che scalciava in giro
con la sua gramigna di zampe
ruppe la tela nel centro
e si buttò nel buio attaccato al suo filo
«il golem! il golem» e il mare si tirò indietro
la nave dei pirati incespicò sulla sabbia
e nel palco delle sue vele sdraiate
l'argento dei cefali e delle triglie
si esibì in ginnastiche sepolcrali.
«Il golem! il golem!» gli animali feroci
vaganti in un quadro senza prospettive
si ritirarono nei castoni degli anelli
e i più aggressivi ai lati dei portoni gentilizi;
sgretolò il corpo di squame della sirena
lasciando vedere che non era
che un sostegno per balconi di museo.
«Il golem! il golem!» e i campi sciorinarono

So it came to pass that a fearsome
golem arose
and traveled the bewildered roads:
it chose the twilight, which more than any hour
resembles falsehood and confusion.
Its deformities were those
of a star interrupted and left to macerate
in the viscid sores of neglect:
it was corroded by grim sidereal waters.

In hands like a tunnel worker's
the golem carried
golden cases and boxes tied with silk ribbons
lest the innocent victims
see the instruments of torture;
from a window it took a reverential cloth
embroidered with silver cones
and made a scarf for hiding
the monstrosity of its transenna shoulders.

"The golem! the golem!" and the spider kicking
with its weed-like legs
ripped the web in the middle
and dove in the dark hanging by its thread
"the golem! the golem!" and the sea drew back
the pirate ship faltered on the sand
and on the stage of distended sails
the silver of the mullet and goatfish
performed sepulchral gymnastics.
"The golem! the golem!" the wild beasts
wandering in a picture without perspectives
withdrew into the settings of gems
with the most aggressive moving to the sides of the noble portals;
the scaly body of the siren crumbled
showing that it was only
a pillar for museum terraces.
"The golem! the golem!" and the fields displayed

i loro grilli e le loro lucertole
e si vide un grande edema verde brulicante;
lo scarabeo stercorario, impaurito,
s'attaccò al corallo tondo
della collana di una bàlia.
«Il golem! il golem!»

Raziel, che ogni giorno rincuorava Bella
che tesseva una mantellina d'ortiche
chiusa nella torre dell'orologio
(l'orologio sgorgava fuori le sue ore
e i suoi rintocchi: così, lei, non aveva fretta)
prese Bella e la portò dove s'apriva una caverna
la prima del mondo
una tana ancora incrostata
di gamberi e di peccato originale.
Bella che è entrata nella grotta
sa leggere la formula col giusto suono
badando al verso delle lettere
senza commettere errori:
mille cherubini lessicali
ha a un palmo dalla testa,
le girano intorno come un'aureola per santi:
altri cento vanno dal Nome ai suoi occhi
e ogni loro spostamento fa crescere una foresta.

«Il golem! il golem!» urlò una strada
che aveva sempre cantato; e i colombi, scappando,
composero una pagina frastagliata...
E venne un temporale
e piovvero ranocchie e tizzoni e pietre nere.

Quando Bella avrà letto il Nome
il golem sarà una pallina di pomice
ma Bella deve leggere nel modo giusto
scandendo ogni lettera nella preghiera adatta.

Il golem ha calzato due cupole di chiesa!

their crickets and their lizards
and a large swarming green edema was seen;
the dung beetle, frightened,
clung to the round coral
of a wetnurse's necklace.
"The golem! the golem!"

Raziel, each day consoling Bella
who locked in the clock tower
was weaving a cape of nettles
(the clock poured out its hours
and strokes: thus she was in no hurry),
seized Bella and brought her to the opening of a cave
the first of the world
a lair still encrusted
with shrimp and original sin.
Bella who has entered the cave
can read the formula with the right sound
minding the cadence of the letters
without making mistakes:
she has one thousand lexical cherubs
inches from her head,
circling around her like a saint's halo:
one hundred more move from the Name to her eyes
and each shift makes a forest grow.

"The golem! the golem!" cried a road
that had always sung; and the doves, fleeing,
composed a jagged page...
And there came a storm
and it rained frogs and firebrands and black stones.

After Bella has read the Name
the golem will be a small pumice ball
but Bella must read it in the right way
enunciating each letter in suitable prayer.

The golem is wearing two church domes as shoes!

Si è inguantato con due edifici pubblici uguali!
Col suo piscio ha bruciato i giardini verso il fiume!
E non parla!
Ecco: è vicino al quartiere delle giostre:
ha rovesciato dieci carrettini di sorbetti!

Quando Bella avrà finito la sua lettura
il Nome cadrà dal golem.
Il golem scoppierà, resterà di lui una biglia grigia
non più grande d'una bacca di ginepro.
Sammael già gorgheggia da soprano
lo spaventoso canto della frantumazione.

Eccolo! Crolla! ora rimpicciolisce
e rotola: è finito nella vasca
dove i pellegrini si lavano i piedi!

Bella è tornata alla sua mantellina di ortiche.

It is gloved with two matching public buildings!
With its piss it has burned the gardens by the river!
And does not speak!
There: it is close to the carousel district:
it has overturned ten sherbet carts!

When Bella has finished her reading
the Name will fall from the golem.
The golem will burst, leaving only a gray marble
no greater than a juniper berry.
Sammael is already trilling like a soprano
the dreadful song of shattering.

There it is! It is collapsing! now it is shrinking
and rolling: it has landed in the basin
where the pilgrims wash their feet!

Bella has returned to her cape of nettles.

GIULIA NICCOLAI

Così desunto*

Così desunto:
creature che non vogliono crescere
nei crateri lunari.
In un mondo di terra e di acqua, incesto
racchiuso nel corpo che nuota.
(L'impresa dell'unione
o della disunione: l'armonia siderale.)
La descrizione di un paesaggio
mentale, l'unità del desiderio
di esaltare gli opposti.

La forma nitida contrasta*

La forma nitida contrasta
in un tempo di minaccia.
Tra gli elementi negativi
appare l'immagine neutrale,
una ricognizione nello spazio vietato.
La verifica di uno stato rovescia
il riflusso dell'esperienza,
l'urgenza di rompere
e insieme la necessità.

Sintattico e verbale*

Un ordinato spazio verbale e sintattico
ordisce l'inganno dei reperti di oggi:
si rende impraticabile volentieri
con perfetta arbitrarietà e noncuranza.

Associando oggetti ed eventi nell'immaginazione
la buona materia raccolta nei testi
acquista un netto e immediato risalto
una raccapricciante volontà di pensare.

*From *Harry's Bar e altre poesie* (Harry's Bar and other poems, 1981).

GIULIA NICCOLAI

So Inferred

So inferred:
creatures that don't want to grow
in the lunar craters.
In a world of earth and water, incest
contained in the body that swims.
(The enterprise of union
or disunion: sidereal harmony.)
The description of a mental
landscape, unity of the desire
of exalting opposites.

The Clear Form Clashes

The clear form clashes
in a menacing era.
Among the negative elements
the neutral image appears,
reconnaissance in a forbidden space.
The verification of a state inverts
the waning of experience,
both the urgency of shattering
and the necessity.

Syntactic and Verbal

An ordered verbal and syntactic space
plots the deception of today's findings:
renders itself willingly inaccessible
with perfect arbitrariness and disregard.

Associating objects and events in the imagination
the good material collected in the texts
acquires a clear and immediate relief
a horrifying volition of thought.

Seminando frantumi e ritagli
in una specie di dissolvenza incrociata
investe le membrature del testo
(oggetto della propria operazione).

Evidentemente non si può dire
che vuole distruggersi di continuo.

Solo indirettamente*

Un orizzonte di aspettative
un insieme ordinato di risposte.

Dal momento in cui l'idea è già sorta
e formulata
il grado di controllabilità
la verosimiglianza

convergono arbitrariamente
in ipotesi o in teoria
nate nella mente
da un sogno o da un'intuizione.

Sono congetture e confutazioni
e quanto poco però
queste conversioni possono riuscire
è ammesso solo indirettamente.

*From *Harry's Bar e altre poesie* (Harry's Bar and other poems, 1981).

Scattering splinters and clippings
in a sort of slow dissolve
it invests the body of the text
(object of its own operation).

Evidently one cannot say
that it wants to destroy itself continuously.

Only Indirectly

A horizon of expectations
an ordered ensemble of answers.

From the moment the idea is already born
and formulated
the level of controllability
the verisimilitude

converge arbitrarily
in hypothesis or theory
originated in the mind
from dream or intuition.

They are conjectures and confutations
and yet how little
these conversions can succeed
is only indirectly granted.

Harry's Bar Ballad*

(un cocktail per Marcello Angioni)

È sempre imbarazzante per un tedesco chiedere
zwei dry martini
potrebbe chiedere
zwei martini dry
ma se chiede
zwei martini dry
gli danno i martini senza il gin.
È costretto a berseli?
No
perché lui e sua moglie
vogliono zwei dry martini
e NON zwei martini dry.
Potrebbe chiedere
zwei mal dry martini
che tradotto in italiano diventa
due volte tre martini.
Allora gliene danno sei.
Sei un bevitore di dry martini?
Fanno diciotto.
Sei, sei dry martini?
Sei più sei dodici
sei per sei trentasei?
Non voglio né dodici né trentasei martini
voglio del gin perché sono G. N.
Giulia Niccolai.
Des dry martini! Neuf!
Pas des vieux bien sûr madame...
Anche un americano che chiede
nine dry martini
corre il rischio di non riceverne neanche uno
se il barman lo prende per un tedesco.
Dix dix dry martini!
Non je dis pas je dis pas je dis pas!

Settembre 1977

*From Harry's Bar a altre poesie (Harry's Bar and other poems, 1981).

Harry's Bar Ballad

   (a cocktail for Marcello Angioni)
It is always embarrassing for a German to order
zwei dry martini[31]
he could order
zwei martini dry
but if he orders
zwei martini dry
they'll give him the martinis without gin.[32]
Does he have to drink them?
No
because he and his wife
want zwei dry martini
and NOT zwei martini dry.
He could order
zwei mal dry martini
which translated into Italian becomes
two times three martinis.
Then they'll give him half a dozen.
Doz'n that make you a drinker of dry martinis?
That makes thirty-six.[33]
Six, six dry martinis?
Six plus six twelve
six times six thirty-six?
I don't want either twelve or thirty-six martinis
I want gin because I am G. N.
Giulia Niccolai.
Des dry martini! Neuf!
Pas des vieux bien sûr madame…[34]
An American who orders
nine dry martinis[35]
also runs the risk of not getting even one
if the barman takes him for German.
Dix dix dry martini!
Non je dis pas je dis pas je dis pas![36]

September 1977

La storia geografica[*]

>   (a Laura Lepetit)

Vado spesso a Melano
e vivo tra Milano e Mulino di Bazzano
nel senso di
quindici giorni qua e quindici giorni là
e non nel senso di
Piacenza
che sarebbe a metà strada.
Sarebbe ed è
a 60 km. da Milano a 60 km. da Mulino.
Anche Melano è a 60 km. da Milano
ma a 180 da Mulino
essendo Melano a nord di Milano
e Mulino a sud.
Questa poesia la sto cominciando a Brescia.   (Continua)

Me voiçi à Paris.
De la fenêtre de mes amis
je vois le Parc Montsouris.
Je souris même si j'exagère avec la rime
parce que le parc n'est pas mon sourire
c'est une montagne de petits rats qu'on ne voit pas.
Eccomi a Parigi.
Dalla finestra dei miei amici
vedo il Parc Montsouris.
Sorrido anche se esagero con la rima
perché il parco non è il mio sorriso
è una montagna di piccoli topi che non si vedono.
Traducendo in italiano ho eliminato la rima
e sono arrivata a 14 versi come prima.   (Continua)

È viaggiare che porta a fare giochi di parole
o sono i giochi di parole che si fanno viaggiando
o sono le parole che giocano e viaggiando fanno

---

*From *Harry's Bar e altre poesie* (Harry's Bar and other poems, 1981).

The Geographical History

(to Laura Lepetit)

I often go to Melano
and I live between Milano and Mulino di Bazzano
meaning
fifteen days here and fifteen days there
and not meaning
Piacenza
that would be midway.
It would be and is
60 km. from Milano 60 km. from Mulino.
Melano is also 60 km. from Milano
but 180 from Mulino
because Melano is north of Milano
and Mulino south.
I am beginning this poem in Brescia.   *(To be continued)*

Me voiçi à Paris.
De la fenêtre de mes amis
je vois le Parc Montsouris.
Je souris même si j'exagère avec la rime
parce que le parc n'est pas mon sourire
c'est une montagne de petits rats qu'on ne voit pas.
Here I am in Paris.
From my friends' window
I see the Parc Montsouris.
I smile even if I take my rhymes too far
because the park is not my smile
it is a mountain of little mice that are nowhere seen.
Translating into Italian I have eliminated the rhyme
and arrived at 14 lines like the last time.   *(To be continued)*

It is travel that leads to creating word games
or it is word games that are created traveling
or it is words that play and in traveling create

e dove portano.
Si vede si vede eccome si vede
che sto traducendo Gertrude Stein.
Ma se sono portata a fare giochi di parole in proprio
se continuo a viaggiare e a scrivere poesie
come si farà a vedere finita la mia traduzione di
The Geographical History of America.
Beh l'inizio c'è già nel titolo e io sono a buon punto.
Ora per un po' sto ferma a Milano
vado avanti con la storia
e anche la poesia   (Continua)

Frisbees sulla luce*

Lucio
dice che i Frisbees
sono delle Polaroid interiori.
Questa definizione
è per me
illuminante.

Dico a Livia Candiani:
«Forse non sentiamo affinità
per Gozzano
perché lui è consapevole
di essere alla fine del lume a petrolio
e noi siamo già elettricità».

Joan Arnold
mi telefona l'anagramma
che le è venuto con Giulia Niccolai:
gioia luci lanci.
Che splendore pirotecnico,
Napule, triccheballacche e putipù!
Penso con gioia
al mio segno zodiacale
il Sagittario

From Frisbees (poesie da lanciare) (Frisbees [poems for launching], 1994).

and lead where.
It's obvious it's obvious it's certainly obvious
that I am translating Gertrude Stein.
But if I'm driven to create my own word games
if I keep traveling and writing poetry
how will we get to see the completion of my translation of
The Geographical History of America.
Well the beginning is already there in the title and I'm at a
          good point.
Now I stop for a while in Milano
I go on with history
and poetry too is   *(To be continued)*

Frisbees on Light

Lucio[37]
says that the *Frisbees*
are *internal Polaroids.*
I find
this definition
illuminating.

I say to Livia Candiani[38]:
"Maybe we don't feel an affinity
with Gozzano[39]
because he is aware
that he is at the oil lamp's end
while we are already electricity."

Joan Arnold
phones me with the anagram
she got from *Giulia Niccolai:*
gioia luci lanci.[40]
What pyrotechnic splendor,
Napule, triccheballacche and *putipù!*[41]
Happily, I think
about my zodiac sign
Sagittarius

che lancia le sue frecce
verso le luci delle stelle
(quando punta in alto).

Ma anche a livello più basso
terra-terra e quotidiano
i Frisbees sono pur sempre
poesie da lanciare...

«Non esageriamo,
non montiamoci la testa,
cuci ali angioli, piuttosto!»
mi dice Maurizio Brignone.
«Icarus, I presume?» chiedo.

Uno di quei magici
giochi di specchi
— argento e luce riflessa —
che è per me la poesia:
Barbara Kleiner
— che sta traducendo i Frisbees in tedesco —
dopo aver letto quello in cui dico
di essere Sagittario ascendente Acquario,
mi annuncia felice:
«E io sono Acquario ascendente Sagittario».
(Ora sono certa che il libro per Droschl
andrà in porto. Eccome!)

Morale: i Frisbees
dovrebbero uscire
in U. S. A. e in Austria
prima che in Italia.
Sarà che il Sagittario
sa lanciare lontano
e non vicino?

Comunque sia, ci voleva, eccome se ci voleva quella
bella specularità tra le due date di nascita per farmi pro-
vare un po' di fiducia. Una volta tanto, signori, solo

launching its arrows
toward the light of the stars
(when aiming high).

But also at a lower level
down-to-earth and daily
the *Frisbees* are still
poems for *launching*...

"Let's not exaggerate,
let's not get swollen-heads,
how about *cuci ali angioli!*"
says Maurizio Brignone.[42]
"Icarus, I presume?" I ask.[43]

One of those magical
mirror tricks
— silver and reflected light —
which poetry is for me:
Barbara Kleiner
— who is translating the *Frisbees* into German —
after reading the one in which I say
I am Sagittarius with Aquarius ascendant,
happily announces:
"And I am Aquarius with Sagittarius ascendant."
(Now I am certain that the book for Droschl
is a done deal. Yes indeed!)

Moral: the *Frisbees*
should come out
in the U. S. and in Austria
before Italy.
Could it be that Sagittarius
can launch long distances
and fails at short ones?

In any case, that beautiful specularity between the two
dates of birth was necessary, necessary indeed, to give me
a little faith. Once in a while, folks, only

una volta tanto.
Proprio oggi invece, guardando e ascoltando al Teatro
dell'Arte *il gruppo indiano di Tholu Bomalatta (il tea-*
tro delle ombre giganti dell'Andra Pradesh),
«...portano i loro sacchi di ombre sulla testa
e cominciano a cantare e a suonare...
I sari per lo schermo
sono forniti dal sindaco del villaggio,
i pali dalla gente del paese,
la luce dal barbiere...»
proprio oggi,
guardando e ascoltando qui a Milano
le ombre dell'Andra Pradesh,
ho sentito che esse rappresentavano la gioia
la gioia pura
la gioia istintiva
la gioia totale
una GIOIA GIGANTE
la G I O I A tout court!

E tu, te la ricordi la gioia?

Dicembre 1985

once in a while.
But just today, at the *Teatro dell'Arte,* watching and
listening to the Indian group Tholu Bomalatta (the theater
of giant shadows of the Andra Pradesh),
"...they carry their sacks of shadows on their heads
and begin to sing and play...
The *saris* for the screen
are provided by the village mayor,
the poles by the village people,
light by the barber..."
just today,
here in Milan, watching and listening
to the shadows of the Andra Pradesh,
I felt that they stood for joy
pure joy
instinctive joy
total joy
a GIGANTIC JOY
J O Y tout court!

And you, do you remember joy?

December 1985

PIERA OPPEZZO

Iterazione*

Le parole non si flettono più.
Si snodano in una iterazione
che non precisa il senso delle cose
ma ci avverte ampiamente
di un loro possibile futuro.

Esigenza*

Questo presente costantemente in difetto
verso l'uomo e la sua evoluzione
esige chiaramente un'interrogazione senza sosta
o non ci eviterà il rischio di restare fusi
nel piombo di una risposta definitiva.

Progetto*

Sezione per sezione attentamente
come un oggetto plastificato, ad esempio,
risultante tale quale il progetto
costruirsi il giorno e viverlo
col solo diritto di identificarsi in esso.

Mondo confezionato*

Mondo attualmente esaurito figurativamente
su scatole tubetti risvolti
interno d'autobus cantieri,
il suo uomo rimbalza presente dovunque
con maniera di vivere
tanto insistentemente manierata

inevitabile ma non ancora ineccepibile
tanta intensa maniera
nell'attuale mondo confezionato
con qualità d'apparenza altamente reclamizzate

*From *L'uomo qui presente* (The man here present, 1966).

PIERA OPPEZZO

Iteration

Words no longer inflect.
They meander in an iteration
that doesn't specify the sense of things
but fully informs us
of their possible future.

Demand

This present that constantly fails
man and his evolution
clearly demands an unceasing interrogation
or it won't spare us from the risk of remaining cast
in the lead of a definitive answer.

Project

Carefully section by section
like a plasticized object, for instance,
that turns out precisely like the project:
to build the day for oneself and live it
entitled only to identifying with it.

Ready-Made World

World currently expended figuratively
on boxes tubes flaps
interior of busses building yards,
the man of this world present everywhere
bounces about in a manner of living
so insistently mannered

inevitable but not yet irreprehensible
such an intense manner
in the current ready-made world
with highly advertised qualities of appearance,

ovvero un falso autentico rispetto alla natura
e più stipato di fatti e oggetti
e dove anche l'incapacità
ha limiti quasi definiti.

V. «Melanctha non aveva una casa, né un'occupazione
regolare, ormai. La vita stava appunto cominciando per lei.»*

No senza senso mai più
urlò quasi lo sguardo un po' allucinato
come quando c'è un vuoto sì
troppe volte m'accorgo
                              d'esserci per stare
dentro questo rullio
                    ancora

    m'oppongo io
    non ho niente di speciale da fare
    ma ho da fare
    insinuò verso chi minacciava
    nervoso perché incerto

Melanctha siamo d'accordo
continua ridendo correndo
con un po' di saliva inumidisce le labbra
intanto pensando trafficando
si ripete ricorda
              ho imparato la differenza
la realtà l'apparenza

    Emily l'hai detto
                  il buon senso
    la più opaca follia dice
    mentre continua il rullio
    lei allontanandosi un po'
    scomparendo tornando
    osservando cose già viste
    manovrando il respiro

*From *Le strade di Melanctha* (Melanctha's roads, 1987).

an authentic fake in respect to nature
one overpacked with facts and objects
where even incapacity
has quasi-defined limits.

V. "Now Melanctha Had neither Home, nor Regular Occupation. Life Was Just Beginning for Her."

No   never again without sense
she almost screamed   her gaze slightly dazed
as if facing a void   yes
too many times I realize
                    I am still here
only to stay inside
             this rocking

       I object   I
       have nothing special to do
       but I have things to do
       she suggested to those who were menacing
       and nervous because uncertain

Melanctha   we agree
she continues laughing running
with a little saliva she moistens her lips
meanwhile thinking busying about
she repeats to herself recalls
                  I have learned the difference
reality appearance

       Emily you said it
                common sense
       the most opaque folly   she says
       while the rocking continues
       she   wandering a little
       disappearing returning
       observing things already seen
       maneuvering her breath

ma dove vai
vuole sapere qualcuno   insiste
cercando di trattenerla

io non mi chiedo dove vado
però m'accorgo dove sono
e qui tutto quanto   ogni tanto
lo so sembra ammirevole
sopportando
benpensando
no   ripete allontanandosi di più
e ancora pronuncia parole
e infine scompare

Melanctha   è sicuro
succede sempre qualcosa se vuoi
afferma cercandola
trovandola
forse qualcosa di morbido   sì
l'ozio e un po' di spazio
è tanto e ancora poco
precisa
mai accontentandosi

e nel tempo ancora
Melanctha sei convinta   mai più
modula secondo il ritmo
dondolandosi con lei sul trapezio
nel circo tutto il buio le luci
l'odore
il calore
il sudore

sì   di tanto in tanto
mi capita una vertigine
risponde a chi osserva il suo esercizio
ansioso diffidente pauroso

                        but where are you going
        someone wants to know   insists
        trying to hold her back

I don't ask myself where I am going
still I realize where I am
and here everything   every so often
seems admirable of course
enduring
            conforming
no   she repeats wandering further
and again utters words
and finally disappears

Melanctha   it is certain
when you want something to happen it always will
she asserts looking for her
                        finding her
perhaps something soft   yes
idleness and a little space
it's a lot and still not much
she specifies
                never being satisfied

and still in time's domain
Melanctha are you convinced   never again
she modulates according to the rhythm
swinging on the trapeze with her
in the circus with all the darkness the lights
the smell
            the heat
                    the sweat

        yes   from time to time
        I get dizzy
        she answers those watching her exercise
        with anxiety diffidence fear

è certo evidente
conclude rallentando
               sorridendo
come sia allegro difficile
voglio dire eccitante e poco facile
il pericolo evitare
ovvero
       non fermarsi per andare

it is certainly evident
she concludes slowing down
                    smiling
how cheerful difficult
I mean exciting and not very easy
it is to avoid danger
that is
      not stopping in order to go

DACIA MARAINI

ho sognato un porco*

ho sognato di cucinare un porco al forno
ho sognato di cucinare un porco al forno
poi il porco è ritornato
poi il porco è ritornato
aveva gli occhi stanchi questo porco
e i piedi feriti per il troppo camminare.
Cosa fai porco di dio?
cosa fai porco di dio?
Faccio carne per chi me la chiede
faccio carne per chi me la chiede.
E tu donna di dio
non fai carne per chi te la chiede?
Io ho il cuore in salamoia, porco di dio,
e ha un buon sapore di rosmarino.
Dopo più tardi di sera
sopra un tavolo tondo
un uomo bellissimo
dagli occhi di giada
mangiava dentro un piatto
di smalto bianco
delle zampe di porco
e un cuore di donna.

l'uomo dalle gambe lunghe*

l'uomo dalle gambe lunghe
oggi non mi parla
occhi gocciolanti e
naso schiacciato
un furiere incontaminato
come in un film di Herzog
ho messo la mia testa
tagliata, nuda, sul piatto

*From *Dimenticato di dimenticare* (Having forgotten to forget, 1982).

DACIA MARAINI

I Dreamt a Pig

I dreamt of cooking roast pig
I dreamt of cooking roast pig
then the pig returned
then the pig returned
he had tired eyes this pig
and injured feet from too much walking.
What do you do pig of god?
what do you do pig of god?
I make meat for those who ask
I make meat for those who ask.
And you woman of god
don't you make meat for those who ask?
I have a heart in brine, pig of god,
and it is flavored with rosemary.
Later in the evening
at a round table
a beautiful man
with jade eyes
was eating pig's feet
and a woman's heart
from a dish
of white enamel

The Man with Long Legs

the man with long legs
doesn't speak to me today
dripping eyes
and flattened nose
an untainted quartermaster
as in a Herzog film
I put my head
severed, nude, on the platter

amore se questo è amore[*]

amore se questo è amore
dalla parte solitaria della montagna
dalla parte scura della luna
dalla parte viola del mare
da una parte sola e solamente
con i segni del sonno esterefatto
se questo è amore amore mio
mi taglio subito un capezzolo
e te lo mando per posta

storie famigliari[*]

«cammina come te tuo padre»
dice e mi fiata nell'orecchio
e io vado avanti pestando l'erba
fra rosmarini polverosi e
albicocchi bacati in un
pomeriggio gonfio d'umido
improvvisamente lo vedo
seduto in mezzo alle dalie
uno squarcio all'inguine
dove gli hanno iniettato
il veleno dopo morto
per non svegliarsi nella tomba
fra le dita un rosario
lui ateo e fascista
«Tuo nonno hai visto»!
dice e punta il dito, gli occhi
mangiati dai moscerini
quelle prugne gialle e gonfie
proprio vicino all'acciottolato
dove da bambina giocavo
ammaliata dai lombrichi
mangiando formiche vive
mi masturbavo contro un albero

[*]From Dimenticato di dimenticare (Having forgotten to forget, 1982).

Love If This Is Love

love if this is love
from the solitary side of the mountain
from the dark side of the moon
from the violet side of the sea
from one side alone and only
with the traces of an astonished sleep
if this is love my love
I will slice off my nipple at once
and send it to you by post

Family Stories

"your father walks like you"
he says his breath in my ear
and crushing the grass I go on
among dusty rosemary and
worm-eaten apricot trees in the
damp swollen air of an afternoon
suddenly I see him
seated among the dahlias
a gash in his groin
where they injected him
with venom after he died
to keep him from awaking in his tomb
a rosary between his fingers
he, an atheist and fascist
"it's your grandfather, don't you see!"
he says and points his finger,
the gnat-eaten eyes
those swollen yellow plums
so near the cobbles
where I used to play as a little girl
mesmerized by the earthworms
eating live ants
I would masturbate against a tree

dalla corteccia ramata
«è bellissimo tuo padre»
dice il mio ragazzo malizioso
dolente girandosi sulle gambe
in un'ora si è divorato le
unghie a sangue, l'immagine
del nonno si è sciolta
nell'afa del pomeriggio
mio padre mi precede piano
ignaro di me e delle disgraziate
storie famigliari, va incontro
alla sua giovane moglie con
un sorriso che gli conosco bene:
di solidità e noia d'amore

io sono due*

io sono due
è chiaro ora
sono due più uno
meno uno e fanno due
che due volte sono
nata e due volte morta
due volte mi sono persa
forse una volta di più
perché due e una sono tre
le volte che ho sbattuto
e una volta ho anche vomitato
ma erano forse due
dato che sono in quattro
a tirarmi per i piedi
mentre dormo con voce di drago
e una volta sola ho amato
ma saranno duecento le volte
che ho toccato l'allegria
però non duecento volte sono nata

---

*From *Viaggiando con passo di volpe* (Traveling with fox steps, 1991).

of copper bark
"your father is so handsome"
says my malicious boyfriend
shifting sorely on his legs
in one hour he has bitten his
nails to the bone, grandfather's
image has dissolved
into the sultry afternoon
my father slowly precedes me
unaware of me and our wretched
family stories, he goes toward
his young wife with
a smile I know well:
of solidity and the tedium of love.

I Am Two

I am two
it is clear now
I am two plus one
minus one makes two
since two times I was
born and two times I died
two times I was lost
perhaps one time more
because two and one are three
times that I crashed
and one time I also vomited
but it was perhaps two
since there are four
pulling me by my feet
while I sleep with the voice of a dragon
and one time only I loved
but it must be two hundred times
I touched happiness
but not two hundred times I was born

perché al centonovantanove
mi sono stufata ed ecco
dall'una al due mi sono scordata
e se una non fosse due sarebbe zero
ma l'una sono io e l'altra due
perciò prendimi come sono
di una due e di due una

ho passato la notte*

ho passato la notte
a girarmi fra lenzuola marce
in un groviglio di sogni
una sola ciliegia sul piatto
mentre il vento sale,
per il tuo futuro
sono un sasso d'acqua dolce
aspetto di ricevere
un tuo bacio di fortuna,
forse domani
su un guscio di noce
attraverseremo le acque sporche,
non mi chiamare madre
ci sono troppe frecce
nell'arco che tu imbracci
giocherai a carte
di fronte alla marina
nella luce unta della sera
quanta gelosia sprecata
c'era già vento
o forse no, era scemato,
ho passato la notte
aspettando di dormire
con te, dentro un sogno acquatico

*From *Viaggiando con passo di volpe* (Traveling with fox steps, 1991).

because at one hundred and ninety-nine
I got fed up and here
from the one to the two I forgot
and if one were not two she would be zero
but I am the one and the other two
therefore take me as I am
of one two and of two one

I Spent the Night

I spent the night
tossing between rotten sheets
in a tangle of dreams
only one cherry on the plate
while the wind rises,
for your future
I am a stone in fresh water
I wait to receive
your improvised kiss,
perhaps tomorrow
on a nutshell
we will cross the soiled waters,
do not call me mother
there are too many arrows
in the bow you draw
you will play cards
in front of the marina
in the oily light of the evening
so much wasted jealousy
it was already windy
or perhaps not, it had abated,
I spent the night
waiting to sleep
with you, inside a watery dream

la tua faccia non ha nome[*]

la tua faccia non ha nome
la tua voce non ha suono
il tuo treno non ha numero
il tuo viaggio non ha orari
ma io so che verrai
con quella faccia
con quella voce
con quel treno
alla fine del tuo lungo viaggio

limone, acqua calda e un grumo di sangue[*]

limone, acqua calda e un grumo di sangue
dentro quelle tazze bianche
dal filo giallo e celeste
che nel fondo appariva
una donnina danzante
e forse pure un mandorlo d'oro,
limone acqua calda e un grumo di sangue
tu sali da profondità
ingommate, carico di zuccheri
e di essenze tiepide
hai un buon sapore di menta
«noi che siamo amici», mi fai,
ma cos'è l'amicizia
dicevo, dicevi, ci eravamo detti,
in un mondo di inezie
quanto sciatta e quanto scolorita
si mostra quella cosa rubata e nascosta
che è il sentimento d'affetto!

[*]From *Viaggiando con passo di volpe* (Traveling with fox steps, 1991).

Your Face Has No Name

your face has no name
your voice no sound
your train no number
your journey no schedule
but I know that you will come
with that face
with that voice
with that train
at the end of your long journey

Lemon, Hot Water and a Blood Clot

lemon, hot water and a blood clot
inside those white cups
with yellow and blue thread
a little dancing woman
popping up at the bottom
and perhaps a golden almond tree,
lemon hot water and a blood clot
you ascend from gummed
depths, loaded with sugar
and warm essences
you taste like mint
"we who are friends," you say to me,
but what is friendship
I said, you said, we had said to each other,
in a world of trifles
how shabby and how faded
appears that stolen and hidden thing
which is affection!

una piccola donna dagli occhi di medusa*

una piccola donna dagli occhi di medusa
due alette mercuriali alle caviglie
un fiocco rosso fra i capelli
che porta corti, alla garçonne,
mi è stata sorella e poi madre
ma il suo latte era amaro
abbiamo camminato e camminato
sotto i tigli in amore
dentro un turbinio di semi volanti
che fai ora fra tante madonne
dipinta su dipinti ufficiali
gioiosa su gioie carnali?
il tempo corre, pulce di mare
la mezzanotte è arrivata, mia garçonne,
e la tua scarpina è ancora in mano al principe

*From *Viaggiando con passo di volpe* (Traveling with fox steps, 1991).

A Little Woman with Medusa Eyes

a little woman with medusa eyes
two mercurial winglets on her ankles
a red bow in her hair
that she wears short, like a pageboy,
she was sister to me then mother
but her milk was bitter
under the linden trees in love
we walked and walked
inside a whirlwind of flying seeds
what are you doing now with all these madonnas,
painted on official paintings
joyful on carnal joys
time flies, sand flea
midnight has arrived, my pageboy,
and your little shoe is still in the prince's hand

JOLANDA INSANA

Conoscermi?*

da tre ore faccio i conti
e non mi torna la spesa del pane
e dell'attesa

— *conoscermi...?*
— *non è mica vietato*
— *conoscermi...sai che ti dico...comincia da te*
— *io per me ho già finito*
— *ah, a me basterebbe conoscermi/conoscerti solo un poco,*
   un poco così, quanto un indice e un pollice strettamente
   congiunti stringono
— *non è difficile*
— *dici dunque che l'invisibile, l'inconoscibile è clarito,*
   luminoso et etiam bello
— *certo*
— *ma allora mi sai spiegare perché io spalanco la pupilla*
   sempre sul buio e di luminoso vedo solo un punto, piccolo
   come un punto fermo, e mi viene il sospetto che la pupilla
   si ricordi della luce e se la sogni al buio...
— *chiacchiere, tu non mi ami*

com'è vicina la tua casa
attraverso mezza Roma e in un attimo sono da te

c'è tanto caldo
e il vino è buono
è sempre novello il vino delle tue terre

*From *Il collettame* (The consignment, 1985).

JOLANDA INSANA

To Know Me?[44]

For three hours I have been doing accounts
and the cost of bread and waiting
doesn't square

— to know me...?
— sure it's not forbidden
— to know me...tell you what...begin with yourself
— as far as I'm concerned I've already finished
— ah, for me it would be enough to know myself/know
          you just a little,
     this little, only as much as a tightly joined forefinger
          and thumb
     can clasp
— it's not difficult
— you are saying then that the invisible, the unknowable is
          resplendent,[45]
     luminous et etiam beautiful[46]
— sure
— but then can you explain to me why I always open my pupil
     onto the darkness and why the only luminous thing I see is a
          dot, small
     as a full stop, and I suspect that the pupil
     remembers the light and dreams of it in the dark...
— nonsense, you don't love me

your place is so close
I cross half of Rome and I'm there in a moment

it's so hot
and the wine is good
the wine of your land is always young

dentro l'arancera
i ragazzi per gioco tracciano un cerchio
e non ci saltano dentro

l'amai quel giorno perché avevo mal di denti
il giorno appresso perché aveva mal di denti

vorrei che si vivesse un'altra volta
per non sentire più
si vive una volta sola

poche pochissime le moltissime parole
tatuate sopra il corpo che partono dall'onfalòs
e si sperdono in un urlo nella ramaglia senza fiore
mio padre — chi se lo ricorda —
urlava per non essere ascoltato

— S. P.   1932–1963, suicida
— V. W.   1882–1941, suicida
— M. C.   1892–1941, suicida
— K. B.   1900–1941, suicida
— A. S.   1928–1974, suicida

— basta…smettila con tutti questi suicidi, è un'ossessione
— non sono suicidi
— va bene…sono morti…ho capito…ma è un'ossessione lo stesso
— no, non hai capito: sono suicide, femmine, di genere femminile,
    plurale, senti: Silvia Plath, Virginia Woolf, Marina Cvetaeva,
    Karin Boye, Anne Sexton…
— ti prego, basta, è ossessivo
— ma no, io lo faccio per scaramanzia, capisci?
— non capisco

inside the orangery
the children draw a circle for fun
and don't jump in it

I loved him that day because I had a toothache
the next day because he had a toothache

I wish we lived once more
so as not to hear anymore
that we live only once

few very few the very many words
tattooed on the body starting from the *onfalòs*[47]
and getting lost in a howl in the flowerless branches
my father — who remembers him —
howled so he wouldn't be heard

— S. P.   1932–1963, suicide
— V. W.   1882–1941, suicide
— M. C.   1892–1941, suicide
— K. B.   1900–1941, suicide
— A. S.   1928–1974, suicide

— enough…stop it with all these people who committed
         suicide, it's an obsession
— they are not people who committed suicide
— all right…they are dead people…I got it…but it's still an
         obsession
— no, you didn't get it: they are women who commit-
  ted suicide, females, of feminine gender,
  plural, listen: Sylvia Plath, Virginia Wolf, Marina Cvetaeva,
  Karin Boye, Anne Sexton…
— please, enough, it's obsessive
— not at all, I do it superstitiously, don't you get it?
— I don't get it

— *vedi: sono tutte donne, tutte con la loro stanza faticosamente*
conquistata e qualche volta manco quella…tutte poetesse o
scrittrici, come vuoi chiamarle, e tutte, dico tutte, e sono
tantissime, morte suicide…ci sarà una ragione, non sarà mica
un caso che…
— *capisco, d'accordo, ma che c'entra la scaramanzia?*
— *ah, c'entra…non voglio fare la loro stessa fine*

Excerpts from
La parabola del cuore*

. . . .

non riesco a riacciuffare il tuttocorpo effuso
dalla clausura della parlata monca e nel rintocco
del sangue il lutto è defraudato
ma quando dico di queste cose è di un'altra che parlo
di un'altra che finge di non parlare

. . . .

il tutto che mi abita è un niente
se lo estrapolo dai suoi contorni certi
e lo scorporo dal fianco che frange il fragile momento
e posso pensare quanto voglio ma non riuscirò a pesare
quanto ardo e sento il male del corpo taglieggiato

. . . .

— *che vuoi Sibilla?*
— *sono voce e non voglio smorire*
— *parla-parla intanto che io ti smielo e svolo*

. . . .

l'impeto dell'assenza fu così forte nell'impatto dello specchio
che ne fui risucchiata e dissennata ma per fortuna

From La clausura (The cloistering, 1987).

— you see: they are all women, all with their own room
        laboriously conquered and sometimes not even
        that…all women poets or writers, whatever you want
        to call them, and all, all of them, and they are
        so many, killed themselves…there must be a reason, it
                can't be
        by chance that…
— I get it, O.K., but what has superstition got to do with it?
— ah, it does…I don't want to end up the same way

Excerpts from
The Parabola of the Heart

. . . .

I am unable to recapture the allbody poured
from the cloister of maimed speech and in the toll
of blood mourning is cheated
yet when telling of these things it is of another I speak
of another who pretends not to speak

. . . .

the whole that inhabits me is nothing
if I extrapolate it from its sure contours
and disincorporate[48] it from the flank that fractures the
        fragile moment
and I can ponder as much as I want but can't manage to weigh[49]
how much I burn and feel the hurt of the overtaxed[50] body

. . . .

— what do you want Sibyl?
— I am voice and don't want to slip away
— keep talking while I unhoney you and steal away

. . . .

the impetus of absence was so strong in the impact of the mirror
that I was swallowed up and deranged by it but fortunately

la mente dimentica molto e troppo getta nel secchio dei rifiuti
e nessuna precauzione prende per non essere ingannata
e nulla tralascia e tutto brucia e cosí vive e sbanda
e rapita da nuovi e padroni sensi
si tappa occhi e orecchi per sentire e vedere meglio
la terra alla deriva

ripesto la stessa immagine nel mortaio e si riflette
integralmente allo specchio fuori della mente
che sgodendo si scorda del corpo e lo disanima tutto
come se fosse un altro
e dico che questo è raccoglimento per non dire pazzia
che fa paura
   ho perso il tatto e il gusto e tutto accadde cosí in fretta
e questo è quanto dura di breve pena
e dura a lungo

....

non so sotto quale legge vivo e perché incolpevole
fuoriesco dalla forata muraglia compitando
le sillabe saltate e affreno la discordia dei linguaggi
per ricomporre il guasto dell'immagine
e però è serrata nell'antro la Sibilla
che nessuno vede e tutti sentono
e non intendono

si prega di non bestemmiare in silenzio

quale scambio con i foraggiatori di grazia
che non conoscono perturbazione
e per i fiati loro continuano a respirare fino ad altezze
impraticabili per chi si sbroda e cola in parola
e non c'è potenza che risuoni all'invocazione

di possesso manco a parlarne

the mind forgets plenty and tosses too much in the trash
and it takes no precaution against deceit
and leaves out nothing and burns everything and so lives and skids
and ravished by new and ruling senses
turns a blind eye and deaf ear to better hear and see
the shore adrift

again I pound the same image in the mortar and it is reflected
entirely in the mirror outside the mind
that overenjoying[51] disregards the body and disheartens it
               completely
as if it were another
and I say that this is collectedness not to say madness
which is frightening
      I lost touch and taste and it all happened so fast
and this is what lasts of brief pain
and it lasts a long time

. . . .

I don't know under which law I live and why guiltless
I spill from the riddled wall spelling out
the skipped syllables and curbing the discord of languages
to mend the damaged image
but the Sibyl is shut in the cave
seen by no one and heard by all
and misunderstood

please do not curse in silence

what sort of exchange with those foddering grace
who don't know perturbation
and minding their own breaths keep breathing reaching heights
inaccessible to those who stain themselves dripping with words
and there is no power resounding at the invocation

let alone possession

se è questo che vuoi mi mozzo la mano e te ne faccio dono
bellezza cannibalica ma non espongo il sacrificio
perché non so che farmene della verità svergognata
o con quale colpa ricorrere alle madri per il primo cilicio
e dunque mi riprendo la mano e ti carpiono

. . . .

Excerpts from
La colica passione*

. . . .

nessuna paura di perdere la sanità
io che mai fui sana ma seppi il mortale
sostentamento in parole di necessaria sostanza

non lo amo ma non è una ragione per distruggerlo
questo mio corpo incoerente mai sazio né beato
e dunque lo allevo e lo tutelo come madre
e lo rattoppo e strappo alle grinfie della figlia

. . . .

La tappezzeria del cuore†

che strano questo nunzio che arriva
e porta l'alba e mi acceca e oscura la forma

il nunzio della notte non usa specchi
e denuncia cosa porta

mi piace la tappezzeria che copre il cuore
e sto altrove quando appiano e rastrello e non pulsa
lo stesso stupore per servitù e ardore

il mare non c'era più

*From *La clausura* (The cloistering, 1987).
†From *Medicina carnale* (Carnal medicine, 1994).

if this is what you want I'll cut off my hand and it's yours to keep
cannibalistic beauty but I won't exhibit the sacrifice
because I don't have any use for shamed truth
or know for which sin I should turn to the mother for
          the first cilice
and therefore I'll take back my hand and souse you[52]

....

Excerpts from
The Colic Passion

....

no fear of losing my sanity
I who was never sane[53] but discovered the mortal
sustenance in words of necessary substance

I don't love it but that's no reason for destroying it
this body of mine incoherent never sated or blissful
and therefore I raise it and protect it as a mother
and patch it and wrench it from the clutches of the daughter

....

The Tapestry of the Heart

How strange is this herald who arrives
and brings dawn and blinds me and obscures form

the herald of night does not use mirrors
and reveals what he brings

I like the tapestry that covers the heart
and I am elsewhere when leveling and raking as equal wonder
doesn't beat for servitude and ardor

the sea was no longer there

profumo per ampolla sturata svapora
il vigore di dentro
perché i pensieri neonati rompono la barriera
dei denti e sfondando il riparo delle labbra
si sfogano in parole

il desiderio impazientemente espresso
esce dalla sua eccitante dimora
senza compenso per la dissipazione

l'avversario non ha fine né modo
e obbligato a camminare in punta di piedi
lungo la circonferenza del cerchio
seguiterà e mai conseguirà che io mi fermi
o mi diparta
nulla mai essendo pronto e a tutto essendo pronta
dappoiché null'altro mi appartiene
tranne gli affetti miei
ma l'aria è stata avvelenata
e io m'aspettavo d'invitare amici a udire
organi e tamburi

e ho dovuto amputare l'insalata che in primavera
dentro una boatta avevo seminato
e non è acqua che basti al tormento d'infiammazione
poiché questa è già malattia e non più sete
e però la fantasia intollerante di riposo si slancia
e va attorno con somma licenza e capriccio
lietissima delle cose nuove
per non eccitare in casa propria altre tragedie

considerata nudamente la natura dell'evento
s'abbassa e rimpicciolisce
e in questo momento sono chi apre il frigorifero
e ha fame e non ha pensato alle provviste
quando soffiò vento malato

la ragione avrà fatto abbastanza
quando sia giunta a raffreddare abuso di ignizione

perfume through uncorked cruet
vigor evaporates from within
because newborn thoughts break the barrier
of teeth and bursting open the shelter of lips
find relief in words

desire impatiently expressed
leaves its exciting dwelling
without compensation for the dissipation

the adversary has neither end nor means
and obliged to walk on tiptoe
along the circumference of the circle
will continue and will never make me stop
or depart
as nothing is ever ready and I am ready for anything
since nothing else belongs to me
except my affections
but the air has been poisoned[54]
and I was expecting to invite friends to listen
to organs and drums

and I had to amputate the lettuce that I had planted
         in a tin in Spring
and there is no water sufficient for the torment of inflammation
because this is already sickness and no longer thirst
but the imagination intolerant of rest rushes off
and most pleased with new things
roams with the utmost liberty and whim
so as not to excite other tragedies in its own home

having considered nakedly the nature of the event
it drops and shrinks
and in this moment I am the one who opens the refrigerator
and is hungry and didn't think of provisions
when sick wind blew

reason will have done enough
when it manages to dampen abuse of the ignition

scacciando il plasma dalle pareti
e rimuovendo commozione all'ingiuria

nemica della moderazione mi sottometto volentieri
a mancare di agi e scelgo ballata grande
di lungo ritornello a quattro versi
non avendo la lingua a cintura

e occultamente dal fondo ribollendo
vanno gli interni accidenti insino a tanto
che irraggiamento trabocca e la vita presente
fa battaglia per covare il suo necessario calore

ad onta d'ogni abbaiatore

Excerpts from
Il radicamento*

....

non sente nessun bisogno d'innalzare pergole
e si mette in ginocchio
per curare il seme buono che germoglia
perché riconosce le erbe tossiche e anche i fiori
e non farebbe mai una frittata di ranuncoli
ma prepara insalate di foglie di fragola tenerelle

e si stringe stretta al petto reggendosi in piedi
quando soffia malo vento e sturati rigurgitano
gli sfiatatoi delle anime bolle

alla moltiplicazione del pesco
più d'ogni altro conviene
l'innesto a occhio dormiente[55]

volendo godere maggior frutto e di maggior durata
zappa la vigna tre volte l'anno
e la netta dagli erbaggi che tolgono alimento

e ariosamente ordina i rami

*From *L'occhio dormiente* (The sleeping eye, 1997).

dispelling plasma from the walls
and removing emotion from the injury

enemy of moderation I willingly submit
to the loss of comforts and choose a grand ballad
with a long refrain in four verses
because I don't have a girdled tongue

and the inner accidents keep boiling
secretly from the bottom until
irradiation overflows and the present life
battles to nurse its necessary fire

despite any backbiter[56]

Excerpts from
The Rooting

....

she doesn't feel the need to erect pergolas
and kneels down
to care for the good seed that sprouts
because she recognizes toxic herbs as well as flowers
and would never make an omelet with buttercups
instead she prepares salads with tender strawberry leaves

and hugs her chest tightly remaining on her feet
when bitter wind blows and unplugged vents
overflow with bubbling souls

most fitting
is the grafting of a dormant bud
for the multiplication of the peach tree

as she wants to enjoy more and more lasting fruit
she hoes the vineyard three times a year
and rids it of the greens that sap nutrition

and airily orders the branches

Excerpts from
L'urlo di Abû Nuwàs*

....

di stupore in stupore
stupore prima dell'arrivo
a ogni ritorno
stupore che varca limiti e spezza vincoli
poi che né la vista né la testa
può testimoniare del quanto e come
che segreti segretamente sa vedendo con altri occhi
e raggiunto non ha spiegazione né definizione il segreto
perché non è idea di vino
che si costituisce nel vigneto

la vigna me la sono sognata

stupore che cresce
pasta della mente lievitata
a dismisura mantecata
sfrollata e intossicata
smania la mente che non mente
e mai inganni monta
e guarda perché non vede
e con le unghie si strappa la pelle

a nozze spergiure né risposta
né sponda

ubriaca di feccia che sprizza
e contro ogni evidenza viene a galla
più di nulla so vantarmi
nel racconto di trippaglie troppo alto
per il limitato sapere della mente
poi che lusinga e rampogna concilia il sonno
alle pupille del narciso
petulante innanzi a tanto languore

---

*From *L'occhio dormiente* (The sleeping eye, 1997).

Excerpts from
The Scream of Abû Nuwàs[57]

....

from wonder to wonder
wonder before arriving
at each return
wonder that exceeds limits and breaks bonds
since neither sight nor mind
can bear witness to the how and how much
that knows secrets secretly seeing with other eyes
and the secret has no explanation or definition having
    been reached
because it is not the idea of wine
that is constituted in the vineyard

I dreamt the vineyard

wonder that grows
batter of the mind leavened
excessively mixed
overripened and poisoned
the mind that doesn't lie is frenzied
and never mounts deceptions
and watches since it doesn't see
and rips off its skin with its claws

to perjured nuptials neither response
nor shore

drunk with dregs that gush
surfacing against all evidence
I can no longer boast of anything
in the tale of tripe too grand
for the mind's limited knowledge
since enticement and rebuke induce sleep
in the pupils of the narcissus
importunate before so much languor

contemplato e contemplante
a sé fece mostra di sé
e l'anima balbetta
perde la cima della corda
e non ha salvaguardia contro l'imbecillità
(ma se non si muove adesso
quando si muoverà?

ascolto e metto l'emozione a bagnomaria
rinunciando agli averi che non ho e recidendo
il legame del cuore
mi libero d'ogni gravame ma so che non è così

....

contemplated and contemplating
to himself he displayed himself
and the soul stutters
loses the end of the rope
and has no safeguard against stupidity
(but if it doesn't move now
when will it move?

I listen and put emotion in a double boiler
renouncing possessions I don't have and rending
the bonds of the heart
I free myself of every burden but I know I lie

....

ANNA CASCELLA

la dimenticanza non è*

la dimenticanza non è
la mia materia, seme incarnato
invece è la memoria, porta del cielo
anche e vecchia storia — mantello
pesante e mongolfiera, corpo ampio
capace di chimera, sofferenza certa
ma gestante di natura e memoria
smemorante di quello che in dolore
poi riaffiora, spore di fiore,
piante di memoria.

difficile con te*

difficile con te
il vortice il gorgo
l'affondare: cauto
ti tieni in mare ad
onde corte e spesso
lo ripeti il navigare
e le sirene anche hanno
arie di signore a
un trattenimento ad
evitare la furia, lo
sgomento, solo un tè
in un fermento di
qualche cima o fiocco
dove pure sarebbe dolce
naufragare.

*From *Tesoro da nulla* (Trifling treasure, 1990).

ANNA CASCELLA

Forgetfulness Is Not

forgetfulness is not
my material, memory
is instead seed incarnate, door to the sky
and also old story — heavy
mantle and montgolfier, broad body
capable of chimera, suffering that is certain
yet pregnant with nature and memory
incognizant of that which in sorrow
resurfaces, spores of flowers
plants of memory.

Difficult with You

difficult with you
the vortex the whirlpool
the sinking: cautiously
you keep course in a sea with
small waves and routinely
repeat your sailing
and even your sirens have
the air of ladies
attending a reception to
avoid the fury, the
dismay, only a tea
in a turmoil of
a few cables or jibs
where being wrecked
would yet be sweet.[58]

finanche il tuo fuggire è un po' speciale*

finanche il tuo fuggire è un po' speciale
con quelle donne
di carta patinata, quegli inserti di
carne vellutata, quelle foto, quei
culetti bianchi, quegli stivali
neri, ah
che amanti pazienti, certosine,
bambine nude vestite malandrine in
effigie ma devote
nel dar clemenza fino all'ultimo
sfoggio in camicette orlate
di volpino, le gambe un po' allargate
un sorrisino
a te
a chiunque, o a quel bambino
che felice si perde all'apertura,
intravedendo tra l'orlo della calza e la seta,
velata, una sostanza.

Poi giustamente hai un sospetto che
in tanta perfezione
anche sul luogo accogliente si posi
una polvere un poco derelitta, una mancanza
d'uso, una sconfitta, un invito al non esserti
perduto
riposi allora l'insieme delle amanti
sul divano del mese di febbraio, costanti dolci
immote, mai incalzanti,
gli ripieghi i seni e i fianchi
in quei fogli di carta, addormentate

Oggi chi sa, potrebbe
funzionare il tuo
immaginoso amore il tuo volare
su donne un poco amazzoni e un poco piccole sante ardite
ah, le tue amiche

*From *Tesoro da nulla* (Trifling treasure, 1990).

Even Your Escape Is a Bit Special

even your escape is a bit special
with those glossy paper
women, those inserts of
velvety flesh, those photos, those
white little asses, those black
boots, ah
what patient, Carthusian lovers,[59]
naked little girls dressed little scoundrels
in effigy but devout
in displaying mercy until the final
exhibition in blouses trimmed
with fox, their legs slightly spread
a little smile
for you
for anyone, or for that little boy
who is happily lost at the opening,
glimpsing between the stocking's hem and the silk,
a veiled substance.

Then you justly suspect that
in so much perfection
even the welcoming site may be covered by
a somewhat derelict dust, a lack
of use, a defeat, an invitation not to be
lost
then again you lay down the lovers' ensemble
on February's couch, constant sweet
motionless, never insistent,
you fold back their breasts and hips
in your sheets of paper, asleep

Today who knows, it might
work, your
imaginative love your flight
over women part amazon and part little daring saint
ah, your girlfriends

il nomade del cielo*

il nomade del cielo
caduto dai giardini
aveva in sé la rosa
scomposta scarmigliata
che gli premeva dentro
bucava gli intestini
ulcerava le carni
tentando da ogni antro
sia bocca ano ventricoli
o la mano
di uscirgli in sbocco
fiotto manto

nei depositi del cuore†

nei depositi del cuore
e nelle vene ingrossate
(dall'uso) — nella fatica
della circolazione (riposa)
la tensione del dolore —
la conoscenza del tempo
(frantumata) la parvenza
dell'essere — il senso
di esistere, di tessere —

*From *Tesoro da nulla* (Trifling treasure, 1990).
†From *Piccoli Campi* (Small fields, 1996).

The Nomad of the Sky

the nomad of the sky
having fallen from the gardens
harbored the disheveled
ruffled rose
that inside pressed against him
pricked his intestine
ulcerated his flesh
trying from every antrum
be it mouth anus ventricles
or the hand
to emerge from him in spittle[60]
stream mantle

In the Deposits of the Heart

in the deposits of the heart
and in the veins enlarged
(by use) — in the strain
of circulation (rests)
the pressure of pain —
the cognizance of time
(shattered) the semblance
of being — the sense
of existing, of weaving —

(ad un malato d'adolescenza)*

(ad un malato d'adolescenza)
per favore
rimettiti presto
facciamo meglio
l'amore — giriamoci
nella coperta celeste
credimi l'unica (cosa)
è credere che rimarremo
intoccati dal tempo —
che l'anno il momento
ci lasceranno
nati ancora — e capaci,
vorrei meglio spiegarti
come non sia illusione
la mia — romanzo rosa
di periferia degradata
dal male (non troppo) —
ma solo sentire —
e un poco patire...
solo un poco — lo spazio
che la ragione
intesse al luogo
febbrile —

*From *Piccoli Campi* (Small fields, 1996).

(To One Afflicted with Adolescence)

(to one afflicted with adolescence)

please
get well soon
let's do a better job
of making love — let's roll over
in the sky blue blanket
believe me the only (thing)
is to believe that we'll remain
untouched by time —
that the year the moment
will leave us
born again — and able,
I'd like to better explain
how mine is not
an illusion — romance novel
of city outskirts degraded
(not too much) by evil —
but only feeling —
and some suffering…
only some — the space
that reason
weaves for the feverish
place —

MARIELLA BETTARINI

Frammento alla madre*

Raccoglie in grembo tutte le fatiche
la donna, sempre:
nelle cocche del grembiale.

Mia madre le raccoglie nel pensiero.

Settembre 1963

Di Padreterni ce n'è uno solo*

Di Padreterni ce n'è uno
solo e io non sono neppure
il suo angelo custode
che scenda per tirarti fuori
dalla buca nella quale sei caduto,
ma solo uno, semplicemente,
il cui potere più grande è quello
di non averne e la cui più autentica
allegria quella
di stare a guardare il mondo
e dirne qualcosa tra noi
— problema autentico in mezzo
a tanti pseudo-problemi —
e cambiare le bende
all'uomo ferito — opera
non 'bella', ma la bellezza
non risolve —
e lasciarsi defraudare
da tutti — perché la sorgente
in un fiume è perenne e un uomo
non è mai un semplice ruscello
che alla prima canicola secchi.

29 maggio 1968

*From *Tre lustri e oltre (Antologia poetica 1963–81)* (Three lustra and be-
yond [poetic anthology 1963–81], 1986).

Mariella Bettarini

Fragment for the Mother

In her lap woman gathers all labors:
in the folds of her apron
she gathers them, always.

My mother gathers them in thought.

September 1963

There Is Only One Almighty

There is only one Almighty
God and I am hardly
his guardian angel
descending to pull you
from the hole where you fell,
I am one, simply,
whose greatest power is to
have none, whose most authentic
happiness is to
watch the world
to speak about it amongst ourselves
— authentic problem in the middle
of many pseudo-problems —
to change the bandages
of the wounded man — not a
"beautiful" work, but beauty
does not resolve —
and to let herself be cheated
by everyone — because the spring
in a river is perennial and a man
is never a simple stream
dry at the first wave of heat.

29 May 1968

Il leccio*

Il geranio ha bisogno
d'acqua. Ma all'acqua non importa
se è un geranio o un lillà:
chi crederà di tenermi tra i denti
mentre ride e prepara cose
da contrappormi, non mi avrà
più; ecco io sono una pecora che possiede
altri foraggi, una
che non riesce ad intrupparsi,
che non si rassegna di come va
il mondo e che per questo parla
con la morte con mezzi medianici, le cadono
gli oggetti di mano, vaga con il sacco dei semi
che le è stato dato all'ingresso
e cerca il campo ed esamina che terra c'è
— se roccia o terra —, prova la concentrazione
in acqua dei minerali, il grado
di siccità o pioggia, misura il lavoro
e si pone all'opera senza séguiti
né baldacchini,
        attacca il blocco,
annaffia, sarchia, ara e semina e non teme
se il campo di fronte ha già la spiga
che si è fatta alta e un altro il fiore denso
perché può darsi che la sua semente non dia
grano né fiore, ma sparto o erba medica
o un unico leccio
in mezzo a una piana secca.

                                23 giugno 1968

*From Tre lustri e oltre (Antologi a poetica 1963–81) (Three lustra and be-
yond [poetic anthology 1963–81], 1986).

The Holm Oak

The geranium needs
water. But water does not care
if it is a geranium or a lilac:
they will not have me anymore, those
who believe they hold me in their teeth
laughing and preparing to counter
me; see, I am a sheep who possesses
other fodder, one
not able to join the ranks,
who does not resign herself to the ways of
the world and so speaks
with death through a medium's means, drops
objects from her hands, wanders with the sack of seeds
she was given at the entrance
and searches for the field examining what earth there is
— rock or dirt — tests the concentration
of the minerals in water, the degree
of draught or rain, measures the work
and sets in without entourage
or baldachins,
                    attacks the block,
waters, hoes, plows, and sows, and does not worry
if the opposing field has ears
that have already grown tall or another dense blooms
because it may be that her seed does not give
either wheat or flower, but esparto or alfalfa
or a single holm oak
in the midst of a dry plain.

23 June 1968

Il nome*

Il mio nome schiumato dal
setaccio, con pesciolini e stelle
di mare; il mio nome ilare,
che non è me, che non mi rappresenta,
un nome sconveniente,
fangoso (brandello da avvoltoio).

Su altre piste muovo
il mio carro; fuori da Firenze, d'Italia, fuori
dal mondo, senza più
ragionevolezza, ma per questo
irriducibile,
ferita nel centro del ventre
come da un taglio cesareo da cui
esca finalmente l'io
che andavo cercando.

9 luglio 1968

Biografia*

Poi firmo un armistizio, ascolto le voci
che dicono «zitto!» al bambino; una cosa
è sicura: la giustizia non emana più
dal re, né da nessuno altro su questa Terra.
Ma poi questi sono discorsi
che vanno e vengono, discorsi che non entrano
nel vivo del tema: o ci si consola da sé
o non si può essere consolati;
ora la mia «consolazione» è che sono
una terra vestita di ventisette strati, un tronco
con ventisette anelli, ventisette
vite e morti in capo e — se ho ancora voglia
di giocare con i numeri e rovescio le cifre (1942) —
ecco, scopro l'America.

*From Tre lustri e oltre (Antologia poetica 1963–81) (Three lustra and beyond [poetic anthology 1963–81], 1986).

The Name

My name skimmed by the
sieve, with small fish and sea
stars; my cheerful name,
that isn't me, that does not represent me,
an unseemly name,
muddy (scrap for vultures).

On other trails I take
my wagon; outside Florence, Italy, outside
the world, no longer
reasonable, but because of this
irreducible,
wounded in the center of my belly
as if by a cesarean cut
delivering the self
for which I was searching.

9 July 1968

Biography

Then I sign an armistice, I listen to the voices
that yell "shut up!" to the child; one thing
is certain: justice no longer emanates
from the king, nor from anyone else on this Earth.
But then these are arguments
that come and go, arguments that don't go
to the heart of the issue: either you console yourself
or you cannot be consoled;
now my "consolation" is that I am
a land dressed in twenty-seven layers, a trunk
with twenty-seven rings, twenty-seven
lives and deaths in my head and — if I still feel like
playing with numbers and I reverse the figures (1942) —
voilà, I discover America.

E poi un boato e siamo sulla luna
— generazione che cresce ormai sui sassi
del Mare della Tranquillità, venuta su
da fuoco e fumo, apprendimento
della parola e sua perdita, presa d'aria
e presa di gas, vita che nasce dal nero
di bombe, oceani spalancati
e colombi morti — senza troppe speranze ma già
non più disperata.

Maggio 1969

Se la natura parla a tutta gola*

Se la natura parla a tutta gola
è chiaro che tremo; se mi guardo
nello specchio lungo della vecchiaia
è chiaro che penso; se chi chiama
è l'amore (ed esso chiama a festa, a morto,
con grida terribili, a tempo e del tutto
fuori tempo) sono terrificata.

Tirata per i capelli, c'è la faccia
dei girasoli che mi arringa,
c'è disavanzo
tra me e me, tra la mia carne e la carne
cumulativa e io sono ormai
quello che mangia e quello
che non ha più fame di nulla.

nel momento in cui il corpo annega*

nel momento in cui il corpo annega
inutile conoscere il peso dell'acqua
o che volume sposti il corpo.
        Se riaffiora la follia
la spingo giù ma se è l'uomo che affiora
gli butto una corda e amen.

*From *Tre lustri e oltre* (*Antologia poetica 1963–81*) (Three lustra and beyond [poetic anthology 1963–81], 1986).

And then a boom and we are on the moon
— generation that now grows on the rocks
of the Sea of Tranquillity, raised
on fire and smoke, acquisition
of the word and its loss, air intake
and gas intake, life born from the blackness
of bombs, gaping oceans
and dead pigeons — without many hopes but already
no longer despairing.

May 1969

If Nature Bellows

If nature bellows
of course I tremble; if I look at myself
in the long mirror of old age
of course I think; if it is love
that is calling (and it calls in celebration and mourning,
with terrible cries, in time and entirely
out of time) I am terrified.

I am dragged by the hair, there are faces
of sunflowers haranguing me,
there is deficit
between me and me, between my flesh and the cumulative
flesh and I am now
the one who eats and the one
no longer hungering.

In That Moment When the Body Drowns

in that moment when the body drowns
futile to know the weight of water
or what volume the body may shift.
If folly resurfaces
I push it down but if it is man who surfaces
I throw him a rope and amen.

*A volte gioco per alleggerire il peso
delle battaglie il cui numero
sale di giorno in giorno.*

*

*intanto l'annata cresce e io
diminuisco ma pezzi riaffiorano
nella corrente, cammino
fin dove incontro le acque
e quaggiù mi spengo.*

> *La mia lotta
tra movimento e ciclo, forma aperta e forma
chiusa, acqua da vaso comunicante e acqua
che esce sangue che esce sangue.*

Ci lascino amare chi vogliamo: l'acqua*

*Ci lascino amare chi vogliamo: l'acqua
se piove il vento se tira vento la veglia
il sonno e quello che so io, il fenicottero
e il coleottero, cieli mani e la faccia
candida-candita
          la faccia
di marmellata affettiva.*

*«Queste sono le mappe per capire le cose, queste
sono le cose».*
          *Non è che abbiamo capito tutto.
Certe cose non le abbiamo capite
                    altre
sono state coperte dal brusio di una folla
nella quale non vedo bene.*

---

*From *Tre lustri e oltre (Antologia poetica 1963–81)* (Three lustra and be-
yond [poetic anthology 1963–81], 1986).

At times I play to lessen the weight
of battles whose numbers
increase from day to day.

★

meanwhile the year grows and I
diminish but pieces resurface
in the current, I walk
to the point where I meet the waters
and here below I die out.

My struggle
between movement and cycle, open and closed
form, water from communicating vessels and water
that comes out blood that comes out blood.

Let Us Love As We Choose: Water

Let us love as we choose: water
if it is rainy wind if it is windy the wake
the sleep and that which I know, the phoenicopterus
and the coleopteron, skies hands and the face
candid-candied
                    the face
of affective jam.

"These are the maps for understanding things, these
are the things."
                    It is not that we have understood everything.
There are certain things we didn't understand
                                        others
have been covered by the buzz of a crowd
where my sight is poor.

dico che il grillo lo scorpione
la cavalletta*

dico che il grillo lo scorpione la cavalletta
hanno più forze di me di cui non vale più
parlare né in questo modo né in altri
dato che del soggetto si è parlato anche troppo
e conviene parlare dell'oggetto
a chiare lettere chiare note a chiarissime
                                  grida

poiché i boschi hanno già preso tutti fuoco
e la cenere che rimane sono fatti
da raccontarsi più crudamente con le mani
attorno ai ginocchi dando un calcio soave
a questo mondo perché si metta a camminare.

Epilogo (a doverosa distanza)*

    ma sai che cosa c'è
al fondo di tutto?
                c'è che ti ignoro
(nel presente)
            che ti faccio crescere
barbe di rami spini o raganelle e che
riaffiori (ma impallidito)
nella teca di un mio padre che
tengo morto a ridosso e da questo
(e da te) mi salvano ironia
e riccia perversità
di un legame anguilloso e solenne
che — no — non ti prevede
                     tu ri-parlante
(grillo)
      ombra
di un'ombra
         embolo di un padre
che ho cacciato

*From *Tre lustri e oltre (Antologia poetica 1963–81)* (Three lustra and be-yond [poetic anthology 1963–81], 1986).

I Say That the Cricket the Scorpion the Grasshopper

I say that the cricket the scorpion the grasshopper
have more strength than me, and I'm no longer worth
talking about neither in this way nor others
since plenty has been said about the subject
and it is better to speak of the object
in clear letters clear notes in the clearest
                                        cries

because the woods have already caught fire
and the remaining ashes are facts
to be recounted more crudely with hands
around knees while giving a gentle kick
to this world so that it begins walking.

Epilogue (at the Proper Distance)

   but you know what's
at the bottom of everything?
                    it's that I ignore you
(in the present)
                    that I make you grow
beards of branches thorns or tree toads and that
you resurface (turned pale)
in the reliquary where I keep
a father hovering and entombed and from this
(and from you) I am saved by the irony
and bristled perversity
of an eely and solemn bond
that — no — does not include you
                                    you re-iterating
(cricket)[61]
            shadow
of a shadow
                    embolus of a father
I chased away

            paraninfo
di un no *definitivo*
                    tramonto
di un errante possibile (che divaga
che sbaglia che s'incaglia)
                    tragedia
tutta quanta strozzata nel suo «alt!»
                            segnale
di un errore
            simulacro
di amore mendicato e orsùdunque
cattivo
        di amore malriposto
                            di colore
d'arrosto
        di padre
troppo tosto
            di bruciato
sembiante
        di passante passato
                            di
qualcosa che (stante)
se n'è andato

From **La casa del poeta***

VI

mia casa (lo sapevi?) — mia casa
la parola
            mia unica
ragione — mia casa
viva e sola
            magione — nido — ostello
ricovero — ristoro
riparo — covo — ombrello
consolazione — polo

*From *Case, luoghi, la parola* (Homes, places, the word, 1998).

                    paranymph
of a definitive *no*
                    waning
of an errant possibility (that wanders
that blunders that runs aground)
                              tragedy
all strangled in its "stop!"
                    indicator
of an error
            simulacrum
of love begged for and come-on-then
bad
      of misplaced love
                        of the color
of roast
          of an over-tough
father
        of a burnt
demeanor
              of passing past
                        of
something that (staying)
has left

From **The Poet's Home**

VI

my home (did you know?) — my home
the word
          my sole
reason — my home
alive and alone
                    abode — nest — hostel
retreat — relief
shelter — den — umbrella
consolation — pole

LUCIANA NOTARI

Chi ogni volta rinnega*

Chi ogni volta rinnega
la forma desiderata
ama troppo il desiderio,

se il desiderio è troppo grande
ogni forma sarà
per la sua imperfezione negata.

Una forza
si riconosce sempre, l'egoismo.

Il corpo e l'anima†

Quello che so
lo so con le mie membra,
fatica delle mani e fuoco agli occhi,
stretta allo stomaco di vuoto
e scudisciate rapide al respiro.
L'anima non è astrale, rarefatta,
percorre stretta al corpo la sua strada,
s'intriga forte dentro l'esperienza,
dilaga nelle cose, in confidenza;
batte nei cigli glabri di ogni rospo
e sale nella linfa verticale
dell'albero, germoglio sotto il cielo.

Ed ora che il dolore è oltre il dosso
l'anima sta a suo agio
e si rispecchia
in ogni coda nuda fino all'osso.

---

*From *Animanimalis* (Animalsoul, 1991).
†From *La vita è nella vita* (Life is in life, 1994).

Luciana Notari

If One Always Denies

If one always denies
the desired form
then desire is loved too much,

if desire is too great
each form will be
denied for its imperfection.

One force
is readily apparent: selfishness.

Body and Soul

What I know
I know with my limbs,
my toiling hands and burning eyes,
I know it from the sinking in my stomach
and the rapid lashing of my breath.
The soul is not astral, rarefied,
it travels close to the body
is tightly entangled in experience,
flows into things, on familiar terms;
beats in a toad's glabrous eyes
and rises in the vertical lymph
of a tree, budding under the sky.

And now that sorrow is beyond the hill
the soul, at ease,
mirrors itself
in every tail, stark-naked.

Scarto*

Sullo scarto incolmabile
di voci e desideri
si stampano le orme
scendendo a tratti
al centro della strada
e gli occhi oltrepassano
la folla
attratti da una luce
di segreta origine ma forte.

Quello scarto incolmabile
feroce
che rende me
pietosa madre
dell'albero e del seme
del pelo elettrico
di tutti gli animali
di piuma implume
che nasce già violata.

La parola nuota con fatica
trasporta a terra le scorie
le piccole tracce dall'oscuro
le annusa le riplasma ricompone
attenta stringe in mano per fissare
la forma quasi piena
carente di sublime.

*From *La vita è nella vita* (Life is in life, 1994).

Distance

Footprints tread
the unfathomed distance
between voices and desires
descending at intervals
onto the middle of the road
and the eyes move beyond
the crowd
drawn by a light
of secret yet forceful origin.

That unfathomed
fierce distance
which makes me
compassionate mother
of the tree and seed
of the electric hair
of all animals
of unfledged feather
born already violated.

With difficulty the word swims
bringing dross to the shore
small traces from darkness
it smells reshapes recomposes them
carefully holding them, fixed
on the almost full form
which lacks the sublime.

Aspra stagione metropolitana*

Aspra stagione metropolitana,
grigia, riarsa, incenerita;
ai bordi d'un'aiuola incatramata
tracima rinnegata la Natura, la Vita.

Paesaggio invernale*

Sui bordi d'autostrada i passerotti
alle ruote s'immolano festosi.
La briciola si tinge un poco in rosso
come rubino di gracile allegria.

Estasi breve*

Per "Le domaine d'Arnheim"

Qui la montagna si congiunge al mare,
la neve sposa vena tintinnante,
il silenzio freme di rumore che solo
altro silenzio sa ascoltare…

L'amore annuncia sempre un altro amore,
lago che suppone fiumi e mare, la nube,
pioggia e pianto ed aria fine.

L'amore annuncia sempre un nuovo altrove,
misterico e feroce, estasi breve.

Giugno 1997

*From *Aiuole di città* (Urban flowerbeds, 1997).

Harsh Metropolitan Season

Harsh metropolitan season,
gray, parched, burnt to ashes;
repudiated Nature, Life, overflows
at the borders of a tarred flower bed.

Winter Landscape

On highway edges the sparrows
offer themselves to the wheels.
The crumb turns a bit red
like a ruby of frail joy.

Brief Ecstasy

For "Le domaine d'Arnheim"[62]

Here the mountain joins the sea,
the snow marries the jingling vein,
the silence quivers with noise that only
another silence can hear...

Love always announces another love,
like a lake which assumes rivers and sea, cloud,
rain and tears and pure air.

Love always announces a new mysterious
and fierce elsewhere, brief ecstasy.

June 1997

BIANCAMARIA FRABOTTA

La penombra spacca il bosco in due distinti versi*

La penombra spacca il bosco in due distinti versi.
Il primo verde è chiaro alto e slanciato
corre da sé verso l'aperta porta alle parole
il sottobosco è scuro verde tronca radice.
Sta in fondo e non si ruba.
Nemmeno l'aeree macchine volanti di Leonardo.

Erosione dell'utopia o rigore della pazienza?*

Erosione dell'utopia o rigore della pazienza?
Rispondere è sostituire il bianco al nero.
Prova tu che ami il disordine
delle tinte, le onde morte dell'etere
lèccane il nero di grassa dolce colla
e sulla lingua spergiura ti resterà neo nata
l'altra metà della domanda, l'inesprimibile bianco
(non la domanda ma la risposta è il nostro nobile
            privilegio)
essere leggibile per tutti e per me indecifrabile.

È vero. Non come te poeta io sono*

È vero. Non come te poeta io sono
io sono poetessa e intera non appartengo a nessuno.
Da me, come da te la pura stella dell'inizio del mondo
è lontana la menzogna primaria, vestita di nero e
            maschile nella voce.
Con mia madre io ho altri problemi
anche se oggi ti rendo l'onore delle armi
il fuoco sacro dell'imitazione.
Vicino alla morte e a morire è la
corolla spampanata di questa coppa di veleni
la verità si fa più semplice e facile da ricordare.
Chi di noi dunque per primo ha perso la memoria?

*From Il rumore bianco (The white noise, 1982).

BIANCAMARIA FRABOTTA

The Dim Light Splits the Woods in Two Distinct Lines

The dim light splits the woods in two distinct lines.
The first green is clear tall and soaring
it runs by itself toward the open door of speech
the underwood is dark green severed root.
It remains at the bottom and can't be stolen.
Not even Leonardo's aerial flying machines.

Erosion of Utopia or Rigor of Patience?

Erosion of utopia or rigor of patience?
To answer is to put white in the place of black.
Try, you who love the confusion
of colors, the dead waves of ether
lick its black of greasy sweet glue
and on your perjured tongue there will remain newly born
the other half of the question, the inexpressible white
(not the question but the answer is our noble
          privilege)
to be legible for all and for me indecipherable.

It Is True. I Am Not a Poet the Way You Are

It is true. I am not a poet the way you are
I am a poetess and whole I do not belong to anyone.
From me, just as from you, the pure star of the beginning
          of the world
the primary lie is distant, dressed in black and
          masculine in its voice.
With my mother I have other problems
even though today I grant you the honors of war
the sacred fire of imitation.
Close to death and to dying, it's the
overblown corolla of this cup of poisons
truth becomes simpler and easy to remember.
Which one of us then was the first to lose our memory?

From **Eloisa**

> E pensare che quello che ti
> chiedo è ben poco,
> e per te facilissimo!

> (Eloisa a Abelardo, *Lettera 2ª*)

I

Qui dimora l'intero e tu disperso
ci ragioni. Che io canti, piú buia
sordidamente, ombra piú pesante
del marmo che mi riposa non conta.
Una sola rondine non mi ti rende
la stagione perduta
e io troppo tempo ho abitato in te
come la ragnatela in un tronco morto

al limite di una terra promessa
non cogliendomi (fu soltanto evocazione
addestramento allo stupro
il fantastico frutto dell'occidente)
mi hai nominata piú bianca della luce
nido di un'idea intricata, torpida fantasia,
pupilla cieca del tuo occhio.

Si sfilava il sibilo dalla teoria lunga
delle stanze: davanti alla porta chiusa
sarò la sorella di quei meli che fuori
si spogliano lisciando a sangue i sensi
e solo la sera ne spegne il tocco.
Un triangolo è divino quando ogni punta è Dio
e ogni lato un'esca. Non c'è veglia piú amara
per me che sono lontano dalla festa.

Le parole non ti costavano molto, ricordi?
scivolano via per filo e per segno
come canoe fluiscono sul filo della corrente.

*From *Il rumore bianco* (The white noise, 1982).

216

From **Heloise**

> *And to think that what I*
> *ask of you is so little,*
> *and for you so very easy!*

(*Heloise to Abelard,* Second Letter)

I

Here dwells the whole and scattered
you ponder over it. That I sing, darker
sordidly, shadow heavier
than the marble quieting me does not matter.
My lone swallow won't bring you
the lost season
and I have lived in you too long
like a cobweb in a dead tree trunk

at the limit of a promised land
refusing to pick me (it was only evocation
training for rape
the fantastic fruit of the West)
you named me whiter than light
nest of an intricate idea, torpid fantasy,
blind pupil of your eye.

The whistle unraveled from the long procession
of rooms: before the closed door
I will be sister to those apple trees that outside
strip themselves stroking the senses raw
only the evening extinguishes their touch.
A triangle is divine when each point is God
and each side bait. There is no vigil more bitter
for me as I am far from the feast.

Words did not cost you much, remember?
gliding away through every detail
flowing like canoes on the current.

Non c'era rapida che ne scuotesse il corso
scorresse anche fino al mare il discorso
del tuo sogno soltanto noi ne scontavamo il costo.

Ma subito potessi smemorarmi
annottassero ovunque le pupille degli uomini desti
in un mondo di dormienti
un bestiario delicatamente miniato dallo stilo di chi può
almeno fin quando arriverò
placida onda di lago a lambirti
i piedi di umide e molli zolle di prato
almeno fin là dove arriva l'essere
e il chierico si fa pierrot
la canaglia un'ariosa città
ogni passante un amico, un evento
allora
l'acqua coprirà il prato e ogni traccia di nome.

Dianae sumus in fide[*]

Grazie tante no. Della grazia
farò a meno. Imparerò
piuttosto la svagata
lezione della viatrice Diana
non Juno Luna Trivia
intriganti e faccendiere
ma l'ambidestra regina
del labirinto dei pazzi
la sterile dimentica amica
dell'anatomia dei vizi
che non ignora
i diletti tratti della differenza
e scarta il meglio, un parto
fortuito fortunosamente liquido
un ramoscello di vita che
nel testacoda del secondo millennio
non so da dove esca

*From *Appunti di volo e altre poesie* (Flight notes and other poems, 1985).

No rapid could shake their course
even if your dream's discourse
had run as far as the sea we alone paid its cost.

If only at once I could lose my memory
if only everywhere the pupils of waking men grew dark
in a world of sleepers
bestiary delicately illuminated by the stylus of the one who can
at least till I arrive
calm wave of lake to lap
your feet, turf of soft, moist meadow
at least to the point where being arrives
and the cleric becomes a pierrot
the rabble an airy city
every passerby a friend, an event
then
water will cover the meadow and every trace of name.

Dianae sumus in fide[63]

Thanks but no. I will do
without grace. I will learn
instead the heedless
lesson of wayfaring Diana
not Juno Luna Trivia[64]
schemers and meddlers
but the ambidextrous queen
of the madman's labyrinth
sterile unmindful friend
to the anatomy of defects
who does not ignore
the beloved traits of difference
and discards the best, a fortuitous
tempestuously liquid delivery
a twig of life issuing
in the spin-out of the second millennium
from where I don't know

se con te non parto
triviale dissipatrice
selvaggia Artemide
dispensami dal rito dovuto
all'altra tua guancia nascosta
salvami dall'infida goccia di Selene
fomentatrice del diluvio
insegnami la danza del sentiero
che mi tiene a distanza
perfino da te Hecate
che occulti il centro
giochi d'ala e non mi neghi
una licenza di caccia una faccia di bronzo
e intorno alla testa una frangetta
dicono proprio adatta a tener testa
al vizio sadomasochista di Ilithya
dicta lumine luna
aiutami a tirare a secco la rete
bulbo gonfio e impudico soltanto
se fra i pesci guizza del mare
aiutami a razzolare
i grumi duri fra le perle
beccare il verme al volo
festeggiare con agile abbrivio
il martirio del libero arbitrio.

Miopia*

Mi presti i tuoi occhi per guardarti?
A chi negheresti una lente nitida pulita?
Sui denti scoperti l'urto dell'acqua lustrale
il rimbalzo fra i rami di un volubile raggio
sotto la gronda una rissa di candide colombe.
Chiunque vorrebbe i tuoi occhi per guardarsi.

*From *Appunti di volo e altre poesie* (Flight notes and other poems, 1985).

if I don't leave with you
trivial[65] squanderer
wild Artemis
dispense me from the rite that is owed
your hidden other cheek
save me from the treacherous drops of Selene
fomenter of the deluge
teach me the dance of the path
that keeps me at a distance
even from you Hecate
who conceal the center
who rely on the wing and don't deny me
a license for hunting a brazen face
and my hair in a bob
just right they say for standing against
the sadomasochistic vice of Ilithyia[66]
dicta lumine luna[67]
help me pull in the net
a bulb swollen and indecent only
when darting among the fish of the sea
help me pick
at the hard clumps among the pearls
peck the worm in mid-air
celebrate with agile headway
the martyrdom of free will.

Myopia

Will you lend me your eyes to look at you?
Would you ever deny a clear clean lens?
On bared teeth the blast of lustral waters
the rebounds of a fickle ray through the branches
under the eaves a brawl of candid doves.
We would all like your eyes to look at ourselves.

Naufragio*

Quale forma di te imitare per essere detta tua?
il ginocchio? la testa? il piede nella scarpa di gomma?
o la mano sfusa che un poco trema se con me parli?
Quale parte del tuo corpo essere per essere infine parte di te?

Autoritratto in terza persona†

Ieri vantava l'aderenza allo specchio
la sazietà di piedi ben fatti, patti
in vista di ulteriori concessioni, tempi
piú lunghi magari e il tiro
corretto al selvatico bilancio d'età.
Oggi nutre raminghe speranze di sparire
nelle sembianze di un gatto, un colpo di tosse
il lento vogare di un capello a mezz'aria.
Domani non ci sarà piú tempo
per l'uso pigramente italiano
del verbo, il sereno ottativo
del vorrei essere stato.
Ma divampando potesse essere lei una
combusta orma al fuoco dell'ellisse
temeraria, mite ombra e pur sostanza
di quel sole che non teme eclisse.

---

*From *Appunti di volo e altre poesie* (Flight notes and other poems, 1985).
†From *La viandanza* (The wayfaring, 1995).

Shipwreck

Which form of you should I imitate to be called yours?
the knee? the head? the foot in the sneaker?
or the loose hand that trembles a little when you speak to me?
Which part of your body should I be to be finally part of you?

Self-Portrait in the Third Person

Yesterday she claimed adherence to the mirror
the satiety of well-made feet, agreements
which foresee additional concessions, time
perhaps extended and aim
adjusted for the wild balance of her years.
Today she harbors roaming hopes of disappearing
in the semblance of a cat, a cough
the slow floating of a hair in mid-air.
Tomorrow there won't be time
for the lackadaisical Italian use
of the verb, the serene optative
of the I-would-like-to-have-been.
But if only ablaze she could be a
burnt trace of the fire[68] of the ellipse
reckless, gentle shadow and yet substance
of that sun that does not fear eclipse.

VIVIAN LAMARQUE

C'era un castello*

C'era un castello
e avevo un manto
e sotto il manto avevo bambini.
C'era un castello con intorno giardini
volava il manto
volava il cielo
volava il verde di tutti i giardini.
C'era al castello un re molto bello
che in piedi nell'erba rideva forte.
E il cielo volava
e il sole volava
volava anche il manto con sotto i bambini.

Poesia illegittima*

Quella sera che ho fatto l'amore
mentale con te
non sono stata prudente
dopo un po' mi si è gonfiata la mente
sappi che due notti fa
con dolorose doglie
mi è nata una poesia illegittimamente
porterà solo il mio nome
ma ha la tua aria straniera ti somiglia
mentre non sospetti niente di niente
sappi che ti è nata una figlia.

Volevo sognare il postino*

Volevo sognare il postino
con una lettera in mano
invece ho sognato il postino
senza una mano.

*From *Teresino* (1981).

VIVIAN LAMARQUE

There Was a Castle

There was a castle
and I had a mantle
and I kept children under the mantle.
There was a castle with gardens around it
the mantle was flying
the sky was flying
the green of the gardens was flying too.
There was a castle with a most comely king
who stood in the grass heartily laughing.
And the sky was flying
and the sun was flying
the mantle with the children was flying too.

Illegitimate Poem

The night I made love to you
mentally
I wasn't careful at all
after a little while my mind swelled
and then, you know, two nights ago
after laboring painfully
I gave birth to an illegitimate poem
it will bear only my name
but it has a foreign air, like you
while you suspect nothing at all
a daughter was born to you.

I Wanted to Dream the Mailman

I wanted to dream the mailman
with a letter in his hand
instead I dreamt the mailman
without a hand.

La signora della neve[*]

Nevicava tanto, una signora voleva tanto bene a
   un signore.
La neve si posava sulla città, il bene della signora
   si posava sul signore.
Nevicava di giorno e di notte, di giorno e di notte
   la signora voleva bene al signore.
La città e il signore, semisommersi, subivano la
   neve e il bene immobili, aspettavano la primavera.

La signora dell'ultima volta[*]

L'ultima volta che la vide non sapeva che era l'ultima volta
            che la vedeva.
Perché?
Perché queste cose non si sanno mai.
Allora non fu gentile quell'ultima volta?
Sí, ma non a sufficienza per l'eternità.

Amante neonata[†]

Amante neonata
succhia l'uomomamma perdutamente
ecco il latte buono viene — guardi —
scorre come dalla montagna il fiume
naturalmente.

Il signore di fronte[']

   Era un signore seduto di fronte a una signora seduta di
fronte a lui.
   Alla loro destra/sinistra c'era una finestra, alla loro sinistra/
destra c'era una porta.
   Non c'erano specchi, eppure in quella
stanza, profondamente, ci si specchiava.

---

[*]From Il signore d'oro (The gentleman of gold, 1986).
[†]From Poesie dando del Lei (Poems addressing you formally, 1989).
[']From Il signore degli spaventati (The gentleman of the frightened, 1992).[69]

The Lady of the Snow

It snowed so much, a lady loved a gentleman
   so dearly.
The snow settled on the city, the love of the lady
   settled on the gentleman.
It snowed day and night, day and night
   the lady loved the gentleman.
The city and the gentleman, semi-submerged, immobile
   endured the snow and love, waiting for spring.

The Lady of the Last Time

The last time he saw her he did not know that it was the
           last time he was seeing her.
Why?
Because these things one never knows.
Then he wasn't kind that last time?
Yes, but it was not sufficient for eternity.

Newborn Lover

Newborn lover
sucks the manmamma abandoningly
here the good milk comes — look —
it runs naturally like a river from
a mountain.

The Gentleman in Front

   He was a gentleman sitting in front of a lady seated in
front of him.
   To their right/left there was a window, to their left/
right there was a door.
   There were no mirrors, and yet in that
room, one could see oneself mirrored, deeply.

Il signore nel cuore*

Le era entrato nel cuore.
Passando dalla strada degli occhi e delle
orecchie le era entrato nel cuore.
E lì cosa faceva?
Stava.
Abitava il suo cuore come una casa.

Il signore e la signora*

Sembravano due ma erano una cosa sola.
Anzi sembravano una cosa sola ma erano due.
Anzi erano due e una cosa sola.
Allora quante poltrone ci volevano?
Due.
Quante seggiole?
Due.
Quanti tavoli?
Uno.
Quanti letti?
Uno.
Quanti soli?
Un sole e una luna.
Quante stelle?
Tutte tutte del firmamento le stelle
disponibili (tranne quelle cadenti).

Bambina†

Col punto erba
col punto croce
diligente si cuciva le labbra
faceva il nodo.

*From Il signore degli spaventati (The gentleman of the frightened, 1992).
†From Una quieta polvere (A quiet dust, 1996).[70]

The Gentleman in the Heart

He had entered her heart.
Passing through the street of her eyes and her
ears he had entered her heart.
And what was he doing there?
Staying.
He was living her heart like a house.

The Gentleman and the Lady

They appeared two but they were one thing only.
Better still, they appeared one thing only but were
two. Better still, they were two and one thing only.

Then how many armchairs did they need?

Two.

How many chairs?

Two.

How many tables?

One.

How many beds?

One.

How many suns?

One sun and one moon.

How many stars?

All all of the available stars of the
sky (but not the falling ones, please).[71]

Little Girl

With the satin stitch
with the cross stitch
diligent she sewed her lips[72]
she tied the knot.

Preghiera delle mamme che hanno involontariamente mancato nei confronti dei propri figli[*]

«le poesie possono aspettare
non possono aspettare le persone care.»

Oh lasciati figlio
al mille per mille di interesse
per ognuno di quegli anni risarcire
per quando avevi un anno
per quando avevi due tre sette anni
per gli anni della nostra assenza
per quando avevi un anno
per quando avevi due tre sette anni
per gli anni della nostra assenza
per quando ci chiamavi e non c'eravamo
o c'eravamo ma eravamo perse a noi stesse
o c'eravamo ma non vedevamo
perché stavamo male
perché stavo male stavo male
figlia dolce mia.

Guardando la luna[†]

Oh essere anche noi la luna di qualcuno!
Noi che guardiamo essere guardati, luccicare.
Sembrare, da lontano, la candida luna
che non siamo.

---

[*]From *Una quieta polvere* (A quiet dust, 1996).
[†]From *Corriere della Sera* (17 August, 1998).

Prayer of Mothers Who Unintentionally Failed Their Children

> "poems can wait
> loved ones cannot."

Oh child let yourself
with an interest of a thousand per thousand
for each of those years be compensated
for when you were one
for when you were two three seven years old
for the years of our absence
for when you were one
for when you were two thrce seven years old
for the years of our absence
for when you called us and we weren't there
or were there but were lost to ourselves
or were there but wouldn't see
because we were sick
because I was sick was sick
my sweet daughter.

Looking at the Moon

Oh, to be somebody's moon!
We, who look, to be looked at and shine.
From afar to seem the white moon
we in no way are.

PATRIZIA CAVALLI

Stupita cercavo le ragioni*

Stupita cercavo le ragioni
di quel sogno che fu piacere di baci.
Ma presto giunse il mio rivale
di tutte le notti il mio rivale
e senza sforzo come cosa sua
sottrasse a me
la rara prigioniera.

Nel giardino appena inumidito*

Nel giardino appena inumidito
un sedile appena sbilanciato
una furia appena addormentata.

Tenebroso con la giacca
(sarà un mantello, una coperta,
una piega di minaccia?)

Scale per discendere. E se invece
prendessi un'altra strada,
se invece di ricopiare il percorso
inventassi una capriola?

Alla fontana mi rinfrescai
la bocca, la fronte e i polsi
e fresca fresca cominciai una frase.

Per simulare il bruciore del cuore,
l'umiliazione*

Per simulare il bruciore del cuore, l'umiliazione
dei visceri, per fuggire maledetta
e maledicendo, per serbare castità
e per piangerla, per escludere la mia bocca
dal sapore pericoloso di altre bocche
e spingerla insaziata a saziarsi dei veleni del cibo

*From *Poesie: 1974–1992* (Poems: 1974–1992, 1992).

PATRIZIA CAVALLI

Stunned, I Was Looking for Reasons

Stunned, I was looking for reasons
for dreaming that pleasure of kisses.
But soon my rival arrived
my rival of each night
and without effort as if she were his
he stole from me
the rare prisoner.

In the Just Dampened Park

In the just dampened park
a just unbalanced bench
a just sedated rage.

Gloomy with his jacket
(could it be a mantle, a cover,
a threatening fold?)

Steps going down. And if instead
I took another way,
if instead of retracing the path
I invented a somersault?

At the fountain I refreshed
my mouth, forehead and wrists
and all fresh I began a phrase.

To Simulate the Burning of the Heart,
the Humiliation

To simulate the burning of the heart, the humiliation
of the bowels, to escape cursed
and cursing, to maintain my chastity
and lament it, to exclude my mouth
from the dangerous flavor of other mouths
and push it unsatiated to satiate itself on the poison of food

nell'apoteosi delle cene quando il ventre
già gonfio continua a gonfiarsi;
per toccare solitudini irraggiungibili e lí
ai piedi di un letto di una sedia
o di una scala recitare l'addio
per poterti escludere dalla mia fantasia
e ricoprirti di una nuvolaglia qualunque
perché la tua luce non stingesse il mio sentiero,
non scompigliasse il mio cerchio oltre il quale
ti rimando, tu stella involontaria,
passaggio inaspettato che mi ricordi la morte.

Per tutto questo io ti ho chiesto un bacio
e tu, complice gentile e innocente, non me lo hai dato.

Lontano dai regni*

Lontano dai regni
come è ferma la stanza!
Vieni, respirami vicino,
che io scopra la dolcezza
di molte imperfezioni, qualche dente
in meno qualche ruga in piú e il corpo
appena estenuato dalla noncuranza.

Fra tutte le distanze la migliore possibile*

Fra tutte le distanze la migliore possibile
è quella di un tavolo di normale grandezza,
di ristorante per esempio o di cucina,
dove possibilmente io possa raggiungerti
ma in verità non lo farò.
E fuori la stessa luce di ieri, lo stesso azzurro
aprono altre distanze
e chiedo alla gentilezza delle nuvole
di intervenire, meglio grigie che bianche,
per svelare l'imbroglio degli azzurri
che fingono la grandezza, fingono l'infinito,
la luce effimera — la ladra.

*From *Poesie: 1974–1992* (Poems: 1974–1992, 1992).

in the apotheosis of meals when the abdomen
already swollen continues to swell;
to touch unreachable solitude and there
at the foot of a bed or a chair
or stairs recite my good-bye
to be able to exclude you from my fantasy
and cover you with any bank of clouds
so that your light would not pale my path,
would not disturb my circle from which
I banish you, you accidental star,
unexpected passing that reminds me of death.

For all this I have asked you for a kiss
and you, gentle and innocent accomplice, refused it.

Far from the Kingdoms

Far from the kingdoms
how still is the room!
Come, breathe close to me,
that I may discover the sweetness
of many imperfections, a few less
teeth a few more wrinkles and the body
slightly wasted from neglect.

Of All Distances the Best Possible One

Of all distances the best possible one
is that of a normal sized table,
a restaurant table for instance or one from the kitchen,
where I might still possibly reach you
but in truth I will not.
And outside the same light as yesterday's light and the
          same blue
open other distances
and I ask the kindness of the clouds
to intervene, better gray ones than white,
for disclosing the fraud of the blue
which feigns greatness, feigns the infinite,
the ephemeral light — the thief.

Addosso al viso mi cadono le notti[*]

Addosso al viso mi cadono le notti
e anche i giorni mi cadono sul viso.
Io li vedo come si accavallano
formando geografie disordinate:
il loro peso non è sempre uguale,
a volte cadono dall'alto e fanno buche,
altre volte si appoggiano soltanto
lasciando un ricordo un po' in penombra.
Geometra perito io li misuro
li conto e li divido
in anni e stagioni, in mesi e settimane.
Ma veramente aspetto
in segretezza di distrarmi
nella confusione perdere i calcoli,
uscire di prigione
ricevere la grazia di una nuova faccia.

Dentro il tuo mare viaggiava la mia nave[*]

Dentro il tuo mare viaggiava la mia nave
dentro quel mare mi sono immersa e nacqui.
Mi colpisce la novità della stagione
e il corpo che si accorge di aver freddo.

Di figura in figura trasmigrava amore,
ora si posa e svela la sua forma.
La riconosco in quel veloce crespo
sulla fronte, piccole onde simili
e contrarie — correva in superficie
uno stupore, un cedimento
nella compattezza, e si incrinava
mutando in tenerezza.

[*]From *Poesie: 1974–1992* (Poems: 1974–1992, 1992).

Across My Face the Nights Fall

Across my face the nights fall
and across my face the days fall too.
I see them as they pile up
forming disordered geographies:
their weight isn't always equal,
sometimes they fall from above and form pits,
other times they just lean
leaving a memory slightly in shadow.
A skilled surveyor I measure them
count them and divide them
into years and seasons, into months and weeks.
But in truth I wait
secretly to distract myself
to lose my calculations in the confusion,
to get out of prison
to receive the grace of a new face.

Inside Your Sea My Boat Was Sailing

Inside your sea my boat was sailing
inside that sea I immersed myself and was born.
I am struck by the change of season
and the body that senses the cold.

Love was migrating from figure to figure,
now it lands to reveal its form.
I see it in the quick wrinkling
of forehead, small ripples in one direction
and then another — an amazement,
a collapse of unity, was running
across the surface, cracking
and changing into tenderness.

Se ora tu bussassi alla mia porta*

Se ora tu bussassi alla mia porta
e ti togliessi gli occhiali
e io togliessi i miei che sono uguali
e poi tu entrassi dentro la mia bocca
senza temere baci disuguali
e mi dicessi: «Amore mio,
ma che è successo?», sarebbe un pezzo
di teatro di successo.

Qualcosa che all'oggetto non s'apprende*

Qualcosa che all'oggetto non s'apprende,
un secchio vuoto che non mi raccoglie.
Tenevo i mesi silenziosi in una trama
che doveva risplendere di voce.
Provavo a dire e mi si sfilacciava.
Non è né rete né mantello, è solo schermo,
io non catturo niente e non mi copre
ma separa un silenzio dal silenzio.
Quell'altro suono labirintico e interiore
esercitato in solitudine per strada
e nei risvegli, non risultava,
non mi si mostrava.

---

*From *Poesie: 1974–1992* (Poems: 1974–1992, 1992).

If Now You Knocked on My Door

If now you knocked on my door
and removed your glasses
and I removed mine that are similar
and if you entered inside my mouth
without fearing dissimilar kisses
and said to me: "My love,
what's happened?" we'd have a smashing
theatrical happening.

It Will Not Apprehend the Object

It will not apprehend the object,
it is an empty bucket that won't collect me.
I left my silent months in a weft
meant to be resplendent with voice.
I tried to speak and it frayed.
It is neither net nor mantle, only a screen,
I won't catch anything and it won't cover me
all it does is separate silence from the silence.
That other labyrinthian and interior sound
trained in solitude along the streets
and on awakening, did not appear to me,
did not bare itself.

«*Vado, ma dove? oh dei!*»*

«*Vado, ma dove? oh dei!*»
Sempre al bar, al ristorante, nei musei
a ciondolare anoressica o bulimica
sempre tra le due madri
quella che mi ama falsamente
e mi vorrebbe privare di ogni cibo
e l'altra che mi ama falsamente
e mi vorrebbe uccidere di cibo,
e io costretta a uno dei due eccessi
o l'astinenza o l'incontinenza
e intanto guardo il bel viso di un ragazzo
sempre lontano dai miei veri amori
spinta al turismo da cerberi
infelici viaggiatori.

"I Go, but Where? Oh Gods!"

"I go, but where? oh gods!"
Constantly to the bar, the restaurant, the museums
to hang around, anorexic or bulimic,
constantly between two mothers
she who loves me falsely
and would deprive me of food
the other who loves me falsely
and would kill me with food,
and me tied to one of two excesses
abstinence or incontinence
meanwhile I look at the beautiful face of a boy
constantly far from my true loves
I am pushed to tourism by surly keepers
unhappy travelers.

ROSITA COPIOLI

Euridice*

Teneva in mano la foto di lei, sussurrava:
«Benché la strada sia impercorribile,
ti strapperò di dove sei».
E le labbra mute di lei mormoravano:
«È tua la notte invincibile,
è morte sposata. I tuoi sogni
si disfano come la carne».
«Arcuerò una musica stregata
venendo a te, la parola
che ti ricondurrà
alla nostra casa.»
Ma lei disse, allo scoccare del sole:
«Ormai io sono dove non guardi. E poi,
verresti a me con legacci e fardelli,
con la tua gabbia indosso?»

Sogni marini*

I

C'è un popolo di sogni che mi spinge
il mare nelle notti, d'improvviso.
L'ho visto che levava montagne d'acqua sui
porti, gonfiava cumuli grigi come cavalli,
inghiottiva orizzonti e naufragi.
Vasto e nero comparve una notte
l'Oceano, dilatava le acque altissime
e piatte, a galla nel buio io ero
foglia, scendevo poi non ero che nulla.
Ma colmando l'aurora
l'abisso di raggi simili al sole diritti e
obliqui, essi dan lampi, luccica e
tintinna il dorso del mare. Nelle
pupille si vela l'oro felino che è sparso

---

*From *Furore delle rose* (Fury of the roses, 1989).

ROSITA COPIOLI

Eurydice

Holding her picture in his hands, he whispered:
"Although the road is impassable,
I'll tear you away from where you are."
And her mute lips murmured:
"Yours is the invincible night,
a married death. Your dreams
decay like flesh."
"I will bend a spell-bound music
toward you, the word
that will carry you back
to our house."
But as the sun struck, she said:
"I am now where you are not looking. And besides,
would you come to me with strings and bundles,
bearing your cage?"

Sea Dreams

I

There is a people of dreams[73] driving
the sea into my nights, suddenly.
I have seen them lift a mountain of water into the
harbor, blow gray cumulous clouds into horses,
swallow horizons and shipwrecks.
Vast and black the Ocean appeared
one night, dilating waters high
and flat, and afloat in darkness I was
leaf, descending, then nothing.
But as the dawn fills up
the abyss with vertical and slanting rays,
sun-like the rays flash and
the sea crest sparkles and clinks. In the
pupil the feline gold scattered at the bottom

sul fondo. Allora io credo alla ricchezza
del mare, la ottengo. Tendo le dita
sott'acqua, l'acqua ritrae lembi di
fosforo tra i banchi di secche e
la riva. Al largo, lontano, il
mare ritratto e profondo, divenuto nero
contiene dentro un suo fumo aureo il sole.
Le dita afferrano grandi smeraldi dalla
luce verde, rinchiusi nell'oro, conchiglie
livide come palpebre occhieggiano intorno
alle ancore, interminate secche germinano
tesori ovunque, ne traggo le gemme
intagliate, i diaspri, i berilli, le perle,
cammei e azzurriti non so dove tenerli, e
raccolgo tra ossa e relitti quasi
sfinita un oro di paesi scomparsi, di
uomini e donne sepolti più giù delle rive,
nelle città sottomarine che la bonaccia
a tratti rivela come scogliere.

II

E certo sul mare ho posato i
piedi, scendendo su spade di
luce che dal terrazzo piombavano
verso i tramonti.

Quando a nuoto sott'acqua la
corrente mi portava come il vento,
vedevo le ombre delle barche, le
carene d'acciaio delle navi, le
luci e gli occhi delle stelle
pendere su me, distanti.

Qualche volta la brezza notturna
mi ha dato in sogno gli animali
del mare, un tumulto simile al
silenzio invadeva le acque, io

is veiled. Then I believe in the wealth
of the sea, I receive it. I extend my fingers
under the water, the water withdraws phosphoreal
limbs between sandbanks and
shore. Far away from the coast, the
deep, withdrawn sea, having turned black
holds the sun inside a golden haze.
My fingers grasp large emeralds of
lucent green, enclosed in gold, shells
livid like eyelids peep around
the anchors, boundless banks sprout
treasures everywhere, I take the cut
gems, jaspers, beryls, pearls,
cameos and azurites not knowing where to keep them, and
among bones and wrecks, almost exhausted
I gather a gold of vanished countries, of
men and women buried deeper than the shores,
in underwater cities which now and then
the calm sea reveals like reefs of rock.

II

And certainly on the sea I have set down my
feet, stepping down on blades of
light which plunged from the terrace
toward the sunsets.

While swimming underwater
carried by the current like a wind
I saw the shadows of the boats, the
steel keels of the ships, the
lit eyes of the stars
hanging over me, distant.

At times the night breeze
has brought into my dreams the animals
of the sea, like silence
a tumult invaded the water,

*pescavo le sogliole larghe sotto
la rena, acquattate e brune, gli
sgombri turchini, meduse
pullulavano come campane
vitree, fioriture d'onde.*

*Ho incatenato i sogni al
richiamo del mare. I delfini
vocali nelle notti li sento, celati
dentro conche celesti. Improvvisi
risuonano gli sciacqui delle risacche,
il vento invade il mio letto, mi
scaglia nelle maree
dissolta, assoluta nella carne blu e
profonda del mare.*

Fa' del tuo corpo un cuore*

*«Fa' del tuo corpo un cuore
trasforma il cuore in dolore.»*

«Tu sai cos'è il dolore? lo sai?»

*«È il desiderio della mano tagliata,
della cosa che non vedi.
Trasforma il corpo in occhi e in cuore.»*

*«Allora vedrò solo me stessa.
Vedrò solo la radice invisibile
del dolore.»*

*From *Elena* (Helen, 1996).

beneath the sand I fished for
large sole, hidden and dark,
and deep-blue mackerels, the jelly
fish swarmed like glass
bells, blossoming waves.

I have chained my dreams to the
call of the sea. I hear
the vocal dolphins in the night, concealed
inside sky-blue basins. Suddenly
splashes of the backwash resound,
the wind invades my bed, I'm
thrust into the tides,
dissolved, absolute in the blue
deep flesh of the sea.

Make Your Body a Heart

"Make your body a heart
turn the heart into pain."

"Do you know what pain is? do you know?"

"It is longing for the severed hand,
for the thing you can't see.
Turn your body into eyes and heart."

"Then I will see only myself.
I will see only the invisible root
of pain."

Il cuore e la testa mozzata

Se nel cammino vedi rotolare
una testa mozzata,
domandale, domandale
i segreti del cuore.

Molti sono i fiumi
fangosi o inariditi,
che non portano vene
dal cuore alla testa.

Resta come caverna di fango
l'universo stellato
quando nessuna diga
filtra la mota infinita.

Tu, spirito del mare,
mio sale,
gioiello sigillo della gola,
dove mi ardo di luce, vola,
riconduci il cuore.

*From *Elena* (Helen, 1996).

The Heart and the Severed Head

If on your way you see
a severed head roll by,
ask it, ask it
the secrets of the heart.

Many are the rivers
muddy or parched,
that don't carry veins
from the heart to the head.

The starry universe
becomes a cavern full of mud
if there is no dam
to filter the infinite mire.

You, spirit of the sea,
my salt,
jewel sealing my throat,
where I burn with light, fly,
bring back the heart.

GABRIELLA SICA

Io*

Io non posso avere né tenere in conto un uomo
che non mi aliti col fiato quando ho freddo
che non agiti l'aria intorno a me se ho caldo.

Come posso avere o tenere in conto un uomo
che è dotto altero e s'occupa di rime
se non piange e ride se piango e rido io?

Il fulmine*

Alle nuvole assomigliano le donne
come le acque delle maree lente vanno
e tornano sui tempi fissi della luna.

Minacciosi come fulmini gli uomini
rimbombano nel mondo irati e stolti
simili al tuono prima della guerra.

Vorresti forse adesso fulminarmi?

Nudità*

Un corpo nudo forse
ma un cuore...un cuore
nudo non lo trovo più.

Monotonia*

Associo le ore e le giornate
non ho mai nessuno da baciare.

*From La famosa vita (The famous life, 1986).

GABRIELLA SICA

I

I will not have or value a man
who will not breathe his breath on me when I am cold
who will not stir the air around me if I am hot.

How can I have or value a man
who is erudite prideful and busy with rhymes
if he does not cry and laugh when I do?

The Lightening

Women resemble the clouds
like tidal waters they slowly recede
and return on the moon's fixed time.

Men threatening like lightening
rumble in the world enraged and foolish
similar to the thundering before war.

Perhaps now you would like to strike me?

Nudity

A naked body maybe
but a heart…a naked heart
I can no longer find.

Monotony

I associate hours and days
I don't ever have anyone to kiss.

Per il mare*

Solcando i mari come nella fiaba
quand'eri bambino su nave pirata
senza bussola partito all'alba
alla conquista vai tutta la vita.

Ponza azzurra e Zannone ostica
solitaria Ventotene a ponente
Capri magnifica e Ischia cocente
e la favolosa Procida antica!
Hai trovato l'isola del tesoro?

*

Me misera tu sforzi per un mese
in queste avventurose imprese
strepito e urlo illividita d'ira
corriamo al porto, a solidi ripari!

In due siamo in balìa delle onde
a deriva lontani dalle sponde
le sciagure del burrascoso mare
tra i gorghi scuri dovremo evitare.

Tu appartieni alla gagliarda stirpe
dei prodi marinai e ardimentosi
e morto sarai famoso, o mio eroe!

Io voglio toccare la ferma terra
di tanti frutti e di frumento ricca
e nel mio caldo letto impigrire.

*

Perchè sfidi la collera divina
i venti freddi e la tempesta marina?
Fermati per cercare sole e pace
accanto a me e un bel numero di baci!

*

*From *Vicolo del Bologna* (Bologna's alley, 1992).

On the Sea

Ploughing the seas like the pirate child
of your boyhood fairytale who sailed
at dawn without a compass
you go on a life-long conquest.

Blue Ponza and inhospitable Zannone
to the West solitary Ventotene
magnificent Capri and scorching Ischia
and the fabulous ancient Procida!

Have you found treasure island?

*

For an entire month you force
me, miserable, into this daring course
livid with rage I yell and shout
let's run to the harbor, to solid shelter!

We are both at the mercy of the waves
adrift and far from the shores
calamities of the stormy ocean
amidst dark whirlpools we should shun.

You belong to a bold breed
of courageous, audacious seamen
and you'll be famous, my hero, when dead!

I want to touch the firm ground
so rich in fruits and grains
and rest idly in my warm bed.

*

Why do you defy divine wrath
the cold winds and the tempestuous sea?
Stop and search for the sun and peace
near to me and to countless kisses!

*

Il guizzo del tuo corpo nudo
nel mare placido di luce
nel silenzio mi fa fermare
e sotto il sole mi fa bruciare.

*

O tu valoroso che impavido vai
per il mare misterioso a caccia!

Dici d'essere un vero uomo di mare
se non porti ricci, sai almeno amare?

*

È un refolo di vento
o un soffio del destino
che muove per un momento
i tuoi capelli biondi come un serafino?

*

Sola ti guardo nuotare lento
lontano al largo e senza posa
abbracciato al mare calmo e vasto
al mare come a una raggiante sposa.

*

Ah!... io non sono tenero mozzo!

*

Vorrei limpida liquefarmi
in acqua dolce e calda mutarmi
confondermi alla schiuma delle onde
sgocciolare sulle tue spalle tonde.

*

Volerai giù nel profondo abissale
se levi l'àncora col fortunale

The leap of your naked body
in the placidly lit sea
in the silence it makes me pause
and in the sun it scorches me.

★

Oh you valorous one who goes undaunted
hunting in the mysterious ocean!

You say you are a true seaman
if you won't be bringing sea urchins, can you at least bring love?

★

Is it a gust of wind
or destiny's breath
that for a moment moves
your hair blond as a seraph?

★

Alone I watch you slowly swimming
far from the shore without tiring
embracing the vast, calm sea
as if it were a radiant bride.

★

Ah!… I am no tender ship boy!

★

I wish I could liquefy, turn limpid
into sweet warm water
blend with the foaming breakers
drip on your broad shoulders.

★

You will fly down into abyssal depths
if you sail in a thunderous gale

dal vento sbattuto e dalla corrente
in un tempestoso mare e furente.

Dove vai dunque? Fermati o capitano
e abbi cura della tua vita bella.

Ogni avventura è sogno o l'arcano...

*

Io rivale del cielo e del mare
un canto piano leverò leggera
per narrare le gesta e il suo addio
di bianco marinaio uguale a un dio.

From **Poesie per un bambino***

10.

Vorrei essere acqua di fonte
e scivolare nella tua boccuccia.

Vorrei essere aria fresca e leggera
per stringere il tuo piccolo corpo.

Vorrei soltanto avere corde d'oro
per levare lodi alla tua grazia.

*From *Poesie bambine* (Child poems, 1998).

tossed by wind and currents
in a turbulent and raging sea.

Where are you going then? Stop captain
and tend to your beautiful life.

Every adventure is a dream or the arcane...

*

Rival of the sky and the sea
I will lightly sing a simple melody
to tell of the deeds and farewell
of a white sailor, a god's equal.

From **Poems for a Little Boy**

10.

I wish I were spring water
flowing into your little mouth.

I wish I were light, fresh air
to embrace your little body.

I only wish I had golden chords
to raise my praise to your grace.

PATRIZIA VALDUGA

L'altra simulazione*

L'altra simulazione:
l'animo che non sa curare i sensi
o l'animo curare con i sensi.

Sa sedurre la carne la parola*

Sa sedurre la carne la parola,
prepara il gesto, produce destini...
E martirio è il verso,
è emergenza di sangue che cola
e s'aggruma ai confini
del suo inverso sessuato, controverso.

Mi dispero perché non ho parole*

Mi dispero perché non ho parole
che ad attrarti e a tenerti sian ventose,
né a impaurirti parole-pistole
del pari del vetriolo perniciose;

non ne ho, per colpirti, come mole,
attive, maledette e contagiose,
neanche ne ho armate o di gran mole,
o lievi, per sfiorarti, o voluttuose,

e termometriche, o anche al tornasole,
d'intimità segrete in più curiose,
di contese, in riserve nere, spose

al piacere; nemmeno di insidiose
ne ho, quelle che in cuore sono esplose,
e non lasciano mai intatte le cose.

---

*From *Medicamenta e altri medicamenta* (Medicaments and other medicaments, 1989).

PATRIZIA VALDUGA

The Other Simulation

The other simulation:
the spirit that can't cure the senses
or with the senses cure the spirit.

The Word Knows How to Seduce the Flesh

The word knows how to seduce the flesh,
it prepares the act, it produces fates...
And the verse is agony
urgency of blood oozing
and clotting at the borders
of its sexed, controversial inverse.

I Despair Because I Don't Have Words

I despair because I don't have words
that are suction cups to attract and hold you
or pistol-words to scare you
pernicious no less than vitriol;

I don't have active, wretched and contagious ones
to crush you, like millstones,
nor do I have armed or massive ones,
or light ones, to brush you, or voluptuous,

and thermometric ones, or litmus-testing ones
that are curious about secret intimacies,
or coveted ones, in dark reserve, brides

of pleasure; neither do I have insidious
ones, words that are detonated in the heart,
and never leave things standing.

E bella notte è questa che nel cuore*

E bella notte è questa che nel cuore
si fa per me armatura interiore
e mi scalda del caldo suo calore
perché mi chiuda questo dentro il cuore:

che l'aspettar del male è mal peggiore
e sempre l'uomo è addormentatore,
in me sgocciolerà il suo dolore...
Oh torna a visitarmi mio signore,

del corpo terremoto, e del cuore...
qui ritorna nei giorni del mio fiore
che solo assedi esigono e terrore,

fin che cammini dentro al grande amore,
senza morire come ognuno muore,
immobile e senza peso il cuore.

Perché chi è amato è così sciocco e greve?†

Perché chi è amato è così sciocco e greve?
l'errore è nella causa o nell'effetto?
Voglio un posto di viole e bucaneve...

di biancospini... il mio posto segreto...
Vattene, adesso!... prendi il vaporetto...
non fingiamoci Ofelia con Amleto...

perché è soltanto fiato, sete e fame,
e accoppiamento e malattia e morte...
e del fuoco che a volte mi fa infame

io lo giuro, la colpa non è mia:
non posso farci niente, è la mia sorte...
Vattene adesso, vattene, va' via!

Tirati dietro azzurro, oro e mare,
ma lascia i fiori, lascia qui i miei fiori!
ma dove sono? li vorrei toccare...

*From *Medicamenta e altri medicamenta* (Medicaments and other medicaments, 1989).
†From *Corsia degli incurabili* (Terminal ward, 1996).

And This Is a Beautiful Night That in the Heart

And this is a beautiful night that in the heart
becomes my inner armor
and warms me with its warm warmth
so that I may close this inside my heart:

that waiting is harm worse than harm
and man always casts his charm
in me he'll drip his misery...
Oh my lord come back to visit me,

earthquake of the body, of the heart...
return here in my flowering days
which demand only sieges and terror,

till I walk inside the great love,
without dying like everybody dies,
with a heart immobile and weightless.

Why Are Those Who Are Loved So Dull and Leaden?

Why are those who are loved so dull and leaden?
is the error in the cause or the effect?
I want a haven of snowdrops and violets...

of hawthorns...a haven kept secret...
Go away, now! take the ferryboat...
let's not pretend to be Ophelia with Hamlet...

because it's only thirst, hunger and breath,
and copulation and sickness and death...
and some fire which sometimes makes me loathsome

the fault is not mine, I swear:
I cannot help it, it's my fortune...
Go away now, go away, leave me!

Drag away blue, gold and sea,
but leave the flowers, leave my flowers here!
But where are they? I would like to touch them...

le viole, i bucaneve, i biancospini...
deponimeli qui... non manca molto...
li voglio tutti qui... sopra... vicini...

il tempo adesso è tutto capovolto...
adesso mi amerai? mi amerai molto?
mi si perdona quello che ti ho tolto?

e la malinconia? la mia mestizia?
Fiori sui morti! fiori su chi è vivo!
fiori... misericordia e non giustizia!

Ecco il giorno che dice: «Arrivo, arrivo!»
e io... io mi lamento che non vivo...
Fiori sui morti! fiori su chi è vivo!

Fiori su questi letti di tortura
e fiori sul martirio e sul terrore...
Fiori sul buio che ci fa paura,

fiori su piaghe, fiori su ferite,
fiori sul dolce delirio del cuore,
fiori sulle speranze seppellite!

Fiori sui vivi! Fiori su chi muore!
Beato chi crede ancora nell'amore!

        E beato chi conosce le sue colpe.
        «Orfeo, Orfeo, mi fanno a pezzi qui,
        mi sfigurano, Orfeo, e non ho colpe!»

        schiamazzava Euridice in mezzo ai morti.
        «Orfeo! Orfeo!» si sfogava così.
        «E tu mi lasci qui? morta tra morti?»

        Ma quel coglione, perché si è voltato?
        Lo stile dei poeti è questo qua?
        Che volesse restare disperato?

        sentirsi ancora più «ispirato»? Bah.

Gran risata   Il grande amore, la mortalità...

the snowdrop, the hawthorn, the violet…
lay them down for me…time is running out…
I want them all here…over me…close to me…

now time is upside down, completely…
will you love me now? will you love me wholly?
am I forgiven for all I was taking?

and the melancholy? my sadness?
Flowers on the dead! flowers on the living!
flowers…mercy instead of justice!

Here is the day that says: "I am coming, I am coming!"
and I…I lament that I am not living…
Flowers on the dead! flowers on the living!

Flowers on these beds of torture
and flowers on torment and terror…
Flowers on the darkness that fills us with horror,

flowers on sores, flowers on suffering,
flowers on the sweet delirium of the heart
flowers on buried yearnings!

Flowers on the living! Flowers on the dying!
lucky are those who still believe in love!

> And lucky are those who know their sins.
> "Orpheus, Orpheus, they are tearing me to shreds,
> they are disfiguring me, Orpheus, and I am sinless!"

> Euridyce was cackling among the dead.
> "Orpheus, Orpheus!" she vented so.
> "And you leave me here? dead among the dead?"

> But that schmuck, why did he turn back?
> Is this what poets do?
> Perhaps he wanted to remain in desperation?

> to feel even more "inspiration"? Bah.

Laughing hard   The great love, mortality…

NOTES

1. Menicanti's epigraph refers to a letter that John Keats wrote to Richard Woodhouse, dated October 27, 1818: Letter 118 in *The Letters of John Keats: 1814–1821*, ed. Hyder Edward Rollins, vol. 1 (Cambridge: Harvard University Press, 1958), 386–88.
2. The philosopher Giulio Preti to whom Menicanti was married between 1937 and 1951.
3. Rigel is the *beta* star and Betelgeuse the *alfa* of the Orion constellation. Sirius is the *alfa* of Canis Major, Capella the *alfa* of Auriga. San Juan (St. John of the Cross) was a great Spanish mystic whose written works include *Noche oscura del alma*. In *Noche oscura del alma,* the mystic night is divided into three phases: in the first, still close to the evening, the soul detaches itself from earthly delights (night of the senses), in the second, it is immersed in solitude and the most absolute deprivation (night of the soul), and finally in the third, close to dawn, it already begins to sense its union with God (night of God). [Author's note.]
4. "la favola bella che più non c'illude" echoes lines from Gabriele D'Annunzio's "La pioggia nel pineto" (Rain in the pinewoods): "la favola bella / che ieri / t'illuse, che oggi m'illude" (the beautiful fable / that yesterday / beguiled you, and today beguiles me), which he inverts later in the poem to read "la favola bella / che ieri / m'illuse, che oggi t'illude" (the beautiful fable / that yesterday / beguiled me, and today beguiles you).
5. One of Italy's most famous cycling champions. The Tour refers to the famous Tour de France.
6. Latin: meaning "for ever and ever."
7. Fabrizio del Dongo is the protagonist of Stendhal's *La Chartreuse de Parme* (*The Charterhouse of Parma,* 1839).
8. "Inconsútile": made with one single piece of fabric, without seams; the term is often used to describe the tunic of Christ, which symbolizes the unity of Christianity.
9. "Hendiadys": a rhetorical figure expressing one concept with two words connected by a conjunction.
10. "travagliò" means "afflicted, tormented, troubled." Rosselli's use of the verb evokes the noun *travaglio,* which means "labor," as in the labor of birth, or toil. An alternative translation whould be "labored him." The past participle "travagliata" in the second stanza also conveys both meanings.
11. The Italian "congenitale" appears to combine *congenita* (congenital) and *congeniale* (congenial).
12. The expression "Abissinia della mia anima" (Abyssinia of my soul) seems to play on the paronomasic relationship between "Abissinia" (Abyssinia) and

"abisso" (abyss). One should note the possible historical resonance of the expression, reinforced by the simile "as sad as the soldier at war" in the poem's conclusion. Abyssinia is a former name of Ethiopia. It was considered a promised land by Italy's Fascist regime and conquered in 1936. Italy lost control of the country during World War II, along with the rest of it's overseas empire. In the 1960s, the traditional, apologetic view of Italian colonialism began to be questioned by historians who adopted a more critical approach to Italy's colonial past.

13. "lattante, latitante" literally means "nursling, fugitive."

14. We used "disintegral" to render the neologism "disintegro."

15. The verb *esaudire* is commonly used in relation to the answering of a prayer or the granting of a wish.

16. "stesura" means "drawing up," "drafting," "writing," "draft" but evokes *stesa* which can be translated as "expanse," "tract," "strech."

17. "impermeated" renders the neologism "impermeato." The prefix adds force to the past participle.

18. "crematorizzata" is a neologism derived from *crematorio* (crematory).

19. Mistinguette (Jeanne Bourgeois, 1875–1956) was a famous French singer and actress in the Parisian music halls.

20. "sberciata" is derived from the intransitive verb *sberciare*, which has two meanings: to botch or blunder, and to howl or bellow.

21. "arroteandomi" combines *arrotandomi* (grinding, sharpening myself) and *roteando* (rotating, turning, swirling, rolling).

22. This poem is part of a series entitled "Versi per mia figlia" (Verses for My Daughter).

23. "one thousand regrets for abandoning you." This verse opens a four-part song by Josquin des Prez (d. 1521), a Franco-Flemish composer active at the turn of the sixteenth century.

24. The lines "the insolent woven hands / of the Apocalyptic Cherubs" are in the *Tapisserie de l'Apocalypse,* which is in the [Castle of] Angers and depicts musician angels. [Author's note.]

25. "bigatto" is a northern name for the silkworm. [Author's note.]

26. "which resembles a vestibule": In the Sefer Yesiràh, it is said that the world we live in has been created with the H, which in the Hebrew alphabet resembles a hall. [Author's note.]

27. "will stay face to the ground listening": from Ezekiel's vision. [Author's note.]

28. I had in mind the words and rhythm of a popular Jewish song which I love very much: the *Had Gadja.* The *Had Gadja* ends with a light: the Saint that kills the angel of death. [Author's note.]

29. Bella is kin, if one may say so, of the angel Raziel: Raziel knows the arcane names and Bella can read the Name with the right "pronunciation." Bella is also certainly related to the little princess of Andersen's fairytale "The Wild Swans" who weaves nettles to make tunics that will save her brothers. Like the little princess, Bella works to save others. This golem, more than the golem that stirred discussion among the mystics, is the golem of the legend whose protagonist is the late sixteenth century Praguian Yehudah Low Bezalcel. The legend is based on the thaumaturgy of the tetragrammatic Name (in one instance the creator of the golem forgets to take the Name away from it and then, fearing it may become dangerous, chases it and destroys it). Naturally, the city where my golem moves is the Prague of Gustav Meyerink, which Kafka so liked. The golem of this story, however, is destroyed by a woman, who takes the animating letters from it, "reading" them in that particular way that will deprive the monstrous robot of vital energy: since I was a child, I have always thought that monsters could be defeated by female creatures. [Author's note.]

30. "He who has a yod in his name": according to a Talmudic hypothesis, the future world is created with this small letter. [Author's note.]

31. "Zwei" means "two"; "dry" plays on the homophony between "dry" and the German *drei* which means "three."

32. A dry martini is a cocktail with gin; martini dry is a type of vermouth.

33. Niccolai puns on the word "sei," which means both "six" and "you are." In order to maintain the pun, we have played on the word "dozen." This changes the number from eighteen to thirty-six in the next line.

34. Niccolai plays on the dual significance of the French "Neuf," which means both "nine" and "new": "Dry martinis! Nine [new]! / Certainly not old ones ma'am...."

35. In the original text the line is in English.

36. Niccolai works with the homophony between the French words "dix" and "dis" which makes it possible to hear "dix" as "dis": "Ten [say] ten [say] dry martinis! / No I don't say I don't say I don't say."

37. Lucio Tosi is a friend of Niccolai's, as is Joan Arnold who is referenced later in the poem. "Lucio," related to the noun *luce* (light), introduces the many references to light in this section of *Frisbees*.

38. A contemporary Italian poet.

39. Guido Gozzano (1883–1916) was one of the most influential poets of the movement known as *Crepuscolarismo*. This movement's name, coined in 1912 by the critic G. A. Borgese, is derived from *crepuscolo* (twilight) and alludes to the subdued, intimate, melancholic lyric tone that characterizes the work of the Crepuscolar poets.

40. "joy lights launches." "Lanci" can also be read as the second person singular of the verb *lanciare* (you launch joy lights).

41. Neapolitan dialect: "Napule" means "Naples." "Triccheballacche" and "putipù" are instruments used in Neapolitan folk music.

42. "sew angels' wings." Brignone is a poet. Barbara Kleiner, mentioned in the next stanza, is a translator who lived in Milan and now works in Germany.

43. In the original text the quote is in English.

44. "Conoscermi" can also be translated as "to know myself."

45. "clarito" is an archaic form of *chiarito*. It functions as an adjective rather than as a past participle. The verse echoes Saint Francis of Assisi's (1182–1226) "Il Cantico di Frate Sole" or "Laudes creaturarum" (The Canticle of the Sun, or The Canticle of the Creatures) in which "clarite" refers to the stars and "bellu" [bello/beautiful] to the sun. [Author's note, personal correspondence.] "Il Cantico di Frate Sole" is one of the canonical texts of Italian literature.

46. "luminous as well as beautiful."

47. A combination of the Italian *onfalo* and the Greek *omphalós,* meaning "navel."

48. "scorporo," from *scorporare* (to separate from capital, to separate from a whole), suggests an association with *corpo* (body).

49. In the Italian, Insana plays on the etymological link between *pensare* (to think or ponder) and *pesare* (to weigh), both of which come from the Latin *pensare* (to weigh with care).

50. "taglieggiato," the past participle of *taglieggiare* (to demand a tribute, to extort), evokes by homophony the word *tagliato* (cut, cut off). In correspondence the author indicated that the verse both refers to and reverses the meaning of a famous hendecasyllable by Gaspara Stampa (1523–1554): "viver ardendo e non sentire il male" (to live burning and not feel the hurt). See *Gaspara Stampa, Selected Poems,* edited by Laura Anna Stortoni and Mary Prentice Lillie (New York, Italica Press, 1994), 160–61.

51. "sgodendo" is a neologism created by adding the intensifying prefix *s-* to *godendo* (enjoying).

52. "ti carpiono" evokes the homophonous *ti arpiono* (I harpoon you).

53. This appears to be a pun on Insana's name, which means "insane."

54. "the air has been poisoned" refers to the tragedy and aftereffects of Chernobyl as do the phrases "other tragedies," "sick wind," "ignition," "irradiation." [Author's note, personal correspondence.]

55. Insana seems to be playing on two meanings of *occhio:* "eye" and "bud." The former meaning is evoked by the images of seeing — blinded, shortsighted, and narcissistic sight, or visionary and dreamy perception — which recur throughout the book. The latter meaning becomes apparent in "The

Rooting" and is also evoked by metaphors of planting, growing, and harvesting developed in other poems.

56. Literally, "barker"; figuratively, a slanderer.

57. Abû Nuwàs was an important poet of the early Abbasid period (750–835). The title refers to the scream that Abû Nuwàs let out as his throat was cut.

58. The conclusion echoes the last line of Giacomo Leopardi's "L'infinito": "e il naufragar m'è dolce in questo mare" (and sweet to me is the shipwreck in this sea).

59. The adjective "certosine," referring to the strict order of Carthusian monks or nuns, is used to indicate tremendous patience and laboriousness.

60. "sbocco": outlet, mouth; it is a popular expression for hemoptysis, the expectorating of blood from the larynx, trachea, bronchi, or lungs.

61. "ri-parlante (grillo)" refers to the *grillo parlante* (lit. talking cricket) of *Pinnocchio*. When used in the expression *fare il grillo parlante,* the phrase is equivalent to the English "a know-it-all."

62. "Le domaine d'Arnheim" (1962) is the second of two paintings with the same title by René Magritte (1898–1967). This version, more poetic than the first, depicts a moonlit mountain landscape: the mountain in the background, suggesting an eagle with wings spread, overlooks a nest in the foreground. The nest, containing three eggs, is precariously balanced on a stone balustrade. The title of this work comes from Edgar Allan Poe's tale "The Domain of Arnheim," which describes an imaginary landscape. The painting, however, was not directly inspired by Poe's landscape.

63. "We Are in Diana's Trust" or "We Are under Diana's Protection." This is the first line of poem XXXIV by Catullus.

64. In Roman mythology, Diana was the goddess of the mountains, woods, women, and childbirth. Early on she became identified with the Greek Artemis who possessed similar characteristics and functions. Originally, there was probably no link between Diana and the moon; however, she later assumed Artemis' connection to Selene (Luna) and Hecate. Juno was the goddess of heaven and protector of women and marriage; she was the feminine principle of celestial light associated with the moon; in this aspect she was coupled with Diana. Luna was a goddess of the moon. Trivia (sometimes identified with the Greek Hecate), associated with sorcery, hounds, and crossroads, was goddess of the earth and Hades. In Catullus' poem Diana is referred to as "Juno Lucina," "Trivia," and "Luna."

65. Frabotta may be playing on the Latin etymology of the word "triviale," derived from *trivium*: comp. of *tri-*(three-) and *via* (way, road). Catullus calls Diana "diva triformis" (goddess of the triple form) in his Ode XXII.

66. Worshipped from the very early days of the Bronze age, Ilithyia was the goddess of childbirth. She was later an attendant of Juno, patroness of

marriage. Originally there were two Ilithyias, daughters of Hera, who were responsible for bringing and relieving the pains of labor. This may account for Frabotta's reference to Ilithyia's "sadomasochistic vice."

67. "you who are called moon with light." Here Frabotta echoes another line from Catullus' poem XXXIV: "notho's / dicta lumine Luna" (you are called Moon with spurious light). In what appears to be a feminist revision of Catullus' line, Frabotta eliminates the notion that Luna's light is reflected.

68. The Italian "fuoco" means both "focus" and "fire."

69. Lamarque wrote the love poems in *Il signore d'oro, Poesie dando del Lei* and *Il signore degli spaventati* for her Jungian analyst who gave her "health and [her] childhood." [Author's note, personal correspondence.]

70. The title is an homage to "This Quiet Dust" by Emily Dickinson. *Una quieta polvere* contains a long poem of the same title. Lamarque incorporates into the poem a number of verses from Dickinson's poetry. [Author's note, personal correspondence.]

71. The addition of the word "please" was suggested by the poet.

72. *Cucirsi la bocca* is an idiomatic expression which means "to seal one's lips."

73. The image of a "people of dreams" echoes a passage from the creation myth "The History of the Human Race" by Giacomo Leopardi (1798–1837), which is the first of his *Operette morali (Moral Tales,* 1827). In this myth Jupiter "created the people of dreams, and charged them with deceiving the thoughts of men in various ways, so that they might show men the plenitude of unfathomable happiness, which [Jupiter] could find no way of creating.…" In keeping with his "theory of pleasure" (i.e., that man's desire for infinite happiness is insatiable, disappointment is inevitable, and familiarity breeds nothing but havoc), Leopardi sees the creation of dreams as a divine measure intended to revive the newly created human race's love for life, which, through "familiarity" and disillusionment, it had lost as it aged. See Giacomo Leopardi, *Moral Tales,* tr. Patrick Creagh (Manchester: Carcanet, 1983), 36. In her theoretical writings on the symbolic, archetypical imagination, Copioli appears to distance herself from Leopardi's romantic, absolutist stance, propounding a more positive conception of dreams, symbols and myths as essential to a poetry of "embodied" knowledge, a poetry viewed as an "ideal mythic translation of a culture traced back to its roots" (*Tradizioni della poesia italiana contemporanea* [Rome: Theoria, 1988], 41).

ABOUT THE POETS

MARIELLA BETTARINI (1942–)

Bettarini was born and lives in Florence. She worked as an elementary school teacher for twenty-five years. In the 1960s she began writing literary analyses and cultural commentaries for national journals and newspapers. She is the founder and director of the journal *Salvo imprevisti* (1973–1992), which adopted the title *L'area di Broca* in 1993. Since 1984, she has been editor, with Gabriella Maleti, of the poetry and prose series "Edizioni Gazebo." In addition to her editorial work, Bettarini has written articles on George Bataille, Ralph Waldo Emerson, Pier Paolo Pasolini, feminist poetics, and nineteenth-century poetry. She translated the work of Simone Weil and, with Silvia Batisti, edited *Chi è il poeta?* — a collection of photos and interviews with thirty-three poets. Some of her poems have been translated into French, English, Greek, Rumanian, Russian, and Spanish. Her work is included in various anthologies of contemporary Italian poetry, including *Poesie d'amore* (1986), *The Defiant Muse*, and *Donne in poesia: Incontri con le poetesse italiane*, and has also appeared on the internet site *Testi e Letture*.

Poetry:
Il pudore e l'effondersi. Florence: Città di Vita, 1966.
Il leccio. Florence: I Centauri, 1968.
La rivoluzione copernicana. Rome: Trevi, 1970.
Terra di tutti e altre poesie (1969–70). Caltanissetta–Rome: Sciascia, 1972.
Dal vero (1972–74). Caltanissetta–Rome: Sciascia, 1974.
In bocca alla balena. Florence: Salvo imprevisti, 1977.
Diario fiorentino. Caltanissetta–Rome: Sciascia, 1979.
"Trittico per Pasolini." *Almanacco dello Specchio* n. 8. Intro. by Roberto Roversi. Milan: Mondadori, 1979.
Ossessi oggetti / spiritate materie. Siena: Quaderni di Barbablù, 1981.
Il viaggio / il corpo. Turin: L'Arzanà, 1982.
La nostra gioventù. Caltanissetta–Rome: Sciascia, 1982.
Poesie vegetali. Photos by Gabriella Maleti. Siena: Quaderni di Barbablù, 1982.
Vegetali figure: 1978–1982. Preface by Mario Luzi. Naples: Guida, 1983.
Il viaggio. With Gabriella Maleti. Florence: Gazebo, 1985.
Tre lustri e oltre (Antologia poetica 1963–81). Caltanissetta–Rome: Sciascia, 1986.
Delle nuvole (1986–1988). Photos by Gabriella Maleti. Florence: Gazebo, 1991.
Diciotto acrostici. Florence: Gazebo verde, 1992.

Familiari parvenze (enigmi?). S. Marco in Lamis: Quaderni della Valle, 1993.
Asimmetria. Florence: Gazebo, 1994.
Il silenzio scritto. Florence: Gazebo, 1995.
Zia Vera - infanzia. Florence: Gazebo, 1996.
Case, luoghi, la parola (1993–95). Rome: Fermenti, 1998.
Per mano d'un Guillotin qualunque. Cosenza: Edizioni Orizzonti Meridionali, 1998.
L'armonioso dissenso. Scandicci: Luna e Gufo, 1999.
Haiku di maggio. Florence: Gazebo verde, 1999.

Prose:
Storie d'Ortensia. Rome: Edizioni delle donne, 1978.
Psycographia. Milan: Gammalibri, 1982.
Amorosa persona. Florence: Gazebo, 1989.
Lettera agli alberi. Como: Lietocolle, 1997.

Translations and Critical Work:
"Il pensiero di Ralph Waldo Emerson." *Città di Vita* 23 (1968): 172–77.
Weil, Simone. *Lettera a un religioso.* Trans. Bettarini. Turin: Borla, 1970.
"I poeti sono uomini." *Materiale per gli anna Ottanta.* Vol. I. Messina– Florence: D'Anna, 1975.
"Bataille: L'interdetto e la trasgressione." *Prospetti* 41–42 (1976): 72–74.
"Pasolini tra la cultura e le culture." In Bettarini, et al. *Dedicato a Pasolini.* Milan: Gammalibri, 1976.
"Donne e poesia." *Poesia femminista italiana.* Ed. Laura Di Nola. Rome: Savelli, 1978.
Felice di essere. Milan: Gammalibri, 1978.
"Pasolini, le culture e noi." *Perché Pasolini.* Ed. Gualtiero De Santi, Maria Lenti, and Roberto Rossini. Florence: Guaraldi, 1978.
Chi è il poeta? With Silvia Batisti. Milan: Gammalibri, 1980.
Sturiale, Alice. *Il libro di Alice.* Ed. Bettarini with Leonardo Sturiale and Marta Bigozzi. Florence: Polistampa, 1996; rpt. Milan: Rizzoli, 1997.

CRISTINA CAMPO (Vittoria Guerrini) (1923–1977)

Campo was born in Bologna. She was a prolific translator and wrote both poetry and prose. Her translations include the work of San Juan de La Cruz, Emily Dickinson, John Donne, George Herbert, Ezra Pound, Christina Rossetti, Simone Weil, and William Carlos Williams. Her prose is collected in *Gli imperdonabili* and her poetry and translations (both edited and unedited) are collected in *La Tigre Assenza.* Both books have appeared in French. Selections of her work have been translated into

English in *From Pure Silence to Impure Dialogue*. Campo died in Rome.
Collections of her letters have been posthumously published.

Poetry:

Passo d'addio. Milan: Scheiwiller, 1956.

La Tigre Assenza. Ed. Margherita Pieracci Harwell. Milan: Adelphi, 1991;
   rpt. 1997.

Prose:

Gli imperdonabili. Milan: Adelphi, 1987.

L'infinito nel finito. Lettere a Piero Pòlito. Ed. Giovanna Fazzar. Pistoia: Via
   del vento, 1998.

Lettere a un amico lontano. Milan: Scheiwiller, 1989; rpt. 1998.

Sotto falso nome. Ed. Monica Farnetti. Milan: Adelphi, 1998.

Lettere a Mita. Ed. Margherita Pieracci Harwell. Milan: Adelphi, 1999.

Translations and Critical Work:

Williams, William Carlos. *Il fiore è il nostro segno. Poesie*. Milan: Scheiwiller,
   1958.

Williams, William Carlos. *Poesie*. With Vittorio Sereni. Turin: Einaudi, 1961.

Fiaba e mistero e altre note. Florence: Vallecchi, 1962.

Weil, Simone. *Venezia salva. Tragedia in tre atti*. Trans. with intro. by Campo.
   Brescia: Morcelliana, 1963; rpt. 1987.

"Introduzione." *Storia della città di rame*. Trans. from Arabic by Alessandro
   Spina. Milan: Scheiwiller, 1963.

"La porte magique." *Jorge Luis Borges*. Paris: L'Herne, 1964.

Donne, John. *Poesie amorose, poesie teologiche*. Turin: Einaudi, 1971.

Il flauto e il tappeto. Milan: Rusconi, 1971.

La Grecia e le istituzioni precristiane. Trans. from French by Campo and
   Margherita Pieracci Harwell. Milan: Rusconi, 1974.

Detti e fatti dei Padri del deserto. Ed. Campo and Piero Draghi. Milan:
   Rusconi, 1975.

"Introduzione." *Racconti di un pellegrino russo*. Trans. Milli Martinelli.
   Milan: Rusconi, 1998.

ANNA CASCELLA (1941–)

Cascella was born in Rome. She studied English and American Litera-
ture at the University of Rome, receiving a degree in Modern Letters.
Her first collection of poetry, *Le voglie*, appeared in *Nuovi poeti italiani*
(1980). Selections of *Le voglie* have been subsequently included in such
anthologies as *Poesie d'amore* (1986), *Donne in poesia: Incontri con le poetesse*

273

italiane, Mirafiori blues, and *Poesia Italiana del Novecento* (1990). Later poems have been published in a variety of periodicals — including *Action Poétique, Nuovi Argomenti, Arsenale, Lengua, Next, Galleria, Trame, Tellus, Origini, Lunarionuovo, Poesia,* and *Salvo Imprevisti* — and have been translated in *Fin de Siglo* (Jerez de la Frontera, 1983), *Italienische Lyrik nach 1945* (Tübingen, 1986), *Liberté* (Montréal, 1994), *Lines Review* (Scotland, 1994), *Quimera* (Barcelona, 1994), and *Zehn italienische Lyrikerinnen der Gegenwart* (Tübingen, 1995). She has also published work on the internet site *Poesia Italiana–Italian Poetry.* Cascella's poetry has won various awards. For *Tesoro da nulla* she received the Mondello opera prima and the Laura Nobile. For *Piccoli Campi* she received the Sandro Penna and the Procida, Isola di Arturo - Elsa Morante. Her scholarly work includes studies on Henry James, Eugenio Montale, and F. Scott Fitzgerald. In addition to her poetry and critical publications, she is the author of *Bolero,* a radio-drama produced for Channel Three of Radio RAI. She has also reviewed British and American literature for RAI.

Poetry:
Tesoro da nulla (1983–1989). Milan: Scheiwiller, 1990.
Piccoli Campi. Poesie per "Statuette." Grottammare (AP): Stamperia dell'Arancio, 1996.
L'intelletto delle erbe. Kamen: Rivista di poesia e filosofia 9.15 (January 2000).

Critical Work:
I colori di Gatsby. Lettura di Fitzgerald. Rome: Lithos Editrice, 1995.

PATRIZIA CAVALLI (1947–)

Cavalli was born in Todi (Perugia). She holds a degree in philosophy from the University of Rome and an advanced degree in the arts. She now lives in Rome where she translates works for the theater. Selections of her poetry have appeared in *Poesie d'amore* (1986), *The Defiant Muse, Donne in poesia: Incontri con le poetesse italiane, Italian Poetry since World War II, New Italian Poets, The Vintage Book of Contemporary World Poetry,* and *I sentieri della notte.* In 1999, she won the prestigious Premio Viareggio for her collection *Sempre aperto teatro.* In addition to her poetry, she has written plays for Radio RAI, including *La bella addormentata* (1975) and *Il guardiano dei porci* (1977). Her translations include works by Molière and Shakespeare.

Poetry:
Le mie poesie non cambieranno il mondo. Turin: Einaudi, 1974.

Il cielo. Turin: Einaudi, 1981.

Poesie: 1974–1992. Turin: Einaudi, 1992.

My Poems Will Not Change the World: Selected Poems, 1974–1992. Trans. Barry Callaghan and Francesca Valente. Toronto: Exile Editions, 1998.

Sempre aperto teatro. Turin: Einaudi, 1999.

Prose:

"Racconto." *Paragone* 300 (February 1975); rpt. as "Arrivederci addio," in *Il pozzo segreto,* ed. M. R. Cutrufelli (Florence: Giunti, 1993).

"Ritratto." *Narratori delle riserve.* Ed. Giovanni Celati. Turin: Einaudi, 1992.

Translations:

Molière. *Anfitrione.* Preface by Giovanni Macchia. Milan: Feltrinelli, 1981.

Shakespeare, William. *Sogno di una notte d'estate.* Turin: Einaudi, 1996.

ELENA CLEMENTELLI (1923–)

Clementelli was born in Rome. She graduated from the University of Rome in 1946 with a degree in Spanish literature and a thesis on the myth of Don Juan. In addition to her university work, she received a diploma from the Instituto Español de Lingua y Literatura. Clementelli works at the Italian–Latin American Institute and is a scholar of Spanish, Portuguese, Latin-American, and Anglo-American literature. Her critical work includes book-length studies of Gabriel García Márquez and Natalia Ginzburg. She has also translated and edited the writings of Vicente Blasco Ibáñez and Federico García Lorca, and is the editor of numerous anthologies. She has won awards for both her scholarly work and poetry, including the Calliope (1985), Bari Palese (1990), Piombino Betocchi (1993), and S. Pellegrino. Selections of her poetry have appeared in such anthologies as *The Penguin Book of Women Poets, Italian Poetry Today* (1979), *Poesia italiana del Novecento* (1980), *Poesia erotica italiana del novecento,* and *The Green Flame.*

Poetry:

Il mare dentro. Preface by Elio Filippo Accrocca. Rome: Bestetti, 1957.

Le ore mute. Cittadella di Padova: Rebellato, 1959.

Questa voce su noi. Preface by Aldo Palazzeschi. Parma: Guanda, 1962.

La breve luce. Rome: Edizioni di Novissima, 1969.

Così parlando onesto. Milan: Garzanti, 1977.

L'educazione. Rome: Quaderni di Piazza Navona, 1980.

Vasi a Samo. Foggia: Bastogi, 1983.

Il conto. Poesie 1983–1998. Rome: Empirìa, 1998.

Translations and Critical Work:

Antologia del canto flamenco. Parma: Guanda, 1961.

Otero, Blas de. *Poesie.* Parma: Guanda, 1962.

Goytisolo, Juan. *Le terre di Níjar.* Milan: Feltrinelli, 1964.

Antologia del Blues. With Walter Mauro. Parma: Guanda, 1965; rpt. Rome: Newton Compton, 1994.

Antologia degli Spirituals. With Walter Mauro. Parma: Guanda, 1966; rpt. Rome: Newton Compton, 1994.

Otero, Blas de. *Que trata de España.* Parma: Guanda, 1967.

Fados. Parma: Guanda, 1969.

Allsop, Kenneth. *Ribelli vagabondi nell'America dell'ultima frontiera.* Bari: Laterza, 1969.

Invito alla lettura di Natalia Ginzburg. Milan: Mursia, 1971.

Toynbee, Arnold. *La città aggressiva.* Bari: Laterza, 1972.

Franqui, Carlos. *Il cerchio di pietra.* Parma: Guanda, 1972.

La trappola e la nudità. Lo scrittore e il potere. With Walter Mauro. Milan: Rizzoli, 1973.

Gabriel García Marquez. Florence: La Nuova Italia, 1974; rpt. 1980.

Carpentier, Alejo. *Il ricorso del metodo.* Rome: Editori Riuniti, 1976.

Casares, Adolfo Bioy. *L'avventura di un fotografo a La Plata.* Rome: Editori Riuniti, 1987.

Brugnoli, Renzo. *Don Faustino.* Rome: Ventaglio, 1989.

Ocampo, Silvina. *La penna magica.* Rome: Editori Riuniti, 1989.

Galdós, Benito Pérez. *La donna di denari.* Milan: Frassinelli, 1993.

Lorca, Federico García. *Tutto il Teatro.* Rome: Newton Compton, 1993.

Il fiore della libertà. Un'antologia delle più significative poesie di tutto il mondo che hanno dato voce con coraggio e dolore ai diritti inalienabili degli uomini. With Walter Mauro. Rome: GTE, 1993.

Ibáñez, Vicente Blasco. *Sangue e arena.* Rome: Newton Compton, 1995.

American Folk Songs. With Walter Mauro. Rome: Newton Compton, 1996.

Guevara, Ernesto Che. *Ideario.* Rome: Newton Compton, 1996.

ROSITA COPIOLI (1948–)

Copioli was born in Riccione and lives in Rimini. She studied aesthetics with the critic Luciano Anceschi and has a degree in Classics from the University of Bologna. She graduated with a thesis on Giacomo Leopardi. Copioli has received various awards, including the Viareggio first book prize for *Splendida Lumina Solis,* the Montale for *Furore delle rose,* and the Metauro for *Elena. Splendida Lumina Solis* was translated into English by

Renata Treitel and received the Oklahoma Book Award. Selections of Copioli's poetry have been included in such anthologies as *Care donne* and *Anni '80*. She has written several dramas (forthcoming from Il battello ebbro), some of which have been staged, broadcast on RAI Radio 2, and published in newspapers. In 1988, she organized, with Giuseppe Conte, Roberto Mussapi, Mario Baudino, Tomaso Kemeny, and Stefano Zecchi, "La nascita delle Grazie," an interdisciplinary symposium on the mythical and symbolic imagination. She is a prominent scholar and translator of W. B. Yeats and writes on the history of the Romagna region. From 1979 to 1989 she edited the literary journal *L'altro versante*; she continues to contribute to various journals, including *Yale Italian Poetry*, and writes for such national newspapers as *La Repubblica, Il Giornale,* and *L'Avvenire*.

Poetry:
Splendida Lumina Solis. Forlì: Forum, 1979.
Furore delle rose. Parma: Guanda, 1989.
Elena. Parma: Guanda, 1996.
The Blazing Lights of the Sun: A Bilingual Edition. Trans. Renata Treitel.
　　Los Angeles: Sun & Moon Press, 1996.
Odyssèe au miroir de Saint Nazaire. Saint-Nazaire: M.E.E.T., 1996.

Prose:
I giardini dei popoli sotto le onde. Elena, eros, la metamorfosi. Parma: Guanda,
　　1991.
Il fuoco dell'Eden. Siracusa: Tema celeste, 1992.
Ildegarda oltre il tempo. Rimini: Raffaelli, 1998.

Translations and Critical Work:
Tradurre poesia. Brescia: Paideia, 1983.
Narrare. Rome: Theoria, 1985.
Yeats, William Butler. *Il crepuscolo celtico.* Ed. and trans. Copioli. Rome:
　　Theoria, 1987; rpt. Bompiani, 1993.
"Intervista a Mario Luzi a cura di Rosita Copioli." *L'anello che non tiene:*
　　Journal of Modern Italian Literature (Fall 1988): 55–70.
Tradizioni della poesia italiana contemporanea. Ed. Copioli. Rome: Theoria,
　　1988.
Yeats, William Butler. *Anima Mundi. Saggi sul mito e sulla letteratura.* Ed.
　　and trans. Copioli. Parma: Guanda, 1988; rpt. 1998.
Yeats, William Butler. *La rosa segreta. Tutti i racconti.* Ed. and trans. Copioli.
　　Parma: Guanda 1995.
Adolphe Noël des Vergers, 1804–1867. Un classicista eclettico e la sua dimora a
　　Rimini. Ed. Copioli. Rimini: Associazione Adolphe Noël des Vergers,
　　1996.

Leopardi, Giacomo. *Discorso di un italiano intorno alla poesia romantica.* Ed. Copioli. Milan: Rizzoli, 1998.

BIANCAMARIA FRABOTTA (1946–)

Frabotta was born and lives in Rome. She is a professor of Modern and Contemporary Italian Literature at the University of Rome "La Sapienza." Her early interests were political: with articles and essays, she played an active role in the feminist movement of the 1970s. Such interests are reflected in her poetry and in the novel *Velocità di fuga,* for which she won the 1989 Premio Tropea. In 1995 she was awarded the Premio Montale for *La viandanza.* In addition to her poetry, fiction, and theater, Frabotta has published numerous scholarly works, including historico-political studies on feminism, essays on women's literature, and monographs on Carlo Cattaneo and the poet Giorgio Caproni. She was a member of the editorial staff of *Orsa minore* from 1981 to 1983, and *Poesia* from 1989 to 1991. She has also contributed to the journals and newspapers *Nuovi Argomenti, aut aut, Horizonte, Il Manifesto,* and *L'Espresso,* and to RAI Television. Her poems have appeared in such anthologies as *Poesia degli anni settanta, Poesie d'amore* (1986), *Poesia oggi, Oltre il mare ghiacciato,* and *Poeti italiani del secondo Novecento: 1945–1995.* Her work has been translated in *Italian Poetry 1960–1980, The Defiant Muse, Italian Women Poets of the Twentieth Century, High Tide,* and *The Promised Land.*

Poetry:
Affeminata. Turin: Geiger, 1977.
Il rumore bianco. Milan: Feltrinelli, 1982.
Appunti di volo e altre poesie. Rome: La Cometa, 1985.
Controcanto al chiuso. Lithographs by Solvejg Albeverio Manzoni. Rome: Rossi & Spera, 1991.
La viandanza (1982–1992). Milan: Mondadori, 1995.
Ne resta uno. Florence: Il Ponte, 1996.
High Tide: Translations from the Italian. Trans. Gillian Allnut, et al. European Network for the Translation of Contemporary Poetry. Dublin: Poetry Ireland/Éigse Eireann and The Tyrone Guthrie Centre, 1998.
Terra contigua. Rome: Empiria, 1999.

Prose:
Velocità di fuga. Gardolo: Reverdito, 1989.

Plays:
Esorcismo al chiaro di luna. In *Silhouettes.* Genoa: Edizioni San Marco dei Giustiniani, 1985.

278

Controcanto al chiuso. Rome: Edizioni della Cometa, 1994.
Trittico dell'obbedienza. Intro. by Franca Angelini. Palermo: Sellerio, 1996.

Critical Work:
Carlo Cattaneo. Lugano: Fondazione Ticino Nostro, 1969.
Femminismo e lotta di classe in Italia (1970–1973). Ed. Frabotta. Intro. by
  Frabotta and Giuseppina Ciuffreda. Rome: Savelli, 1973; rpt. 1975.
La politica del femminismo. Ed. Frabotta. Rome: Savelli, 1976.
*Donne in poesia. Antologia della poesia femminile in Italia dal dopoguerra a
  oggi.* Ed. Frabotta. Rome: Savelli, 1976.
Letteratura al femminile. Bari: De Donato, 1980.
Punto a capo. Rome: Edizioni Centro Culturale Virginia Woolf, 1982.
Giorgio Caproni, il poeta del disincanto. Rome: Officina, 1993.

LUCIANA FREZZA (1926–1994)

Frezza was born in Rome. She lived in Rome, Sicily, and Milan, and
studied at the University of Rome with Giuseppe Ungaretti, receiving
a degree in Contemporary Italian Literature with a thesis on Montale.
Her poems have appeared in numerous journals, including *Almanacco
dello Specchio, Arsenale, Botteghe oscure, Carte Segrete, Lettera, Letteratura,*
and *Paragone,* and in such anthologies as *La giovane poesia, Donne in
poesia, Poesia italiana oggi, The Defiant Muse, Poesie d'amore* (1986), and
Europa in versi. Frezza was particularly interested in eighteenth- and
nineteenth-century French writers. Guillaume Appolinaire, Charles
Baudelaire and Stéphane Mallarmé were among the many authors she
translated. She committed suicide on June 30, 1994.

Poetry:
Cefalù e altre poesie. Caltanissetta–Rome: Sciascia, 1958.
La farfalla e la rosa. Milan: Feltrinelli, 1962.
Cara Milano (1960–1966). Vicenza: Neri Pozza, 1967.
Un tempo di speranza (1961–1970). Vicenza: Neri Pozza, 1971.
La tartaruga magica. Preface by Filippo Bettini. Rome: Florida, 1984.
24 pezzi facili. Padova: Biblioteca Cominiana, 1988.
Parabola sub (1985–1987). Preface by Walter Pedullà. Rome: Empirìa, 1990.

Prose:
Il disegno e altri racconti. Rome: Empirìa, 1996.

Translations and Critical Work:
Mallarmé, Stéphane. *Poesie.* Vicenza: Neri Pozza, 1963; rpt. Milan:
  Feltrinelli, 1966.

Laforgue, Jules. *Poesie*. Milan: Lerici, 1965.
Laforgue, Jules. *Un cervello a tre emisferi*. Milan: Accademia, 1972.
Nouveau, Germain. *I baci e altre poesie*. Turin: Einaudi, 1972.
Verlaine, Paul. *Poesie*. Milan: Rizzoli, 1974; rpt. 1986.
Baudelaire, Charles. *I fiori del male*. Milan: Rizzoli, 1980; rpt. 1999.
Giraud, Albert. *Farfalle nere*. Rome: Edizioni dell'Elefante, 1980.
Fargue, Léon-Paul. *Poesie, 1886–1933*. Turin: Einaudi, 1981.
Apollinare, Guillaume. *Alcool, Calligrammi*. Milan: Mondadori, 1986; rpt. 1996.
Proust, Marcel. *Poesie*. Milan: Feltrinelli, 1993.

VERA GHERARDUCCI (1923–)

Gherarducci was born in Bari and, from 1950 onward, lived in Rome. She attended the Academy of Dramatic Arts where she acted in Eduardo De Filippo's theater group. With her husband, film director Vittorio de Seta, she worked on "Banditi a Orgosolo." Her first book of poetry appeared in 1962. Pasolini published her poems in the journal *Nuovi Argomenti* and wrote an introduction for her second book.

Poetry:
Le giornate bianche. Milan: Scheiwiller, 1962.
Giorno unico. Parma: Guanda, 1970.

Film:
Banditi a Orgosolo. Produced by Vittorio de Seta; directed by Franco Ferrara; screenplay and dialogues by Gherarducci. Titanus Films, 1961; rpt. Burbank: Hollywood's Attic, 1996.

MARGHERITA GUIDACCI (1921–1992)

Guidacci was born in Florence. She studied Italian literature at the University of Florence with Giuseppe De Robertis and wrote her thesis on Ungaretti. After a stay in England, where she studied English literature, she returned to Italy, eventually moving to Rome. She taught English and American literature at the University of Macerata and at the Istituto Universitario di Magistero "Maria Assunta" in Rome, and was a frequent contributor to many Italian journals and newspapers, including the Vatican daily *L'Osservatore Romano*. Guidacci published over eighteen volumes of poetry, along with numerous critical studies and translations of English and American writers. Her own poetry has been translated into English, French, and German. Selections of her work have appeared in the anthologies *Quarta generazione, La giovane poesia, Contemporary Italian Poetry, From Pure Silence to Impure Dialogue, Donne in poesia, Donne in poesia: Incontri con le poetesse italiane, The Penguin Book of Women Poets, Italian Poetry Today, Poesia italiana del Novecento* (1980), *Poesie d'amore* (1986), *The Defiant Muse, The Green Flame,* and *Italian Women Poets of the Twentieth Century.* She has won numerous awards, including the Cervia (1965), Biella (1978), and Tagliacozzo (1983). Selections of *Paglia e polvere* have been set to music by Reginald Smith-Brendal of Sussex University.

Poetry:
La sabbia e l'angelo. Florence: Vallecchi, 1946.
Morte del ricco. Florence: Vallecchi, 1955.
Giorno dei Santi. Milan: Scheiwiller, 1957.
Paglia e polvere. Padua: Rebellato, 1961.
Poesie. Milan: Rizzoli, 1965.
Un cammino incerto. Luxembourg: Cahiers d'origine, 1970.
Neurosuite. Vicenza: Neri Pozza, 1970.
Terra senza orologi. Milan: Trentadue, 1973.
Poems from Neurosuite. Trans. Marina La Palma. Berkeley: Kelsey Street Press, 1975.
Taccuino Slavo. Vicenza: La Locusta, 1976.
Il vuoto e le forme. Padua: Rebellato, 1977.
Brevi e lunghe. Vatican City: Libreria Editrice Vaticana, 1980.
L'altare di Isenheim. Milan: Rusconi, 1980.
L'orologio di Bologna. Florence: Città di Vita, 1981.
Inno alla gioia. Florence: Nardini, 1983.
La via Crucis dell'umanità. Florence: Città di Vita, 1984. (A multilingual collection with poems in Italian and translations in English, French, German, and Spanish.)
Liber Fulguralis. With English translations by Ruth Feldman. Messina: Mela stregata, 1986.
Poesie per poeti. Milan: Istituto propaganda libraria, 1987.
Una breve misura. Chieti: Vecchio Faggio, 1988.
Il buio e lo splendore. Milan: Garzanti, 1989.
A Book of Sibyls: Poems by Margherita Guidacci. Trans. Ruth Feldman. Boston: Rowan Tree Press, 1989.
Landscapes with Ruins: Selected Poetry of Margherita Guidacci. Trans. Ruth Feldman. Intro. by Gian-Paolo Biasin. Detroit: Wayne State University Press, 1992.
Anelli del tempo. Florence: Edizioni Città di Vita, 1993.
In the Eastern Sky: Selected Poems of Margherita Guidacci. Trans. Catherine O'Brien. Dublin: Dedalus, 1993.

Le poesie. Ed. Maura Del Serra. Florence: Le lettere, 1999.

Prose:

Prose e interviste. Ed. Ilaria Rabatti. Pistoia: CRT, 1999.

Translations and Critical Work:

Donne, John. *Sermoni.* Florence: Liberia editrice fiorentina, 1946.

Beerbohm, Max. *L'ipocrita beato.* Florence:Vallecchi, 1946.

Dickinson, Emily. *Poesie.* Florence: Cya, 1947.

Monnier, Emmanuel. *L'avventura cristiana.* Florence: Libreria editrice fiorentina, 1950.

Frost, Robert. *Albero alla finestra.* Milan: Scheiwiller, 1956.

Gissing, George. *Sulla riva dello Jonio.* Bologna: Cappelli, 1957; rpt. 1962.

Tu, Fu. *Desiderio di pace.* Milan: Scheiwiller, 1957.

Due anni col pubblico cinematografico. Ricerche ed esperienze. With Luca Pinna and Malcom S. MacLean, Jr. Rome: Edizioni di Bianco e Nero, 1958.

MacLeish, Archibald. *New York.* Milan: Scheiwiller, 1958.

Pound, Ezra. *Patria mia. Discussione sulle arti, il loro uso e il loro furturo in America.* Florence: Centro Internazionale del Libro, 1958.

Antichi racconti cinesi. Bologna: Cappelli, 1959; rpt. 1962.

Guillén, Jorge. *Federico in persona. Carteggio.* Milan: Scheiwiller, 1960.

James, Henry. *Roderick Hudson.* Bologna: Cappelli, 1960.

Conrad, Joseph. *Destino.* Milan: Bompiani, 1961.

Racconti popolari irlandesi. Bologna: Cappelli, 1961.

Twain, Mark. *Vita sul Mississippi.* Rome: Editoriale Opere Nuove, 1962.

T'ao, Ch'ien. *Poema per la bellezza della sua donna.* Milan: Scheiwiller, 1962.

Poeti estoni. Ed. Guidacci. Rome: Abete, 1973.

Studi su Eliot. Milan: Istituto propaganda libraria, 1975.

Studi su poeti e narratori americani. Cagliari: EDES, 1978.

Ioannes Paulus, II [Wojtyla, Karol]. *Il sapore del pane. Poesie.* With Aleksandra Kurczab.Vatican City: Libreria EditriceVaticana, 1979.

Bishop, Elizabeth. *L'arte di perdere.* Milan: Rusconi, 1982.

Aspetti ed eredità della poesia europea dell'Ottocento. Rome: Studium, 1984.

Northangerland e altri studi brontiani. With Anthony Jennings. Rome: Studium, 1988.

Sacre rappresentazioni inglesi. Florence: Libreria editrice fiorentina, 1990.

Dickinson, Emily. *Lettere e Poesie.* Milan: Bompiani, 1997.

ARMANDA GUIDUCCI (1923–1992)

Guiducci was born in Naples. She studied with scholar and anti-fascist leader Antonio Banfi at the University of Milan, graduating with a degree in philosophy. After finishing university she became an active contributor to politically left-wing cultural organizations. With Franco Fortini, Luciano Amodio, and Roberto Guiducci she founded *Ragionamenti,* a Marxist journal dedicated to examining the relationship between contemporary politics and aesthetics. She was a regular contributor to the literary pages of the Socialist party daily *L'Avanti* and wrote for several periodicals, including *Argomenti, Cultura e Realtà, Opinione, Passato e presente,* and *Tempi moderni.* She was also director of the Socialist organization Circolo Turati of Milan. Later she became director of cultural programming for Swiss television. Guiducci won the Premio Cittadella for her verse collection *Poesie per un uomo.* She won Pisa prizes for both *A colpi di silenzio* and *Il mito Pavese.* Particularly noteworthy are the ways in which Guiducci mixes genres, merging anthropological analysis, the travelogue, and fictional techniques with Marxist commentary. In addition to her poetry, she has received international acclaim as a feminist critic. Her scholarship includes work on the Soviet Union, New Guinea, Indonesia, African literature, and Virginia Woolf. Her books have been translated into French, German, Greek, and Spanish. Selections of her poems have appeared in various anthologies, including *Donne in poesia, Italian Poetry Today* (1979), and *The Defiant Muse.*

Poetry:
Poesie per un uomo. Milan: Mondadori, 1965.
A colpi di silenzio. Milan: Lanfranchi, 1982; rev. and expanded, 1990.

Prose:
La mela e il serpente. Autoanalisi di una donna. Milan: Rizzoli, 1974; rpt. 1988.
Due donne da buttare. Milan: Rizzoli, 1976; rpt. 1980.
La donna non è gente. Milan: Rizzoli, 1978; rpt. 1980.
A testa in giù. Milan: Rizzoli, 1984.

Translations and Critical Work:
La domenica della rivoluzione. Milan: Lerici, 1961.
Dallo zdanovismo allo strutturalismo. Milan: Feltrinelli, 1967.
Il mito Pavese. Florence: Vallecchi, 1967.
Invito alla lettura di Pavese. Milan: Mursia, 1972; rpt. 1979.
Rougemont, Denis de. *L'amore e l'occidente.* Trans. Luigi Santucci. Intro. by Guiducci. Milan: Rizzoli, 1977.

All'ombra di Kalì. Milan: Rizzoli, 1979.
La letteratura della nuova Africa. With Lina Angioletti. Rome: Lerici, 1979.
Donna e serva. Milan: Rizzoli, 1983.
Perdute nella storia. Storia delle donne dal I al VI secolo d.c. Florence: Sansoni, 1989.
Medioevo inquieto. Storia delle donne dall'VIII al XV secolo d.c. Florence: Sansoni, 1990.
Virginia e l'angelo. Milan: Longanesi, 1991.
Il Grande Sepik. Il tramonto del primitivo. Milan: Lanfranchi, 1992.
Donne, John. *L'amore e il male.* Milan: Lanfranchi, 1996.

JOLANDA INSANA (1937–)

Insana was born in Messina and lives in Rome, where she is a teacher. Her poetry has appeared in numerous anthologies, including *Poesia femminista italiana, Poesia degli anni settanta, Poesia erotica italiana del novecento, Poesia italiana oggi, The Defiant Muse,* and *Italian Women Poets of the Twentieth Century.* She has received awards for *Fendenti fonici* (Mondello) and *Il collettame* (Rimini Poesia). Insana's scholarly interests include Sappho's poems and Plautus' and Euripides' plays. She has edited Ahmad Shawqi's *La passione di Cleopatra* and Aleksandr Tvardovskij's *Per diritto di memoria.*

Poetry:
Sciarra amara. Parma: Guanda, 1977.
Fendenti fonici. Parma: Guanda, 1982.
Il collettame (1980–1982). Milan: Società di Poesia, 1985.
La clausura. Milan: Crocetti, 1987.
Medicina carnale. Milan: Mondadori, 1994.
L'occhio dormiente: 1987–1994. Venice: Marsilio, 1997.

Translations and Critical Work:
Saffo. *Poesie.* Florence: Estro, 1985.
Shawqi, Ahmad. *La Passione di Cleopatra.* Ed. Insana. Milan: Ubulibri, 1989.
Tvardovskij, Aleksandr. *Per diritto di memoria.* Ed. Insana and Viviana Tutova. Palermo: Acquario, 1989.
Carmina Priapea. Milan: CDE, 1991.
Cappellano, Andrea. *De amore.* Milan: SE, 1992.

VIVIAN LAMARQUE (1946–)

Lamarque was born in Tesero (Trento). She lives in Milan where she teaches secondary school. She has published numerous books of poetry and has translated the work of Baudelaire, Louis-Ferdinand Céline, Jean de La Fontaine, the Grimm brothers, Jacques Prévert, and Paul Valéry. She has also written a number of fables and children's songs and writes for the national daily *Corriere della Sera*. For her first volume of poetry, *Teresino,* she won the Premio Viareggio opera prima. Her other awards include the Premio Tropea for *Poesie dando del Lei,* the Premio Montale for *Il signore degli spaventati,* and the 1996 Pen Club prize for *Una quieta polvere.* Her work has appeared in numerous anthologies, including *Donne in poesia, The Defiant Muse, Poeti italiani del secondo Novecento: 1945–1995,* and *Italian Women Poets of the Twentieth Century.* With Luigi Balestrini she contributed to Tommaso Ottonieri's CD 2. She is a jury member for the Nazionale di Diaristica prize.

Poetry:
Teresino. Milan: Guanda, 1981.
Il signore d'oro. Milan: Crocetti, 1986; rpt. 1997.
Poesie dando del Lei. Milan: Garzanti, 1989.
Il signore degli spaventati. Intro. by Giovanni Giudici. Forte dei Marmi: Pegaso, 1992.
Una quieta polvere. Milan: Mondadori 1996.

Children's Literature:
Il libro delle ninne-nanne. Civisello Balsamo: Paoline, 1989.
La bambina che mangiava i lupi. Milan: Mursia, 1992.
La bambina di ghiaccio. Trieste: EL, 1992
La bambina senza nome. Milan: Mursia, 1993.
Arte della libertà. Il sogno di Sara. Milan: Mazzotta, 1995.
La bambina che non voleva andare a scuola. Varese: La Coccinella, 1997.
Cioccolatina, la bambina che mangiava sempre. Milan: I Delfini Bompiani, 1998.
Gentilmente. Cari giudici, gentili gerani. Milan: Rizzoli, 1998.
Unik, storia di un figlio unico. Milan: I Girini Bompiani, 1999.

Translations:
Prévert, Jacques. *Sole di notte.* Milan: Guanda, 1983.
Valéry, Paul. *Scritti sull'arte.* Milan: Guanda, 1984.
Céline, Louis-Ferdinand. *Storia del piccolo Mouck.* Milan: Rizzoli, 1998.

Other Arts:
Ottonieri, Tommaso. *2.* Milan: Bompiani, 1998.

GABRIELLA LETO (1930–)

Leto was born and lives in Rome. She made her debut in 1975 in Mondadori's poetry series *Almanacco dello Specchio*. Her work has subsequently appeared in Einaudi's *Nuovi poeti italiani* (1980), the anthology *Donne in poesia: Incontri con le poetesse italiane*, and in such journals as *Paragone* and *Nuovi Argomenti*. In 1991 she won the prestigious Premio Viareggio for *Nostalgia dell'acqua*. Her most recent work has been collected in *L'ora insonne* (1997). She has translated the work of such writers as Victor Hugo, Ovid, Propertius, and Stendhal.

Poetry:
Ariette. Lugano: D. Pusek, 1989.
Nostalgia dell'acqua. Turin: Einaudi, 1990.
L'ora insonne. Turin: Einaudi, 1997.

Translations and Critical Work:
Ovidius, Publius Naso. *Le eroidi*. Turin: Einaudi, 1966.
Propertius, Sextus. *Elegie*. Intro. by Antonio La Penna. Turin: Einaudi, 1970.
Hugo, Victor. *Notre-Dame de Paris*. Milan: Mondadori, 1985; rpt. 1995.
Stendhal. *Cronache italiane*. With Maria Bellonci. Milan: Mondadori, 1990.
Ovidius, Publius Naso. *Gli amori*. Turin: Einaudi, 1995.
Ovidius, Publius Naso. *Versi e precetti d'amore*. Intro. by Paolo Fedeli.
    Turin: Einaudi, 1998.
Ovidius, Publius Naso. *Opere I. Dalla poesia d'amore alla poesia dell'esilio*.
    Ed. Paolo Fedeli, trans. Leto and Nicola Gardini. Turin: Einaudi, 1999.

DACIA MARAINI (1936–)

Maraini was born in Florence to leftist parents, ethnologist Fosco Maraini and painter Topazia Alliata. From 1938 until 1947 she and her family lived in Japan. Refusing to recognize Japan's military government, they were interned with nine other Italians in a Japanese camp. After leaving Japan, the family settled in Bagheria, Sicily. References to both places figure repeatedly in her poetry and prose. In the late 1950s Maraini moved to Rome where she met Aberto Moravia and avant-garde writers Alfredo Giuliani and Edoardo Sanguineti. In 1956 she co-founded the journal *Tempo della letteratura*. Along with her countless critical articles, novels, and collections of poetry, Maraini has edited an anthology of modern Japanese poems. Her support for women's rights has been widely recognized, as has her work in film and the women's theater movement in Rome. Her extensive involvement in theater includes over 30 plays,

collaborations with Moravia and Enzo Siciliano, the development of La
Maddalena (a theater group composed entirely of women), and the The-
ater of Centocelle whose primary purpose was to present plays in working-
class neighborhoods. Many of her stories have been adapted for film. These
include Roberto Faenza's 1994 production of *La lunga vita di Marianna
Ucrìa* (entitled *Marianna Ucrìa*) and Maraini and Piera Degli Esposti's adap-
tation of *Storia di Piera*. Maraini's work includes a number of cross-genre
pieces. *Se amando troppo,* her latest collection of poetry, includes a CD
which brings together Maraini's work and the music of Giuseppe Moretti.
Maraini is the recipient of numerous awards, including the prestigious
Premio Campiello (1990) for *La lunga vita di Marianna Ucrìa* and the Premio
Strega for *Buio* (1999). In 1992 she was awarded both the Mediterraneo
and Città di Penne for *Viaggiando con passo di volpe.* Maraini's work has been
translated into over eighteen languages. *Mangiami pure* and *Viaggiando con
passo di volpe* have been translated into English as, respectively, *Devour Me
Too* (1987) and *Traveling in the Gait of a Fox* (1992). Selections of her poetry
are included in *Italian Poetry Today* (1979) and *The Defiant Muse.* In recent
years she has been teaching writing in universities and cultural centers.

Poetry:
Crudeltà all'aria aperta. Milan: Feltrinelli, 1966.
Donne mie. Turin: Einaudi, 1974; rpt. 1977.
Mangiami pure. Turin: Einaudi, 1978.
Dimenticato di dimenticare. Turin: Einaudi, 1982.
Devour Me Too. Trans. Genni Donati Gunn. Montréal: Guernica, 1987;
    rpt. 1990.
Viaggiando con passo di volpe. Poesie 1983–1991. Milan: Rizzoli, 1991.
Traveling in the Gait of a Fox: Poetry 1983–1991. Trans. Genni Gunn.
    Kingston, Ont.: Quarry Press, 1992.
Occhi di Medusa. Rome: Edizione del Giano, 1992.
Se amando troppo. Poesie 1966–1998. Milan: Rizzoli, 1998.

Prose:
La vacanza. Intro. by Alberto Moravia. Milan: Lerici, 1962.
L'età del malessere. Turin: Einaudi, 1963; rpt. 1996.
The Age of Malaise. Trans. Frances Frenaye. New York: Grove Press, 1963.
A memoria. Milan: Bompiani, 1967.
Mio marito. Milan: Bompiani, 1968.
Memorie di una ladra. Milan: Bompiani, 1972; rpt. Milan: Rizzoli, 1993.
Memories of a Female Thief. Trans. Nina Rootes. New York: Transatlantic
    Press, 1974.
Donna in guerra. Turin: Einaudi, 1975; rpt. Milan: Rizzoli, 1998.

Lettere a Marina. Milan: Bompiani, 1981.

Il treno per Helsinki. Turin: Einaudi, 1984.

Isolina. La donna tagliati a pezzi. Milan: Mondadori, 1985; rpt. Milan: Rizzoli, 1995.

The Holiday. Trans. Stuart Hood. London:Weidenfeld and Nicholson, 1986.

Letters to Marina. Trans. Dick Kitto and Elspeth Spottiswood. London: Camden Press, 1987.

Woman at War. Trans. Mara Benetti and Elspeth Spottiswood. New York: Italica Press, 1988.

La lunga vita di Marianna Ucrìa. Milan: Rizzoli, 1990.

The Silent Duchess. Trans. Dick Kitto and Elspeth Spottiswood. London: Peter Owen, 1992.

Bagheria. Milan: Rizzoli, 1993.

Voci. Milan: Rizzoli, 1994; rpt. 1999.

Storie di cani per una bambina. Milan: Bompiani, 1996.

Dolce per sé. Milan: Rizzoli, 1997.

Buio. Milan: Rizzoli, 1999.

Theater:

Il ricatto a teatro e altre commedie. Turin: Einaudi, 1970.

Viva l'Italia. Turin: Einaudi, 1973.

Fare teatro. Materiali, testi, interviste. Milan: Bompiani, 1974.

Don Juan. Turin: Einaudi, 1976.

Dialogo di una prostituta con un suo cliente. Padua: Mastrogiacomo, 1978.

Suor Juana. Turin: La Rosa, 1980.

I sogni di Clitennestra e altre commedie. Milan: Bompiani, 1981.

Lezioni d'amore e altre commedie. Milan: Bompiani, 1982.

Stravaganza. Rome: Serarcangeli, 1987.

Paura e amore. London:World Cinema, Channel 4 Television, 1988; rpt. 1998.

Veronica, meretrice e scrittora. Milan: Bompiani, 1991.

La casa tra due palme. Salerno: Edizioni Sottotraccia, 1995.

Essays, Interviews, Translations, and Critical Work:

La protesta poetica del Giappone. Antologia di cent'anni di poesia giapponese. With Michiko Nojiri. Rome: Officina, 1968.

Witkiewicz, Stanislaw Ignacy. *Commedia ripugnante di una madre*. Trans. Maraini. Roma: Bulzoni, 1970.

Storia di Piera. With Piera Degli Esposti. Milan: Bompiani, 1980.

Il bambino Alberto. Interviste. Milan: Bompiani, 1986.

La bionda, la bruna e l'asino. Milan: Rizzoli, 1987.

Cercando Emma. Gustave Flaubert e la signora Bovary. Milan: Rizzoli, 1993.

E tu chi eri? 26 interviste sull'infanzia. Milan: Bompiani, 1973; rpt. Milan: Rizzoli, 1998.

DARIA MENICANTI (1914–1995)

Menicanti was born in Piacenza and died in Milan in 1995. She graduated from the University of Milan with a thesis on the poetry of John Keats. There she studied aesthetics under the supervision of Antonio Banfi. Menicanti's work with Banfi brought her into contact with a large group of young philosophers, including Enzo Paci, Giulio Preti, and Remo Cantoni. She and Preti married in 1937 and were divorced in 1951. Menicanti's interest in the relationship between philosophy, politics, and literature would evenutally lead her to a meeting with Vittorio Sereni. Sereni was a respected poet of the *linea lombarda* school and had close ties to the publishing house Mondadori. Impressed by her poetry, he brought her work to the attention of Mondadori's editors. In 1964 they published her first collection of verse, *Città come*. Selections of her work have been translated into English in *The Defiant Muse* and *Italian Women Poets of the Twentieth Century*. Her work has also appeared in several Italian anthologies, including *Donne in poesia, Poesia italiana del Novecento* (1980), and *Poesia erotica italiana del novecento*. Over the years, she has contributed to such journals as *Paragone, Inventario, Lunarionuovo, Salvo Imprevisti,* and *Resine*. She has translated works by Nöel Coward, Paul Géraldy, John Keats, Paul Nizan, Sylvia Plath, Betty Smith, Dylan Thomas, and Michael Tournier.

Poetry:
Città come. Milan: Mondadori, 1964.
Un nero d'ombra. Milan: Mondadori, 1969.
Poesie per un passante: 1969–1976. Milan: Mondadori, 1978.
Ferragosto. Acireale: Lunarionuovo, 1986.
Altri amici (1956–1985). Forlì: Forum, 1986.
Ultimo quarto (1985–1989). Milan: Scheiwiller, 1990.

Prose:
Il cuore della ragione. Omaggio a Giulio Preti. Florence: Gabinetto G. P. Vieusseux, 1986.

Translations:
Nizan, Paul. *Aden Arabia*. Preface by Jean-Paul Sartre. Milan: Mondadori, 1961; rpt. Rome: Vascello, 1994.
Nizan, Paul. *La cospirazione*. Milan: Mondadori, 1961; rpt. 1981.

Coward, Nöel. *Amore e protocollo.* Milan: Mondadori, 1962.
Smith, Betty. *Al mattino viene la gioia.* Milan: Mondadori, 1964.
Paris, Jean. *James Joyce.* Milan: Il Saggiatore, 1966.
Plath, Sylvia. *La campana di vetro.* Milan: Mondadori, 1968; rpt. 1979.
Géraldy, Paul. *Toi e moi.* Milan: Mondadori, 1976; rpt. 1986.

ALDA MERINI (1931–)

Merini was born and lives in Milan. She began her career at an early age, appearing in Giacinto Spagnoletti's *Antologia della poesia italiana: 1909–1949.* Since 1965, however, her life and work have been repeatedly disrupted by long stays in psychiatric hospitals. In 1979, following one such period, she returned to writing with a series of poems inspired by her experience as a patient. These are collected in *La Terra Santa,* which was awarded the Librex Montale prize in 1993. In 1996 she won the Premio Viareggio for *Ballate non pagate.* In addition to the collections she has published with large publishing houses, Merini has produced numerous short-run books of verse. Each one is printed on hand-made paper with individual illustrations. She is also the author of various works in prose and has contributed to Luca Ragagnin's CD *3.* Her poetry has appeared in anthologies ranging from *Quarta generazione* and *La giovane poesia* to the recent *Poeti italiani del secondo Novecento: 1945–1995.* Selections of her work have been translated into English in *From Pure Silence to Impure Dialogue, Donne in poesia: Incontri con le poetesse italiane,* and *Italian Women Poets of the Twentieth Century.*

Poetry:
La presenza di Orfeo. Milan: Schwarz, 1953.
Paura di Dio. Milan: Scheiwiller, 1955.
Nozze romane. Milan: Schwarz, 1955.
Tu sei Pietro. Milan: Scheiwiller, 1961.
Destinati a morire. Poggibonsi: Lalli, 1980.
Le rime petrose. Edizione privata, 1981.
Le satire della Ripa. Ed. Giulio de Mitri and Pietro Mandricco. Taranto: Laboratorio Arti Visive, 1983.
Le più belle poesie. Edizione privata, 1983.
La Terra Santa. Milan: Scheiwiller, 1984; rpt. 1996.
Fogli bianchi. Livorno: Biblioteca Cominiana, 1987.
Testamento (1947–1988). Ed. Giovanni Raboni. Milan: Crocetti, 1988.
Vuoto d'amore. Ed. Maria Corti. Turin: Einaudi, 1991.
Ipotenusa d'amore. Milan: La vita felice, 1992; rpt. 1996.
La palude di Manganelli o Il monarca del re. Milan: La vita felice, 1992.

La presenza di Orfeo. Milan: Scheiwiller, 1993. (Also includes *Paura di Dio, Nozze romane,* and *Tu sei Pietro.*)

Titano amori intorno. Milan: La vita felice, 1993.

Ballate non pagate. Ed. Laura Alunno. Turin: Einaudi, 1995.

Aforismi. Milan: Pulcinoelefante, 1996.

Un'anima indocile. Milan: La vita felice, 1996; rpt. 1997.

La volpe e il sipario. Legnano: Girardi, 1997.

Fiore di poesia (1951–1997). Ed. Maria Corti. Turin: Einaudi, 1998.

57 poesie. Milan: Mondadori, 1998.

La poesia luogo del nulla. Poesie e parole con Chicca Gagliardo e Guido Spaini. Lecce: P. Manni, 1999.

Prose:

L'altra verità. Diario di una diversa. Preface by Giorgio Manganelli. Milan: Scheiwiller, 1986.

Delirio Amoroso. Genoa: Il melangolo, 1989.

Il tormento delle figure. Genoa: Il melangolo, 1990.

Le parole di Alda Merini. Viterbo: Stampa Alternativa, 1991.

La pazza della porta accanto. Milan: Bompiani, 1995.

La vita facile. Sillabario. Ed. Guido Spaini and Chicca Gagliardo. Milan: Bompiani, 1996.

Una ferrovia piena di allegria. Rime, testi e disegni dei bambini di Mantova con una favola di Alda Merini. Mantova: Corraini, 1998.

Il ladro Giuseppe. Racconti dagli anni Sessanta. Milan: Scheiwiller, 1999.

Other Arts:

Ragagnin, Luca. *3.* Milan: Bompiani, 1998.

GIULIA NICCOLAI (1934–)

Niccolai was born in Milan to an American mother and Italian father. At an early age she learned to speak Italian and English. Later she learned German and French. Niccolai began her professional career as a photographer, with works appearing in such eminent magazines as *Life, Paris Match,* and *Der Spiegel.* In 1966 she published her first novel and in 1969 her first book of poetry. She was associated with the neo-avant-garde *Gruppo 63,* and in 1970 she founded (with Adriano Spatola) the avant-garde journal *Tam Tam.* In addition to her poetry, Niccolai is known for her many translations. These include the work of Beatrix Potter, Gertrude Stein, and Dylan Thomas. Her own verse is multilingual in nature and is influenced by children's stories, the texts of Stein, and "nonsense" poems such as Lewis Carroll's "Jabberwocky." She has traveled extensively in Asia and is known for her sound performances and visual poetry. Her poems have appeared in several anthologies, including *Poesia degli anni settanta, Poesia italiana oggi, Poesia italiana della contraddizione*, and *Twentieth-Century Italian Poetry* (1993), and have been translated into English in *Italian Poetry Today* (1979), *Italian Poetry 1960–1980, The Defiant Muse, Foresta Ultra Naturam, Poems for the Millennium, The Promised Land*, and numerous U.S. journals. In 1995 she won the Premio Feronia for *Frisbees (poesie da lanciare)*. In the mid-1980s, Niccolai turned to Tibetan Mahayana Buddhism. Her forthcoming book *Esoterico biliardo*, which includes the already published essay "Stein come pietra miliare," is, in Niccolai's words, an "inter-text (memoir, narrative, essay)" that bridges her literary and spiritual experiences.

Poetry:

Humpty Dumpty. Turin: Geiger, 1969.

Greenwich. Turin: Geiger, 1971.

Poema & Oggetto. Turin: Geiger, 1974.

Substitution. With Paul Vangelisti. Los Angeles: Red Hill Press, 1975.

Facsimile. Modena: Tau/ma, 1976.

Russky Salad Ballads & Webster Poems. Turin: Geiger, 1977.

Harry's Bar e altre poesie 1969–1980. Preface by Giorgio Manganelli. Milan: Feltrinelli, 1981.

Singsong for New Year's Adam & Eve. Mulino di Bazzano: Tam Tam, 1982.

Lettera aperta. Udine: Campanotto, 1983.

Frisbees in facoltà. Bergamo: Edizioni El bagatt, 1984.

Frisbees (poesie da lanciare). Udine: Campanotto, 1994.

Prose:

Il grande angolo. Milan: Feltrinelli, 1966.

The Ship in the Fields. Illustrations by Henny and Luciano Boschini. New York: Scroll Press, 1972.

Francobolli francobolli. With Maurizio Osti. Milan: Emme, 1976.

"La via Emilia." In Niccolai et al. *Esplorazioni sulla via Emilia.* Milan: Feltrinelli, 1986.

"Stein come pietra miliare." *Le traduzioni italiane di Herman Melville e Gertrude Stein.* Ed. Sergio Perosa. Venice: Istituto veneto di scienze, lettere ed arti, 1997.

Translations:

Mérimée, Prosper. *La notte di San Bartolomeo.* With Adriano Spatola. Milan: Emme, 1975.

Edwardes, Michael. *Nell'India antica.* Milan: LM, 1975.

Stein, Gertrude. *La storia geografica dell'America, o Il rapporto della natura umana con la mente umana.* Milan: La tartaruga, 1980.

Beisner, Monika. *Centouno indovinelli.* Milan: Emme, 1981.
Potter, Beatrix. *La favola di Ludovico Coniglio.* Milan: Emme, 1981.
Potter, Beatrix. *La favola della Signora Riccio Rotolò.* Milan: Emme, 1981.
Thomas, Dylan. *Il mio Natale nel Galles.* Milan: Emme, 1981.
Potter, Beatrix. *La favola di Tom Miciozzion.* Milan: Emme, [1985].
Cross, Amanda. *Un delitto per James Joyce.* Milan: Interno giallo, 1992.
Neill, Alexander Sutherland. *La nuvola verde.* Milan: Bompiani, 1994.

LUCIANA NOTARI (1944–)

Notari was born in Terni. She graduated from the University of Rome
with a degree in Modern Literature. Since then she has taught junior
high school literature and has worked for the RAI radio series "I luoghi
della cultura" (The Places of Culture). Selections of her poems have
appeared in such anthologies as *Diapason di voci, L'altro Novecento,* and
Melodie della terra. She was awarded the Felsina prize for *Animanimalis*
and the Nuove Scrittrici prize for *Aiuole di città.* She is currently presi-
dent of the Gutenberg Association of Terni and has organized festivals of
contemporary Italian poetry. The anthology *Oltre il mare ghiacciato,* which
Notari edited in 1996, came out of one such event.

Poetry:
Animanimalis. Preface by Umberto Piersanti and Elio Pecora. Forlì:
Forum, 1991.
La vita è nella vita. Preface by Paolo Ruffilli. Venice: Edizioni del Leone,
1994.
Aiuole di città. Pescara: Tracce, 1997.

Critical Works:
Oltre il mare ghiacciato. I poeti e l'oggi. Ed. Notari. Udine: Campanotto, 1996.

ROSSANA OMBRES (1931–)

Ombres was born in Turin. For many years she was the literary critic of
the national newspaper *La Stampa.* Her poems have appeared in some of
the most important twentieth-century Italian periodicals, including
*Almanacco, Botteghe Oscure, L'Approdo, La fiera letteraria, Marcatrè, Nuovi
Argomenti, Paragone, Tempo Presente,* and the Neapolitan daily *Il Giornale,*
and in anthologies such as *Poesia degli anni settanta, Poesia erotica italiana
del novecento, Poesie d'amore* (1986), and *Donne in poesia: Incontri con le
poetesse italiane.* Selections of her work have been translated in *Italian
Poetry Today* (1979), *A Book of Women Poets from Antiquity to Now, The*

Defiant Muse, New Italian Poets, and *The Promised Land.* In 1974 she won the PremioViareggio for *Bestiario d'amore.* She was the first female recipient of the award in the prize's fifty-year history. Ombres also writes extensively for children. She is director of Radar, a literary column for middle schools and, in 1975, published *Le belle statuine,* a collection of poems for children. Her columns appear in *Corriere dei Piccoli,* a publication for children. In addition to her poetry, she is the author of numerous novels and the radio drama *Cosa hai visto dopo la notte.*

Poetry:
Orizzonte anche tu. Florence:Vallecchi, 1956.
Le ciminiere di Casale. Milan: Feltrinelli, 1962.
L'ipotesi di Agar. Turin: Einaudi, 1968.
Bestiario d'amore. Milan: Rizzoli, 1974.
Le belle statuine. Turin: Einaudi, 1975.

Prose:
Principessa Giacinta. Milan: Rizzoli, 1970.
Memorie d'una dilettante. Milan: Rizzoli, 1977.
Serenata. Milan: Mondadori, 1980.
Un dio coperto di rose. Milan: Mondadori, 1993.
Baiadera. Milan: Mondadori, 1997.

PIERA OPPEZZO (1934–)

Opezzo was born inTurin and now lives in Milan. She has been actively involved in the feminist movement. Her work has appeared in such journals as *Linea d'ombra, Nuovi Argomenti, Tam Tam,* and the newspaper *Il Manifesto.* Her poetry has been anthologized in *Donne in poesia, Italian Poetry 1960–1980, Versi d'amore,* and *The Defiant Muse.*

Poetry:
L'uomo qui presente. Turin: Einaudi, 1966.
Sì a una reale interruzione. Turin: Geiger, 1976.
Le strade di Melanctha. Milan: Nuovi autori, 1987.

Prose:
Minuto per minuto. Milan: La tartaruga, 1978.

Translations:
Gibran, Kahil. *Il profeta.* Milan: Mondadori, 1995; rpt. 1998.

AMELIA ROSSELLI (1930–1996)

Rosselli was born in Paris to anti-fascist activists Marion Cave and Carlo Rosselli. Cave was an English woman of Irish descent and Rosselli, an Italian professor of political science and organizer of the resistance group Giustizia e Libertà. Carlo Rosselli was killed by French fascists when Amelia was seven. After his death, the Rosselli family left France for England, eventually travelling to New York. It was in Britain and the United States that Rosselli learned English. She lived in America until 1946, attending college and studying Italian during the summer. She then returned to England where she began studying piano, violin, and music composition. In 1948 she left Britain to settle with her paternal grandmother in Florence. Her mother died a year later when Rosselli was nineteen. After her mother's death, Rosselli moved to Rome to look for work and to continue her education. There she developed an interest in ethnomusicology and electronic music. She published "La serie degli armonici," a critical essay on ethnomusicology with *Il Verri*. In 1964 Garzanti published *Variazioni Belliche,* Rosselli's first book of poems. It included a laudatory introduction by Pasolini. The book had been rejected by four publishers and received attention only after the appearance of Rosselli's work in Italo Calvino and Elio Vittorini's prestigious *Il Menabò*. In 1981 Rosselli won the Premio Pasolini award for work produced between 1950 and 1979. Her poetry has appeared in numerous newspapers and periodicals, including *L'Avanti, Paese Sera, L'Unità,* and *La Stampa,* and in anthologies such as *Poeti italiani del Novecento, Poesia erotica italiana del novecento,* and *Twentieth-Century Italian Poetry* (1993). Selections of her work have been translated in *The New Italian Poetry, The Defiant Muse, Italian Poetry since World War II, Italian Women Poets of the Twentieth Century, The Pip Anthology of World Poetry, Poems for the Millennium,* and *The Promised Land.* Rosselli is now considered one of Italy's foremost experimental writers. Her life, however, was marked by Parkinson's disease, a number of nervous breakdowns, and frequent stays in psychiatric hospitals. She committed suicide in Rome on February 11, 1996.

Poetry:

Variazioni belliche. Ed. Plinio Perilli, intro. by Pier Paolo Pasolini. Milan: Garzanti, 1964; rpt. Rome: Fondazione Piazzolla, 1995.

Serie ospedaliera. Milan: Il Saggiatore, 1969.

Documento (1966–1973). Milan: Garzanti, 1976.

Primi Scritti (1952–1963). Milan: Guanda, 1980.

Impromptu. Intro. by Giovanni Giudici. Genoa: Edizioni S. Marco dei Giustiniani, 1981; rpt. Rome: Mancosu, 1993.

Appunti sparsi e persi (1966–1977). Reggio Emilia: Aelia Laelia, 1983.

La libellula. Milan: SE, 1985. (Reprint of poem written in 1958.)
Antologia poetica. Ed. Giacinto Spagnoletti, intro. by Giovanni Giudici. Milan: Garzanti, 1987.
Sonno-Sleep (1953–1966). With Antonio Porta. Rome: Rossi e Spera, 1989.
Diario ottuso (1954–1968). Intro. by Alfonso Berardinelli. Rome: Istituto Bibliografico Napoleone, 1990; rpt. Rome: Empirìa, 1996.
Sleep. Poesie in inglese. Trans. into Italian by Emmanuela Tandello. Milan: Garzanti, 1992.
Le poesie. Ed. Emmanuela Tandello. Milan: Garzanti, 1997.

Translations and Critical work:
Rosselli, Carlo. *Epistolario familiare.* Ed. Rosselli. Milan: Sugarco, 1979.
Plath, Sylvia. *Le muse inquietanti e altre poesie.* Trans. with Gabriella Morisco. Milan: Mondadori, 1985.
Evans, Paul. *Dialogo tra un poeta e una musa.* Rome: Fondazione Piazzola, 1991.
Maeterlinck, Maurice. *L'uccellino azzurro, fiaba in sei atti e dodici quadri.* Florence: Le Monnier, 1992.

GABRIELLA SICA (1950–)

Sica was born in Viterbo and lives in Rome where she teaches Italian Literature at the University "La Sapienza." She made her poetic debut in 1980 in the literary journal *Prato pagano* with poems later included in her first book, *La famosa vita.* In 1983 her *Poesie per le oche* was published in Mondadori's poetry series *Almanacco dello Specchio.* Her work has since appeared in numerous journals, national newspapers such as *Corriere della Sera,* and such anthologies as *Poesie d'amore* (1986), *The Defiant Muse,* and *L'albero delle parole.* Her awards include the 1986 Premio Brutium Tropea for *La famosa vita* and the 1992 Premio San Pellegrino Terme for *Vicolo del Bologna.* Some of her poems have been translated into English, French, and Rumanian. In addition to her poetry, she has also written prose. *È nato un bimbo* was inspired by the birth of her child, as were the poems in "Poesie per un bambino" included in her latest book, *Poesie bambine.* Sica's contributions to the field of literature have been numerous: from 1980 to 1987, she was director of the journal *Prato pagano;* she has published a book on the art of writing verse; and edited a volume of essays on recent tendencies in Italian poetry. Most recently, she has worked for RAI on six films about poets of the twentieth century.

Poetry:
Poesie per le oche. Almanacco dello Specchio. Milan: Mondadori, 1983.

La famosa vita. Rome: Il melograno, 1986.
Vicolo del Bologna. Forte dei Marmi: Pegaso, 1992.
Poesie bambine. With a letter by Emanuele Trevi. Milan: La vita felice, 1997.

Prose:
Scuola di ballo. Rome: Rotundo, 1988.
È nato un bimbo. Milan: Mondadori, 1990.

Critical Work:
La parola ritrovata. Ultime tendenze della poesia italiana. Ed. Sica and Maria
    Ida Gaeta. Venice: Marsilio, 1995.
Scrivere in versi. Metrica e poesia. Parma: Pratiche editrice, 1996.
Sia dato credito all'invisibile. Prose e saggi. Venice: Marsilio, 2000.

MARIA LUISA SPAZIANI (1924–)

Spaziani was born in Turin where she studied at the university, graduating with a dissertation on Marcel Proust. She has lived in Milan, Paris, and Rome, has written for newspapers such as *La Stampa,* and has taught French Literature at the University of Messina for over twenty-five years. She has also worked for Italian and Swiss radio and television. In 1950 she won the Premio Viareggio for journalism and, in 1954, made her poetic debut with the publisher Mondadori. In 1977 she edited a French edition of Dino Campana's 1914 *Canti orfici,* a major text of the Italian modernist period. She has published critical work on French, Italian, and German literature, and has translated poetry, plays, fiction, and criticism by, among others, André Gide, Wolfgang Goethe, George Sand, Michel Tournier, and Marguerite Yourcenar. She is also the author of short stories and plays. Her poetry has been translated into over sixteen languages. English translations have appeared in *The Penguin Book of Women Poets, Italian Poetry Today* (1979), *A Book of Women Poets from Antiquity to Now, The Defiant Muse, The Green Flame, Italian Poetry since World War II, New Italian Poets,* and *Italian Women Poets of the Twentieth Century.* Her collection *La stella del libero arbitrio* was translated and published as *Star of Free Will* in 1996. In Italy her work has been included in anthologies such as *Quarta generazione, La giovane poesia, Donne in poesia, Poesia italiana del Novecento* (1988), *Poesia erotica italiana del novecento,* and *Poeti italiani del secondo Novecento: 1945–1995.* Spaziani is founder and president of the Centro Internazionale Eugenio Montale in Rome and presides over the Premio Montale. She has won numerous awards, including the 1954 Premio Internazionale Byron for *Le acque del Sabato,* the 1981 Premio Viareggio for *Geometria del disordine,* the 1990 Il Ceppo prize for the "novel-poem" *Giovanna D'Arco,* and the 1999 Premio Grinzane Cavour for her work as a translator. In 1990, 1992, and 1997 she was Italy's candidate for the Nobel Prize.

Poetry:
Le acque del Sabato. Milan: Mondadori, 1954.
Primavera a Parigi. Milan: Scheiwiller, 1954.
Luna lombarda. Vicenza: Neri Pozza Editore, 1959.
Il Gong. Milan: Mondadori, 1962.
Utilità della memoria. Milan: Mondadori, 1966.
L'occhio del ciclone. Milan: Mondadori, 1970.
Ultrasuoni. Lugano: Munt Press, 1976.
Transito con catene. Milan: Mondadori, 1977.
Poesie. Intro. by Luigi Baldacci. Milan: Mondadori, 1979.
Geometria del disordine. Milan: Mondadori, 1981.
La stella del libero arbitrio. Milan: Mondadori, 1986.
Giovanna D'Arco. Milan: Mondadori, 1990; rpt. 1992.
All'America. With four essays by Furio Colombo. Ferrara: La Bautta, 1990.
Torri di vedetta. Milan: Crocetti, 1992.
I fasti dell'ortica. Milan: Mondadori, 1996.
Star of Free Will. Trans. Carol Lettieri and Irene Marchegiani Jones. Toronto and New York: Guernica, 1996.
Sentry Towers. Trans. Laura Stortoni. Berkeley, CA: Hesperia Press, 1996.
La radice del Mare. Naples: Pironti, 1999.
Un fresco castagneto. Rome: Edizioni Il Bulino, 1999.

Prose:
Il mio Sud. Messina: Il Gabbiano, 1989.
Donne in poesia. Interviste immaginarie. Venice: Marsilio, 1992; rpt. 1994.

Theater:
Il dottore di vetro. Libretto for music by Roman Vlad. 1960.
Puccini, Carducci, Weininger. Broadcast in 1979 for the radio series "Io accuso. Chi accusi?" Selection Premio Italia.

Translations:
Yourcenar, Marguerite. *Il colpo di grazia e Alexis.* Milan: Feltrinelli, 1962.
Sand, George. *Francesco il trovatello.* Turin: E.R.I., 1963.
Sully-Prudhomme, René François Armand. *Poesie.* Milan: Feltrinelli, 1964–65.
Toulet, Paul-Jean. *Poesie.* Turin: Einaudi, 1966.
Bellow, Saul. *La vittima.* Milan: Feltrinelli, 1966; rpt. 1978.
Racine, Jean. *Bajazet.* Rome: Lo Faro, 1973.

Goethe, Wolfgang. *Götz von Berlichingen.* Turin: Einaudi, 1973.
Gide, André. *Oscar Wilde.* Florence: Mario Luca Giusti, 1979.
Tournier, Michel. *Le meteore.* Milan: Mondadori, 1979; rpt. Milan: Garzanti, 1995.
Yourcenar, Marguerite. *Novelle Orientali.* Milan: Rizzoli, 1983; rpt. 1987.
Yourcenar, Marguerite. *Fuochi.* Milan: Bompiani, 1984.
Tournier, Michel. *Il gallo cedrone.* Milan: Garzanti, 1986.
Racine, Jean. *Britannico, Bajazet, Atalia.* Milan: Garzanti, 1986.
Tournier, Michel. *Gaspare, Melchiorre e Baldassarre.* Milan: Garzanti, 1989.

Critical Works:
Due poeti. Charles d'Orléans e Sully-Prudhomme. Rome: Lo Faro, 1970.
Racine e il Bajazet. Rome: Lo Faro, 1972; rpt. 1973.
Ronsard fra gli astri della Pléiade. Turin: E. R. I., 1972; rpt. Milan: Mondadori, 1998.
Il teatro francese del Settecento. Rome: Lo Faro, 1974.
Il teatro francese dell'Ottocento. Rome: Lo Faro, 1975.
Il teatro francese del Novecento. Messina: EDAS, 1976.
Storia dell'Alessandrino. Messina: EDAS, 1977.
Campana, Dino. *Chants Orphiques.* Ed. Spaziani. Paris: Seghers, 1977.
Alessandrino e altri versi fra Ottocento e Novecento. Messina: EDAS, 1978.
Racine. Ed. Spaziani. Milan: Garzanti, 1986.

PATRIZIA VALDUGA (1953–)

Valduga was born in Castelfranco Veneto (Treviso) and now lives in Milan. After studying medicine for three years, she completed a degree in Letters at the University of Venice. She is founder of the monthly journal *Poesia,* which she edited for one year, and a contributor to the weekly magazine *Panorama.* Her one-woman show, based on *Donna di dolori,* has been widely performed throughout Italy. Her theatrical work includes translations of Beckett, Céline, Cocteau, and Molière. She has also translated the work of Donne, Mallarmé, Shakespeare, and Valéry. Her poetry has appeared in various anthologies, including *Poesie d'amore* (1986), *La furia di Pegaso, I sentieri della notte, Poeti italiani del secondo Novecento: 1945–1995, Italian Women Poets of the Twentieth Century,* and *Nuovi poeti italiani contemporanei.* She was awarded the Premio Viareggio opera prima for *Medicamenta* and the Clemente Rebora for *La tentazione.*

Poetry:
Medicamenta. Parma: Guanda, 1982.
La tentazione. Intro. by Franco Cordelli. Milan: Crocetti, 1985.

Medicamenta e altri medicamenta. Intro. by Luigi Baldacci. Turin: Einaudi, 1989.

Donna di dolori. Milan: Mondadori, 1991.

Requiem. Per mio padre morto il 2 dicembre 1991. Venice: Marsilo, 1994.

Corsia degli incurabili. Milan: Garzanti, 1996.

Cento quartine e altre storie d'amore. Turin: Einaudi, 1997.

Prima antologia. Turin: Einaudi, 1998.

Translations:

Donne, John. *Canzoni e sonetti.* Milan: SE, 1985; rpt. 1999.

Mallarmé, Stéphane. *Poesie.* Essay by Jacques Derrida. Milan: Mondadori, 1991.

Valéry, Paul. *Il cimitero marino.* Milan: Mondadori, 1995.

Molière. *Il malato immaginario.* Florence: Giunti, 1995.

Molière. *Il misantropo.* Florence: Giunti, 1995.

Shakespeare, William. *Riccardo III.* Turin: Einaudi, 1998.

SELECTED BIBLIOGRAPHY

ITALIAN ANTHOLOGIES

L'albero delle parole. Grandi poeti di tutto il mondo per i bambini. Donatella Bisutti, ed. Milan: Feltrinelli, 1996.

L'altro Novecento. La poesia femminile in Italia. Vittoriano Esposito, ed. Foggia: Bastogi, 1997.

Anni '80. Poesia italiana. Luca Cesari, ed. Milan: Jaca Book, 1993.

Antologia della poesia italiana: 1909–1949. Giacinto Spagnoletti, ed. Parma: Guanda, 1950.

Antologia della poesia italiana. Cesare Segre and Carlo Ossola, eds. Turin: Einaudi, 1997.

Il canto ritrovato. Giovanna De Angelis, ed. Pescara: Tracce, 1995.

Care donne. Elia Malagò, ed. Forlì: Forum, 1980.

Da donna a donna. Poesie d'amore e d'amicizia. Laura Di Nola, ed. Rome: Edizioni delle donne, 1976.

Dal fondo. Carlo Bordini and Antonio Veneziani, eds. Rome: Savelli, 1978.

Dialetti d'Italia. Antologia poetica. Associazione nazionale poeti e scrittori dialettali. Rome: Edizioni Rari Nantes, 1986.

Diapason di voci: omaggio a Sandro Penna. Elio Pecora, ed. Valverde (Catania): Il girasole, 1997.

Le donne della poesia. Oltre il femminile. Domenico Cara, ed. Milan: Laboratorio delle Arti, 1991.

Donne in poesia. Antologia della poesia femminile in Italia. Biancamaria Frabotta, ed. Rome: Savelli, 1976.

Donne in poesia: Incontri con le poetesse italiane. 1988. Maria Pia Quintavalla, ed. Udine: Campanotto, 1992.

Europa in versi. Luce D'Eramo and Gabriella Sobrino, eds. Rome: Il Ventaglio, 1989.

La furia di Pegaso. Poesia italiana d'oggi. Marco Tornar, ed. Milan: Archinto, 1996.

Le futuriste. Claudia Salaris, ed. Milano: Edizioni delle donne, 1982.

La giovane poesia. Saggio e repertorio. Enrico Falqui, ed. Rome: Colombo, 1956.

Gruppo 63. La nuova letteratura. 34 scrittori, Palermo ottobre 1963. Nanni Belestrini and Alfredo Giuliani, eds. Milan: Feltrinelli, 1964.

Gruppo 93. Le tendenze attuali della poesia e della narrativa. Antologia di testi teorici e letterari. Anna Grazia D'Oria, ed. Lecce: P. Manni, 1992.

Letteratura degli anni Ottanta. Fillippo Bettini, Mario Lunetta, and Francesco Muzzioli, eds. Foggia: Bastogi, 1985.

La letteratura emarginata. Walter Pedullà, Silvana Castelli, and Stefano Giovanardi, eds. Cosenza: Lerici, 1978.

Linea lombarda. Sei poeti. Luciano Anceschi, ed. Varese: Magenta, 1952.

Lirici nuovi. Antologia di poesia contemporanea. Luciano Anceschi, ed. Milan: Hoepli, 1943. Rpt. with title *Lirici nuovi. Antologia.* Milan: Mursia, 1964.

Manuale di poesia sperimentale. Guido Guglielmi and Elio Pagliarani, eds. Milan: Mondadori, 1966.

Melodie della terra. Novecento e natura: il sentimento cosmico nei poeti italiani del nostro secolo. Plinio Perilli, ed. Milan: Crocetti, 1997.

Mirafiori blues. Riccardo Duranti and Annalisa Goldoni, eds. Rome: Dip. di Anglistica, Univ. "La Sapienza," 1988.

I Novissimi. Poesie per gli anni '60. Alfredo Giuliani, ed. Milan: Rusconi e Paolazzi, 1961. Turin: Eiunaudi, 1965.

Nuovi poeti italiani. Vol 1. Emilio Faccioli, et al., eds. Turin: Einaudi, 1980.

Nuovi poeti italiani. Vol 2. Alfonso Berardinelli, ed. Turin: Einaudi, 1982.

Nuovi poeti italiani. Vol 3. Walter Siti, ed. Turin: Einaudi, 1984.

Nuovi poeti italiani. Vol 4. Mauro Bersani, ed. Turin: Einaudi, 1995.

Nuovi poeti italiani contemporanei. Roberto Galaverni, ed. Rimini: Guaraldi, 1996.

Nuovi segnali. Antologia sulle poetiche verbo-visuali negli anni '70–'80. Vitaldo Conte, ed. Rimini: Maggioli, 1984.

Oltre il mare ghiacciato. I poeti e l'oggi. Luciana Notari, ed. Udine: Campanotto, 1996.

La parola innamorata. I poeti nuovi 1976–1978. Giancarlo Pontiggia and Enzo Di Mauro, eds. Milan: Feltrinelli, 1978.

Poesia contemporanea: Testi e saggi critici. Guido Rispoli and Amedeo Quondam, eds. Florence: Le Monnier, 1969.

Poesia d'ispirazione cristiana. 1860–1996. Santino Sparta, ed. Rome: Rogate, 1996.

Poesia degli anni settanta. Antonio Porta, ed. Milan: Feltrinelli, 1979.

Poesia del Novecento. Edoardo Sanguineti, ed. Turin: Einaudi, 1969.

Poesia donna: Antologia. Rome: Il nuovo Giornale dei poeti, 1996.

Poesia erotica italiana del novecento. Carlo Villa, ed. Rome: Newton Compton, 1981.

La poesia femminile del '900. Gaetano Salveti, ed. N.p.: Edizioni del Sestante, 1964.

La poesia femminista. Nadia Fusini and Mariella Gramaglia, eds. Rome: Savelli, 1977.

Poesia femminista italiana. Laura Di Nola, ed. Rome: Savelli, 1978.

Poesia italiana (1941–1988). La via lombarda. Giorgio Luzzi, ed. Milan: Marcos y Marcos, 1989.

Poesia italiana contemporanea. 1909–1959. Giacinto Spagnoletti, ed. Parma: Guanda, 1959.

Poesia italiana contemporanea. Giovanni Raboni, ed. Florence: Sansoni, 1981.

Poesia italiana del dopoguerra. Salvatore Quasimodo, ed. Milan: Schwarz, 1958.

Poesia italiana del Novecento. Piero Gelli and Gina Lagorio, eds. 2 vols. 1980. Milan: Garzanti, 1988.

Poesia italiana del Novecento. Elio Pecora, ed. Rome: Newton Compton, 1990.

Poesia italiana del Novecento. Ermanno Krumm and Tiziano Rossi, eds. Milan: Skira, 1995.

Poesia italiana della contraddizione. Franco Cavallo and Mario Lunetta, eds. Rome: Newton Compton, 1989.

Poesia italiana oggi. Mario Lunetta, ed. Rome: Newton Compton, 1981.

Poesia oggi. Massimiliano Mancini, et al., eds. Milan: Angeli, 1986.

Poesie d'amore. Lucia Mesini, ed. Milan: Mariotti, 1998.

Poesie d'amore. Roberta Serra, ed. Milan: Rizzoli, 1998.

Poesie d'amore: l'assenza, il desiderio. Le più importanti poetesse italiane contemporanee presentate da trentasei critici. Francesca Pansa and Marianna Bucchich, eds. Rome: Newton Compton, 1986.

Poesie e realtà '45–'75. Giancarlo Majorino, ed. 2 vols. Rome: Savelli, 1977.

Poetesse del Novecento. Milan: Scheiwiller, 1951.

I poeti degli "anni ottanta." Michele D'Agata and Vincenzo Di Maria, eds. Catania: Edizioni della SSC, 1980.

Poeti della Quinta Generazione. Giovanni Ramella Bagneri, ed. Forlì: Forum, 1983.

Poeti dialettali del Novecento. Franco Brevini, ed. Turin: Einaudi, 1987.

Poeti italiani del Novecento. Pier Vincenzo Mengaldo, ed. Milan: Mondadori, 1978.

Poeti italiani del secondo Novecento: 1945–1995. Maurizio Cucchi and Stefano Giovanardi, eds. Milan: Mondadori, 1996.

Primavera di poesia. Gabriella Sica, ed. Rome: Edizioni Scettro del Re, 1993.

Il pubblico della poesia. Alfonso Berardinelli and Franco Cordelli, eds. Cosenza: Lerici, 1975.

Quarta generazione. La giovane poesia (1945–1954). Piero Chiara and Luciano Erba, eds. Varese: Magenta, 1954.

Rimerotiche. Preface by Lina Wertmüller Job. Rome: Gradiva, n.d.

I sentieri della notte. Figure e percorsi della poesia italiana al varco del millennio. Gualtiero De Santi, ed. Milan: Crocetti, 1996.

Una strana polvere. Altre voci per i nostri anni. Paolo Lagazzi and Stefano Lecchini, eds. Udine: Campanotto, 1994.

Versi d'amore. M. Giovanna Maioli Loperfido, ed. Venice: Corbo e Fiore, 1982.

Verso la poesia totale. Adriano Spatola, ed. Turin: Paravia, 1978.

Via Terra: Antologia di poesia neodialettale. Achille Serrao, ed. Udine: Campanotto, 1992.

Viva la poesia! Marco Marchi, ed. Florence: Vallecchi, 1985.

English-Language Anthologies

A Book of Women Poets from Antiquity to Now: Selections from the World Over. 1980. Aliki Barnstone and Willis Barnstone, eds. New York: Schocken Books, 1992.

Contemporary Italian Poetry: An Anthology. Carlo L. Golino, ed. Berkeley: University of California Press, 1962.

The Defiant Muse: Italian Feminist Poems from the Middle Ages to the Present. Beverly Allen, Muriel Kittel, and Keala Jane Jewell, eds. New York: The Feminist Press, 1986.

The Favorite Malice: Ontology and Reference in Contemporary Italian Poetry. Thomas J. Harrison, ed. and trans. New York: Out of London Press, 1983.

Foresta Ultra Naturam: Verses & Visuals by Emilio Villa, Giulia Niccolai and Luciano Caruso. Paul Vangelisti, ed. San Francisco: Red Hill Press, 1989.

From Pure Silence to Impure Dialogue: A Survey of Post-War Italian Poetry 1945–1965. Vittoria Bradshaw, ed. New York: Gaetano Massa, 1971.

The Green Flame: Contemporary Italian Poetry with English Translations. Alessandro Gentili and Catherine O'Brien, eds. Dublin: Irish Academic Press, 1987.

The Hidden Italy: A Bilingual Edition of Italian Dialect Poetry. Hermann W. Haller, ed. Detroit: Wayne State University Press, 1986.

Introduction to Italian Poetry: A Dual Language Book. Luciano Rebay, ed. New York: Dover, 1969.

Italian Poetry, 1950–1990. Gayle Ridinger and Gian Paolo Renello, eds. Gayle Ridinger, trans. Boston: Dante University of America Press, 1996.

Italian Poetry 1960–1980: From Neo to Post Avant-Garde. Adriano Spatola and Paul Vangelisti, eds. San Francisco: Red Hill Press, 1982.

Italian Poetry: An Anthology from the Beginnings to the Present. Arturo Vivante, ed. and trans. Wellfleet: Delphinium Press, 1996.

Italian Poetry since World War II. Paolo Cherchi and Joseph Parisi, eds. Special issue of *Poetry* 155. 1–2 (Oct.–Nov. 1989).

Italian Poetry Today. Ruth Feldman and Brian Swann, eds. St. Paul: New Rivers Press, 1979.

Italian Poetry Today: A Critical Anthology. Raffaele Perrotta, ed. Sydney: Frederick May Foundation for Italian Studies, University of Sydney, 1980.

Italian Poets of the 20th Century. Giuseppe Nicoletti, ed. Florence: Casalini libri, 1997.

Italian Women Poets of the Twentieth Century. Catherine O'Brien, ed. and trans. Dublin: Irish Academic Press, 1996.

Italy's Ultramodern, Experimental Lyrics: Corpo 10. Justin Vitiello, trans. New York: Peter Lang, 1992.

Modern Poetry in Translation: Italy 26 (Winter 1975). Ruth Feldman and Brian Swann, eds.

The New Italian Poetry, 1945 to the Present: A Bilingual Anthology. Lawrence R. Smith, ed. and trans. Berkeley: University of California Press, 1981.

New Italian Poets. Dana Gioia and Michael Palma, eds. Brownsville: Story Line Press, 1991.

I Novissimi: Poetry for the Sixties. Alfredo Giuliani, ed. David Jacobson, et al., trans. Los Angeles: Sun & Moon Press, 1995.

The Penguin Book of Women Poets. Carol Cosman, Joan Keefe, and Kathleen Weaver, eds. 1978. New York: Penguin, 1988.

The Pip Anthology of World Poetry of the 20th Century. Vol. 1. Douglas Messerli, ed. Los Angeles: Green Integer, 2000.

Poems for the Millennium: The University of California Book of Modern and Postmodern Poetry. Vol. 2. Jerome Rothenberg and Pierre Joris, eds. Berkeley: University of California Press, 1998.

Poeti italiani moderni: Modern Italian Poets. Ferdinando Alfonsi and Sandra Alfonsi, eds. and trans. Catanzaro: Antonio Carrello Editore, 1986.

The Promised Land: Italian Poetry after 1975. Luigi Ballerini, Beppe Cavatorta, Elena Coda, and Paul Vangelisti, eds. Los Angeles: Sun & Moon Press, 1999.

Shearsmen of Sorts: Italian Poetry 1975–1993. Luigi Ballerini, ed. Stony Brook: Center for Italian Studies, State University of New York at Stony Brook, 1992.

Twentieth-Century Italian Poetry: A Bilingual Anthology. Levi Robert Lind, ed. Indianapolis and New York: Bobbs-Merrill, 1974.

Twentieth-Century Italian Poetry: A Bilingual Anthology. Margherita Marchione, ed. and trans. Rutherford: Fairleigh Dickinson University Press, 1974.

Twentieth-Century Italian Poetry: An Anthology. John Picchione and Lawrence R. Smith, eds. Toronto: University of Toronto Press, 1993.

Twentieth-Century Italian Poets. 1992. Giovanna Wedel De Stasio, Glauco Cambon, and Antonio Illiano, eds. Detroit: Gale Research, 1993.

Via terra: An Anthology of Italian Neodialect Poetry. Achille Serrao, Luigi Bonaffini, and Justin Vitiello, eds. Brooklyn: Legas, 1999.

The Vintage Book of Contemporary World Poetry. J. D. McClatchy, ed. New York: Vintage Books, 1996.

CRITICAL STUDIES, HISTORIES OF ITALIAN LITERATURE, AND REFERENCE BOOKS

Anceschi, Luciano. *Le poetiche del Novecento in Italia.* Turin: Paravia, 1972. Venice: Marsilio, 1990.

Aricò, Santo L., ed. *Contemporary Women Writers in Italy: A Modern Renaissance.* Amherst: University of Massachusetts Press, 1990.

Bagnoli, Vincenzo. *Contemporanea. La nuova poesia italiana verso il Duemila.* Padova: Esedra, 1996.

Bàrberi Squarotti, Giorgio, and Anna Maria Golfieri. *Dal tramonto dell'ermetismo alla neovanguardia.* Brescia: La Scuola, 1984.

Barbuto, Antonio. *Da Narciso a Castelporziano. Poesia e pubblico negli anni settanta.* Rome: Edizioni dell'Ateneo, 1981.

Barilli, Renato, ed. *Viaggio al termine della parola. La ricerca intraverbale.* Milan: Feltrinelli, 1981.

Bettini, Fillippo, ed. *Terza ondata. Il nuovo movimento della scrittura in Italia.* Bologna: Synergon, 1993.

Bettini, Fillippo, and Francesco Muzzioli, eds. *Gruppo '93. La recente avventura del dibattito teorico letterario in Italia.* Lecce: Manni, 1990.

Birnbaum, Lucia Chiavola. *Liberazione della donna: Feminism in Italy.* Middletown, Connecticut: Wesleyan University Press, 1986.

Bono, Paola, and Sandra Kemp, eds. *Italian Feminist Thought: A Reader.* Oxford: Basil Blackwell, 1991.

—. *The Lonely Mirror: Italian Perspectives on Feminist Theory.* London and New York: Routledge, 1993.

Braccesi, Lorenzo. *Poesia e memoria. Nuove proiezioni dell'antico.* Rome: "L'Erma" di Bretschneider, 1993.

Camerino, Giuseppe Antonio. *Poesia senza frontiere e poeti italiani del Novecento.* Milan: Mursia, 1989.

Cordelli, Franco. *Il poeta postumo.* Rome: Lerici, 1978.

Corona, Daniela, ed. *Donne e scrittura.* Palermo: La Luna, 1990.

De Robertis, Giuseppe. *Altro Novecento.* Florence: Le Monnier, 1962.

Esposito, Edoardo. *Metrica e poesia del Novecento.* Milan: Angeli, 1992.

Esposito, Vittoriano. *Poesia, non-poesia, anti-poesia del '900 italiano.* Foggia: Bastogi, 1992.

Ferroni, Giulio. *Storia della letteratura italiana. Il Novecento.* Vol 4. Milan: Einaudi Scuola, 1991.

Frattini, Alberto. *La giovane poesia italiana. Cronache e orientamenti.* Pisa: Nistri-Lischi, 1964.

—. *Poesia nuova in Italia. Tra ermetismo e neoavanguardia.* Milan: IPL, 1967.

Fusini, Nadia. "Sulle donne e il loro poetare." *Nuova duf* 5 (Oct.–Dec. 1977): 5–21.

Gaeta, Maria Ida, and Gabriella Sica, eds. *La parola ritrovata. Ultime tendenze della poesia italiana.* Venice: Marsilio, 1995.

Hellman, Judith Adler. *Journeys among Women: Feminism in Five Italian Cities.* New York: Oxford University Press, 1987.

—. "The Originality of Italian Feminism." Testaferri. 15–23.

Jeffries, Giovanna Miceli, ed. *Feminine Feminists: Cultural Practices in Italy.* Minneapolis: University of Minnesota Press, 1994.

Jewell, Keala Jane. *The Poiesis of History: Experimenting with Genre in Postwar Italy.* Ithaca: Cornell University Press, 1992.

Jones, F. J. *The Modern Italian Lyric.* Cardiff: University of Wales Press, 1986.

Kemeny, Tomaso, and Cesare Viviani, eds. *Il movimento della poesia italiana negli anni settanta.* Bari: Dedalo, 1979.

—. *I percorsi della nuova poesia italiana.* Naples: Guida, 1980.

Lanuzza, Stefano. *L'apprendista sciamano. Poesia italiana degli anni settanta.* Messina–Florence: D'Anna, 1979.

Lorenzini, Niva. *Il presente della poesia: 1960–1990.* Bologna: Il Mulino, 1991.

—. *La poesia italiana del Novecento.* Bologna: Il Mulino, 1999.

Luperini, Romano. *L'allegoria del moderno.* Rome: Editori Riuniti, 1990.

Manacorda, Giorgio. *Per la poesia. Manifesto del Pensiero Emotivo.* Rome: Editori Riuniti, 1993.

Mengaldo, Pier Vincenzo. *Giudizi di valore.* Turin: Einaudi, 1999.

Merola, Nicola, ed. *Il poeta e la poesia.* Naples: Liguori, 1986.

Pagnanelli, Remo. *Studi Critici. Poesia e poeti italiani del secondo Novecento.* Daniela Marcheschi, ed. Milan: Mursia, 1991.

Piemontese, Felice, ed. *Autodizionario degli scrittori italiani.* Milan: Leonardo, 1990.

Picchione, John. "Poesia al femminile(?): rabbia, gioco e terapia." Testaferri. 59–70.

Re, Lucia. "(De)Constructing the Canon: The Agon of the Anthologies on the Scene of Modern Italian Poetry." *The Modern Language Review* 87.3 (July 1992): 585–602.

—. "Mythic Revisionism: Women Poets and Philosophers in Italy Today." *Italian Women Writers from the Renaissance to the Present: Revising the Canon.* Ed. with an introduction by Maria Ornella Marotti. Pennsylvania: The Pennsylvania State University Press, 1996. 187–233.

Riggan, William, et al. *Italian Literature Today.* Special Issue of *World Literature Today* 71.2 (Spring 1997).

Russell, Rinaldina, ed. *Italian Women Writers: A Bio-Bibliographic Sourcebook.* Westport, CT: Greenwood Press, 1994.

——. *The Feminist Encyclopedia of Italian Literature*. London: Greenwood, 1997.

Spagnoletti, Giacinto. *Storia della letteratura italiana del Novecento*. Rome: Newton Compton, 1994.

Testaferri, Ada, ed. *Donna: Women in Italian Culture*. Ottawa: Dovehouse, 1987.

Vincentini, Isabella. *Colloqui sulla poesia. Le ultime tendenze*. Rome: Nuova Eri, 1991.

——. *La pratica del desiderio. I giovani poeti negli anni Ottanta*. Caltanissetta–Rome: Sciascia, 1986.

——. *Varianti da un naufragio. Il viaggio marino dai simbolisti ai postermetici*. Milan: Mursia, 1994.

West, Rebecca, and Dino S. Cervigni, eds. *Women's Voices in Italian Literature*. Special Issue of *Annali d'Italianistica* 7 (1989).

Wilson, Katharina M., ed. *An Encyclopedia of Continental Women Writers*. New York and London: Garland Publishing, 1991.

Wood, Sharon. *Italian Women's Writing 1860–1994*. London: Athlone, 1995.

Zagarrio, Giuseppe. *Febbre, furore e fiele. Repertorio della poesia italiana contemporanea 1970–1980*. Milan: Mursia, 1983.

Zamboni, Chiara. "Il linguaggio della poesia, il linguaggio del corpo." *Luna e l'altro*. Supplement to *Nuova Duf* 16 (Spring 1981): 73–81.

Zanzotto, Andrea. *Aure e disincanti nel Novecento letterario*. Milan: Mondadori, 1994.